HOLIDAY & CELEBRATIONS

Taste of Home

© 2018 RDA Enthusiast Brands, LLC.
1610 N. 2nd St., Suite 102, Milwaukee
WI 53212-3906

**INTERNATIONAL STANDARD
BOOK NUMBER:** 978-1-61765-786-3

**INTERNATIONAL STANDARD
SERIAL NUMBER:** 1535-2781

COMPONENT NUMBER:
118000054H

COVER PHOTOGRAPHER:
Grace Natoli Sheldon

SET STYLIST: Melissa Franco
FOOD STYLIST: Lauren Knoelke

PICTURED ON FRONT COVER:
Reindeer Cake, p. 2

PICTURED ON BACK COVER:
Apple-Gouda Pigs in a Blanket (p.
32); Cranberry Party Punch (p. 32);
Ugly Sweater Cookies (p. 39); Orange
Lemonade (p. 206); Fruit & Cheese
Kabobs (p. 209); Chicken Salad
Party Sandwiches (p. 205); Roasted
Citrus & Herb Turkey (p. 102); Pearl
Onion Broccoli Bake (p. 99); Unicorn
Cake (p. 180); Rainbow Shortbread
Cookies (p. 179)

Printed in U.S.A.

1 3 5 7 9 10 8 6 4 2

Come One, Come All!

Celebrating means being with the ones you love most. It's this special art of togetherness that makes the moments, both big and small, meaningful and memorable. It's easy to serve up a big helping of comfort and joy all year long with the extraordinary recipes, enticing menus, fun party themes, easy decor tips and other sensational ideas inside this stunning edition of *Taste of Home Holiday & Celebrations* cookbook. From main attractions and sides to appetizers and desserts, we've gathered up 285 culinary creations to help you celebrate in good taste. You'll also find beautiful photos, helpful how-to's and timelines, simple crafts and creative gift-giving ideas. Let the party begin!

SUBMIT YOUR RECIPE!

Would you like to see one of your family recipes featured in a *Taste of Home collection?*

Visit **tasteofhome.com/submit** to share your story and recipes.

On the Cover!

Layered cakes have always been classic holiday party-pleasers, but this reindeer that charms our cover takes Christmas dessert to a whole new level! With its shiny red nose, gingerbread antlers, chocolate-dipped ears and other magical touches, it's guaranteed to stop everyone in their tracks—and will have them asking for another slice!

Loving the reindeer theme? See page 63 for adorable Chocolate Reindeer Cookies. Stack St. Nick's cookie plate even higher with any one of the kid-friendly cookie recipes in the Kids in the Kitchen chapter, starting on page 60. We think Santa, Mrs. Claus, the elves and all the reindeer would approve!

REINDEER CAKE

Let your imagination take flight with this enchanting triple-layer cake. These fun decorating ideas are perfect for beginner and advanced bakers alike. No special skills or fancy equipment required!
—Lauren Knoelke, Milwaukee, WI

Prep: 1 hour • **Bake:** 25 min. + cooling
Makes: 20 servings

- 2¼ cups cake flour
- 1½ cups sugar
- 3½ tsp. baking powder
- ½ tsp. salt
- ½ cup unsalted butter, cubed
- 4 large egg whites, room temperature
- ¾ cup 2% milk, divided
- 1 tsp. clear vanilla extract
- ½ tsp. almond extract
- ⅓ cup red and green jimmies

BUTTERCREAM
- 6 oz. dark chocolate, chopped
- ¼ cup heavy whipping cream
- 6 large egg whites
- 1½ cups sugar
- ½ tsp. cream of tartar
- ½ tsp. salt
- 2 cups unsalted butter, cubed
- 1½ tsp. vanilla extract
- ½ cup baking cocoa

1. Preheat oven to 350°. Line bottoms of three 6-in. round baking pans with parchment paper; grease and flour pans.

2. In a large bowl, whisk the flour, sugar, baking powder and salt. Beat in butter until crumbly. Add egg whites, one at a time, beating well after each addition. Gradually beat in ¼ cup milk and extracts; beat on medium until light and fluffy, for about 2 minutes. Gradually beat in remaining milk. Gently fold in jimmies.

3. Transfer batter to prepared pans. Bake until a toothpick inserted in center comes out clean, 25-30 minutes. Cool in pans 10 minutes before removing to wire racks; remove paper. Cool completely.

4. For buttercream, in a microwave, melt chocolate with cream until smooth, stirring every 30 seconds. Set aside to cool slightly. In a heatproof bowl of a stand mixer, whisk egg whites, sugar, cream of tartar and salt until blended. Place over simmering water in a large saucepan over medium heat. Whisking constantly, heat mixture until a thermometer reads 160°, 8-10 minutes.

5. Remove from heat. With the whisk attachment of stand mixer, beat on high speed until cooled to 90°, about 7 minutes. Gradually beat in butter, a few Tbsp. at a time, on medium speed until smooth; beat in vanilla and chocolate mixture. Gradually beat in the cocoa through a sifter.

6. Spread frosting between layers and over top and sides of cake. Following tips on the next page, decorate as desired. Store in refrigerator.

Rudolph the Red-Nosed Cake

Follow these easy tips to turn your frosted cake into an adorable reindeer. It's so much fun, you may find yourself humming the classic Christmas tune as you decorate!

To create ears, using your favorite cutout cookie dough, cut two 2-in. hearts and bake. While still warm, mold baked cookies onto the curve of a large metal spoon; let stand until cool. Spray with edible gold mist; let dry. Dip edges in melted chocolate. Once set, place ears on top of cake.

To create antlers, using your favorite cutout cookie dough, cut two shapes with a gingerbread boy cookie cutter. Stretch into antler shapes and bake. Pipe melted chocolate over cooled cookies for texture. Once set, spray with edible gold mist. Once dry, place antler on top of cake.

To create mane, using paste food coloring, tint leftover buttercream frosting into colors of your choice. Using decorator tips of your choice, pipe designs on top of cake in between antlers and ears. Add store-bought meringues.

To create eyes, pipe melted chocolate onto parchment paper; refrigerate until set. Once set, attach to front of the cake.

To create nose, dip a vanilla wafer into melted red candy coating disks; let dry. Once dry, place nose on front of cake.

Add edible gold pearl sprinkles around base of cake. Available from *wilton.com*.

Two Cakes in One!

See page 180 for a unicorn cake based on the same recipe!

Table of Contents

'TIS THE SEASON

It's the most wonderful time of year, so relish every moment by celebrating with family and friends. Whether hosting formal dinners or casual get-togethers, you'll create memories with the sensational recipes and holiday hints found here. Set a buffet of simply scrumptious appetizers, bake Christmas cookies with little ones, and make everything merry and bright when you usher in the happiest season of all!

5-Star Classics

Thumb through your big box of recipes and you're sure to find a gem or two that always wins accolades. Here's a sampling of unbelievably delectable appetizers, main dishes, sides and desserts, all befitting of a celebratory occasion. One taste and you'll see why each of these is worthy of five stars and will earn a permanent spot in your holiday repertoire.

Cranberry Glazed Ham (p. 13) **Green Beans & Caramelized Onions** (p. 9)

GREEN BEANS &
CARAMELIZED ONIONS

GREEN BEANS & CARAMELIZED ONIONS

Brown sugar, bacon and cider vinegar dress up green beans and onions. They have a fresh, crisp flavor and never fail to please holiday guests.
—Jill Heatwole, Pittsville, MD

Prep: 10 min. • **Cook:** 40 min.
Makes: 8 servings

- 4 bacon strips, chopped
- 2 large onions, cut into ½-in. wedges
- 2 lbs. fresh green beans, trimmed
- 3 Tbsp. cider vinegar
- 1 to 2 Tbsp. brown sugar
- ¼ tsp. salt
- ¼ tsp. pepper

1. In a large skillet, cook the chopped bacon over medium heat until crisp, stirring occasionally. Using a slotted spoon, remove bacon to paper towels, reserving 2 Tbsp. drippings in pan.
2. In drippings, saute the onions over medium heat until softened. Reduce the heat to medium-low; cook onions until deep golden brown, for 30-40 minutes, stirring occasionally. Stir in the vinegar and brown sugar.
3. In a pot of boiling water, cook green beans, uncovered, until crisp-tender, 4-7 minutes; drain. Add to onions; cook 1 minute, tossing to combine. Stir in bacon; sprinkle with salt and pepper.

BRIE WITH APRICOT TOPPING

One of our favorite quick and tasty appetizers is baked brie. This one features a dried apricot topping, but don't be shy when it comes to experimenting with other dried fruits, such as cherries or figs.
—*Taste of Home* Test Kitchen

Takes: 25 min. • **Makes:** 8 servings

- ½ cup chopped dried apricots
- 2 Tbsp. brown sugar
- 2 Tbsp. water
- 1 tsp. balsamic vinegar
  Dash salt
- ½ to 1 tsp. minced fresh rosemary or ¼ tsp. dried rosemary, crushed
- 1 round Brie cheese (8 oz.)
  Assorted crackers

1. Preheat the oven to 400°. In a small saucepan, combine first five ingredients; bring to a boil. Cook and stir over medium heat until slightly thickened. Remove from heat; stir in rosemary.
2. Trim rind from top of cheese. Place cheese in an ungreased ovenproof serving dish. Spoon apricot mixture over cheese. Bake, uncovered, until cheese is softened, 10-12 minutes. Serve warm with crackers.

CONTEST-WINNING FESTIVE TOSSED SALAD

With its unique medley of fruits, this salad has become a Christmas tradition at our house. Our three grown daughters look forward to it every year.
—Jauneen Hosking, Waterford, WI

Takes: 15 min. • **Makes:** 10 servings

- ⅓ cup red wine vinegar
- 2 Tbsp. lemon juice
- ½ cup sugar
- 2 Tbsp. finely chopped onion
- ½ tsp. salt
- ⅔ cup canola oil
- 2 to 3 tsp. poppy seeds
- 10 cups torn romaine
- 1 medium pear, chopped
- 1 medium apple, chopped
- 1 cup shredded Swiss cheese
- ½ to 1 cup chopped cashews
- ¼ cup dried cranberries

1. For dressing, place first five ingredients in a blender; cover and process until blended. While processing, gradually add oil in a steady stream. Add poppy seeds; pulse just until combined.
2. To serve, place remaining ingredients in a large bowl. Toss with dressing.

POTLUCK SAUSAGE-STUFFED MUSHROOMS

Pennsylvania is often referred to as the Mushroom Capital of the World. This recipe is a delicious appetizer and always the hit of the party here.
—Beatrice Vetrano, Landenberg, PA

Prep: 15 min. • **Bake:** 20 min.
Makes: 12 servings

- 12 large fresh mushrooms
- 2 Tbsp. butter, divided
- 2 Tbsp. chopped onion
- 1 Tbsp. lemon juice
- ¼ tsp. dried basil
  Salt and pepper to taste
- 4 oz. bulk Italian sausage
- 1 Tbsp. chopped fresh parsley
- 2 Tbsp. dry bread crumbs
- 2 Tbsp. grated Parmesan cheese
  Thinly sliced green onions, optional

1. Preheat oven to 400°. Remove stems from the mushrooms; place the caps in a greased 15x10x1-in. pan. Finely chop stems; wrap in paper towels and squeeze to remove moisture.
2. In a skillet, heat 1½ Tbsp. butter; saute onion and stems over medium-high heat until tender. Stir in lemon juice, basil, salt and pepper; cook until juices are almost evaporated. Cool slightly.
3. Combine sausage, parsley and onion mixture; spoon into mushroom caps. Mix bread crumbs and cheese; sprinkle over tops. Dot with remaining butter.
4. Bake until sausage is cooked through, 15-20 minutes, basting occasionally with the pan juices. If desired, top with sliced green onions.

ZESTY MARINATED SHRIMP

These easy shrimp look impressive on a buffet table and taste even better. The zesty marinade has a wonderful spicy citrus flavor. I especially like this recipe because I can prepare it ahead of time.
—Mary Jane Guest, Alamosa, CO

Prep: 10 min. + chilling
Makes: about 4½ dozen

- 12 lemon or lime slices
- ½ cup thinly sliced red onion
- 1 Tbsp. minced fresh parsley
- ½ cup canola oil
- ½ cup lime juice
- ½ tsp. salt
- ½ tsp. dill weed
- ⅛ tsp. hot pepper sauce
- 2 lbs. peeled and deveined cooked shrimp (26-30 per lb.)

Place first eight ingredients in a large bowl; toss with shrimp. Refrigerate, covered, 4 hours, stirring occasionally. Drain shrimp before serving.

ROASTED GARLIC MASHED POTATOES

Try these creamy spuds for a classic dinner side that's lighter than most other mashed potatoes. I use reduced-fat cream cheese and fresh garlic to flavor.
—Nikki Dolan, Largo, FL

Prep: 15 min. • **Bake:** 30 min. + cooling
Makes: 6 servings

- 1   whole garlic bulb
- 1   tsp. canola oil
- 2¼ lbs. red potatoes (about 8 medium), cut into 1-in. pieces
- 1   pkg. (8 oz.) reduced-fat cream cheese, cubed
- ¼   cup 2% milk
- ½   tsp. salt
- ¼   tsp. pepper

1. Preheat oven to 425°. Remove papery outer skin from garlic bulb, but do not peel or separate the cloves. Cut off top of garlic bulb, exposing individual cloves; brush with oil. Wrap bulb in heavy-duty foil. Bake until garlic cloves are softened, 30-35 minutes. Unwrap and cool 10 minutes.
2. Meanwhile, place potatoes in a large saucepan; cover with water. Bring to a boil. Reduce heat; cook, uncovered, until potatoes are tender, 10-15 minutes.
3. Squeeze the garlic cloves into a bowl; mash with a fork until smooth. Drain the potatoes; return to pan. Add garlic; mash potatoes to desired consistency, gradually adding remaining ingredients.

SIRLOIN ROAST WITH GRAVY

This recipe is perfect for my husband, who is a meat-and-potatoes kind of guy. The peppery fork-tender roast combined with rich gravy creates a tasty centerpiece for any meal.
—Rita Clark, Monument, CO

Prep: 20 min. • **Cook:** 3½ hours
Makes: 8 servings

- 1   beef sirloin tip roast (3 lbs.)
- 2   garlic cloves, minced
- 1   to 2 Tbsp. coarsely ground pepper
- ¼   cup reduced-sodium soy sauce
- 3   Tbsp. balsamic vinegar
- 1   Tbsp. Worcestershire sauce
- 2   tsp. ground mustard
- 2   Tbsp. cornstarch
- ¼   cup cold water

1. Rub roast with garlic and pepper; place in a 3-qt. slow cooker. Mix the soy sauce, balsamic vinegar, Worcestershire sauce and mustard; pour over roast. Cook, covered, on low until the roast is tender, 3½ to 4 hours.
2. Remove roast; keep warm. Strain the cooking juices into a small saucepan; skim the fat. Mix cornstarch and water until smooth; stir into cooking juices. Bring to a boil; cook and stir gravy until thickened, 1-2 minutes. Cut roast into slices; serve with gravy.

Santa Belt Napkin Rings

Bright red napkins that resemble Santa's suit—how jolly! Just cinch them up with handcrafted napkin rings made from black ribbon and gold glitter card stock. To make each ring, punch or cut a square from the card stock. Using a pencil, mark two vertical lines in the center that are as long as the width of the ribbon. Use a craft knife to cut the slits, then thread the ribbon through the slits and tie it around a napkin.

SIRLOIN ROAST WITH GRAVY

CARAMEL PRALINE-TOPPED CHEESECAKE

Cheesecake can be stunning with a pretty wafer crust, creamy center and gooey caramel-pecan topping cascading down the sides. This is one for the keeper files.
—Laurel Leslie, Sonora, CA

Prep: 30 min. • **Bake:** 55 min. + chilling
Makes: 12 servings

- 1½ cups crushed vanilla wafers (about 45 wafers)
- ¼ cup sugar
- ¼ cup butter, melted
- 16 whole vanilla wafers

FILLING
- 3 pkg. (8 oz. each) cream cheese, softened
- 1 cup sugar
- ½ cup sour cream
- 1 tsp. vanilla extract
- 3 large eggs, lightly beaten

TOPPING
- 25 caramels
- 2 Tbsp. milk
- ½ cup chopped pecans, toasted

1. Preheat oven to 325°. Mix crushed wafers and sugar; stir in melted butter. Press onto bottom of a greased 9-in. springform pan. Arrange vanilla wafers around sides of pan, rounded sides out, pressing gently into crust.
2. In a large bowl, beat the cream cheese and sugar until smooth. Beat in sour cream and vanilla. Add eggs; beat on low speed just until blended. Pour over crust. Place pan on a baking sheet.
3. Bake until center is almost set, 55-60 minutes. Cool on a wire rack 1 hour. Refrigerate overnight, covering when completely cooled.
4. Remove rim from pan. In a microwave, melt caramels with milk; stir until smooth. Drizzle caramel over cheesecake; sprinkle with pecans.

Freeze option: Wrap individual portions of cheesecake in plastic wrap and place in a resealable plastic freezer bag. Seal bag and freeze. To use, thaw in the refrigerator.

Note: To toast nuts, bake in a shallow pan in a 350° oven for 5-10 minutes or cook in a skillet over low heat until lightly browned, stirring occasionally.

"My grandmother served this sweet potato casserole at Thanksgiving. The puffy marshmallow topping gives the dish a festive look, and traditional spices enhance the flavor."

—EDNA HOFFMAN, HEBRON, IN

MALLOW-TOPPED SWEET POTATOES

Prep: 40 min. • **Bake:** 45 min.
Makes: 12 servings

- 4 lbs. sweet potatoes (about 5 large), peeled and cut into 1-in. pieces
- 1 cup 2% milk
- 6 Tbsp. butter, softened
- ½ cup packed brown sugar
- 1 large egg
- 1½ tsp. ground cinnamon
- 1½ tsp. vanilla extract
- ¾ tsp. ground allspice
- ½ tsp. salt
- ¼ tsp. ground nutmeg
- 10 large marshmallows, halved lengthwise

1. Preheat oven to 350°. Place sweet potatoes in a 6-qt. stockpot; add water to cover. Bring to a boil. Reduce heat; cook, uncovered, until tender, 15-20 minutes. Drain potatoes; place in a large bowl.
2. Beat the potatoes until smooth. Add next nine ingredients; beat until blended.
3. Spread into a greased shallow 2½-qt. baking dish. Bake, uncovered, until heated through, 40-45 minutes. Increase oven setting to 425°.
4. Top casserole with marshmallows. Bake until marshmallows are lightly browned, 3-4 minutes.

TEST KITCHEN TIP

Sweet Potato Secrets

When purchasing sweet potatoes, select those that are firm with no cracks or bruises. If stored in a cool, dark, well-ventilated place, they will remain fresh about 2 weeks. If the temperature is above 60°, they'll sprout sooner or become woody. Once cooked, sweet potatoes can be stored up to 1 week in the refrigerator.

CHAMPAGNE-BASTED TURKEY

I prepare this turkey every Thanksgiving. I recommend it for Christmas and other holidays, too. The secret is to use lots of fresh sage and parsley and to keep basting. The result is a tender, flavorful bird.
—Sharon Hawk, Edwardsville, IL

Prep: 20 min. • **Bake:** 3 hours + standing
Makes: 16 servings (1⅔ cups gravy)

- ¼ cup butter, softened
- 1 tsp. salt
- 1 tsp. celery salt
- ¾ tsp. pepper
- 1 turkey (14 to 16 lbs.)
  Fresh sage and parsley sprigs, optional
- 2 medium onions, chopped
- 1½ cups minced fresh parsley
- ½ tsp. dried marjoram
- ½ tsp. dried thyme
- 2 cups champagne or other sparkling wine
- 1 cup condensed beef consomme, undiluted
- 1 Tbsp. butter
- 1 Tbsp. all-purpose flour

1. Preheat oven to 325°. Mix first four ingredients. Place turkey on a rack in a roasting pan, breast side up; pat dry. Rub butter mixture over outside and inside of turkey. If desired, place sage and parsley sprigs in cavity. Tuck wings under turkey; tie drumsticks together.
2. Roast, uncovered, 30 minutes. Toss onions with parsley, marjoram and thyme; add to roasting pan. Pour in champagne and consomme. Roast, uncovered, until a thermometer inserted in thickest part of thigh reads 170°-175°, 2½ -3 hours, basting occasionally with the pan juices. (Cover loosely with foil if turkey browns too quickly.)
3. Remove turkey from oven; tent with foil. Let stand 20 minutes before carving.
4. Meanwhile, strain pan juices into a bowl. In a small saucepan, melt butter. Stir in flour until smooth; gradually add strained juices. Bring to a boil; cook and stir until thickened, 1-2 minutes. Serve with turkey.

CRANBERRY GLAZED HAM

That showstopping entree you've been hoping for is right here, and it only takes five ingredients to make. The sweet and tangy cranberry glaze pairs beautifully with succulent ham.
—Joni Peterson, Wichita, KS

Prep: 5 min. • **Bake:** 1 hour 35 min.
Makes: 16 servings

- 1 boneless fully cooked ham (5 lbs.)
- 1 can (14 oz.) whole-berry cranberry sauce
- ½ cup maple syrup
- ¼ cup cider vinegar
- 1 to 1½ tsp. ground mustard

1. Preheat oven to 325°. Line a roasting pan with foil. Place the ham on a rack in prepared pan. Bake, covered, 1 hour.
2. Meanwhile, in a small saucepan, whisk the remaining ingredients until blended. Remove 1 cup mixture for glaze; reserve remaining mixture for sauce. Brush ham with some of the glaze mixture. Bake, uncovered, until a thermometer reads 140°, 35-45 minutes, brushing every 10 minutes with remaining glaze.
3. Warm reserved sauce mixture over medium heat, stirring occasionally; serve with ham.

7-LAYER
GELATIN SALAD

Ingredients (Mocha Yule Log)

5 large eggs, separated
½ cup cake flour
¼ cup baking cocoa
¼ tsp. salt
1 cup sugar, divided
½ tsp. cream of tartar

FILLING

1½ tsp. instant coffee granules
1 cup heavy whipping cream
½ cup confectioners' sugar

FROSTING

⅓ cup butter, softened
2 cups confectioners' sugar
⅓ cup baking cocoa
1 Tbsp. brewed coffee, cooled
1½ tsp. vanilla extract
2 to 3 Tbsp. 2% milk

1. Place egg whites in a small bowl; let stand at room temperature 30 minutes.
2. Meanwhile, preheat oven to 350°. Line bottom of a greased 15x10x1-in. pan with parchment paper; grease paper. Sift flour, cocoa and salt together twice. In a large bowl, beat the egg yolks until slightly thickened. Gradually add ½ cup sugar, beating on high speed until thick and lemon-colored. Fold in flour mixture.
3. Add cream of tartar to egg whites; with clean beaters, beat on medium until soft peaks form. Gradually add remaining sugar, 1 Tbsp. at a time, beating on high after each addition until sugar is dissolved. Continue beating until soft glossy peaks form. Fold a fourth of the whites into the batter, then fold in remaining egg whites. Transfer the batter to prepared pan, spreading evenly.
4. Bake until top springs back when lightly touched, 12-15 minutes (do not overbake). Cool 5 minutes. Invert onto a tea towel dusted lightly with cocoa. Gently peel off paper. Roll up cake in the towel jelly-roll style, starting with a short side. Cool cake completely on a wire rack.
5. For filling, in a bowl, dissolve coffee granules in cream; beat until it begins to thicken. Add sugar; beat until stiff peaks form. Unroll cake; spread filling over cake to within ½ in. of the edges. Roll up again, without towel; trim ends. Transfer to a platter, seam side down. Refrigerate cake, covered, until cold.
6. For frosting, beat all ingredients until smooth. Spread over cake. Using a fork, make lines in frosting to resemble tree bark. Refrigerate until serving.

7-LAYER GELATIN SALAD

My mother makes this colorful gelatin salad to accompany our Christmas dinner each year. Choose different flavors to create special color combinations for particular holidays or gatherings.
—Jan Hemness, Stockton, MO

Prep: 30 min. + chilling • **Makes:** 20 servings

4½ cups boiling water, divided
7 pkg. (3 oz. each) assorted flavored gelatin
4½ cups cold water, divided
1 can (12 oz.) evaporated milk, divided
1 carton (8 oz.) frozen whipped topping, thawed
Sliced strawberries and kiwifruit, optional

1. In a small bowl, add ¾ cup boiling water to one gelatin package; stir 2 minutes to completely dissolve. Stir in ¾ cup cold water. Pour into a 3-qt. trifle or glass bowl. Refrigerate until gelatin is set but not firm, about 40 minutes.
2. In a clean bowl, dissolve another gelatin package into ½ cup boiling water. Stir in ½ cup cold water and ½ cup milk. Spoon over the first layer. Refrigerate until gelatin is set but not firm.
3. Repeat five times, alternating plain and creamy gelatin layers. Refrigerate each layer until set but not firm before adding the next layer. Refrigerate layered gelatin, covered, overnight. Serve with whipped topping and, if desired, fruit.
Note: Recipe may also be prepared in a 13x9-in. dish coated with cooking spray; follow recipe as directed. Cut into squares before serving.

MOCHA YULE LOG

This dessert is guaranteed to delight your holiday guests, especially chocolate lovers, with its yummy cocoa cake, mocha filling and frosting. I garnish it with marzipan holly leaves and berries, but you can also top it with shaved chocolate and a light dusting of confectioners' sugar.
—Jenny Hughson, Mitchell, NE

Prep: 65 min. + chilling
Bake: 15 min. + cooling
Makes: 12 servings

Seasonal Surf & Turf

The presents are wrapped, the cookies are baked, and the lights on the tree are twinkling with a warm glow. Christmas is the time to break out your most impressive recipes and prepare a feast fit for the season. If you're looking for something elegant, try this menu's classic pairing of land and sea. Accompanied by succulent sides and a gorgeous dessert, this will be your most memorable holiday yet.

Rosemary Garlic Shrimp (p. 22) **Gruyere Mashed Potatoes** (p. 24) **Seasoned Ribeye Roast** (p. 24)

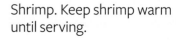

Christmas Countdown

The fresh-baked aroma of **sweet, warm cookies** set out for St. Nick. **Kids hanging their stockings** with delightful anticipation. These merry sights can only mean one thing— **Christmas is here!** Let your holiday season shine brighter than ever with these festive and flavorful ideas. Turn to this handy guide to help plan your feast from start to finish.

A FEW WEEKS BEFORE

☐ Prepare two grocery lists—one for nonperishable items to buy now and one for perishable items to buy a few days before Christmas.

TWO DAYS BEFORE

☐ Buy remaining grocery items.

☐ Prepare the jalapeno vodka for the Pomegranate Cocktail. Cover and refrigerate vodka for 2-3 days.

☐ Prepare the dressing for the Lemon Artichoke Romaine Salad. Refrigerate.

☐ Bake the cake layers for the Black Walnut Layer Cake. Freeze or store in an airtight container.

☐ Bake the Dinner Rolls. Freeze or store in an airtight container.

☐ Bake the Blue Cheese Thins. Store in an airtight container.

☐ Wash china, stemware and table linens.

THE DAY BEFORE

☐ Prepare the Greek Olive Tapenade. Cover tapenade and refrigerate.

☐ Prepare the Parsnip & Celery Root Bisque. Allow to cool completely and do not add garnishes. Cover the bisque and refrigerate.

☐ Prepare the Peppermint Patty Cream Pie. Cover and refrigerate until ready to serve.

☐ Set the table.

CHRISTMAS DAY

☐ About 3-4 hours before dinner, remove the Dinner Rolls and Black Walnut Cake layers from the freezer to thaw.

☐ About 3-4 hours before dinner, prepare the Gruyere Mashed Potatoes. Allow to cool. Cover and refrigerate.

☐ About 2 hours before dinner, prepare and bake the Seasoned Ribeye Roast. Keep warm until serving.

☐ About 45 minutes before dinner, prepare and broil lobster tails. Keep warm until serving.

☐ About 30 minutes before dinner, prepare the Bacon-Wrapped Figs, Vegetable Brown Rice, and Bacon-Onion Green Beans. Keep dishes warm until serving.

☐ About 20 minutes before dinner, prepare the Rosemary Garlic Shrimp. Keep shrimp warm until serving.

RIGHT BEFORE DINNER

☐ As guests arrive, prepare the Pomegranate Cocktails using the chilled jalapeno vodka.

☐ As guests arrive, toast baguette slices in the oven. Serve with Greek Olive Tapenade.

☐ Frost the Black Walnut Layer cake. If desired, garnish with additional walnuts and orange slices. Remove pie from the refrigerator.

☐ Remove the salad dressing for the Lemon Artichoke Romaine Salad from the refrigerator and shake well. Prepare salad and toss with dressing. Sprinkle the salad with cheese.

☐ Remove mashed potatoes from the refrigerator and warm in the oven just before serving.

☐ Remove the bisque from the refrigerator and warm on the stovetop. Sprinkle with chives and pomegranate seeds just before serving.

☐ Warm dinner rolls in the oven just before serving.

BLUE CHEESE THINS

I grew up in the South with cheese straws at most potlucks and meals. These use blue cheese for a bit of twist. They are wonderful to munch before the meal. They can also be crumbled and added to soups or salads.
—Kim Fabrizio, Burien, WA

Prep: 15 min. + chilling
Bake: 15 min./batch + cooling
Makes: about 3 dozen

- 1¼ cups crumbled blue cheese
- ½ cup butter, softened
- 1½ cups all-purpose flour
- 3 tsp. poppy seeds
- ½ tsp. salt
- ½ tsp. garlic powder
- 3 to 6 tsp. water

1. In a large bowl, beat blue cheese and butter until blended. Whisk together the flour, poppy seeds, salt and garlic powder; gradually beat into the creamed mixture. Gradually stir in enough water to form a soft dough.
2. Divide dough in half; shape each into a 5½-in. long roll. Wrap in plastic; refrigerate until firm, about 1 hour.
3. Preheat oven to 350°. Unwrap and cut dough into ¼-in. slices. Place 2 in. apart on parchment paper-lined baking sheets. Bake until edges are lightly browned, 13-15 minutes. Remove from pans to wire racks to cool.

POMEGRANATE
COCKTAIL

POMEGRANATE COCKTAIL

This spicy and sweet sipper gives you a little fix of jalapeno flavor minus the heat. Start a couple of days ahead to flavor the vodka.
—Melissa Rodriguez, Van Nuys, CA

Prep: 10 min. + chilling • **Makes:** 8 servings

- 2 jalapeno peppers, halved lengthwise and seeded
- 1½ cups vodka
- 6 to 8 cups ice cubes
- 3 cups pomegranate juice
- 3 cups Italian blood orange soda, chilled
  Lime wedges

1. For jalapeno vodka, place jalapenos and vodka in a glass jar or container. Refrigerate, covered, 2-3 days to allow flavors to blend. Strain before using.
2. For each serving, fill cocktail shaker three-fourths full with ice. Add 3 oz. pomegranate juice and 1½ oz. jalapeno vodka; cover and shake until condensation forms on outside of shaker, 10-15 seconds. Strain into a cocktail glass; top with 3 oz. soda. Serve with lime wedges.

BACON-WRAPPED FIGS

This is the first bacon-wrapped fig recipe I made. I like that the figs and walnuts have very similar nutritional values, making this recipe a high energy appetizer or snack.
—Shelly Bevington, Hermiston, OR

Takes: 30 min. • **Makes:** 2 dozen

- 24 dried figs, trimmed
- 24 walnut halves
- 12 bacon strips, halved crosswise
- ⅓ cup grated Parmesan cheese

1. Preheat oven to 375°. Cut a slit lengthwise down the center of each fig; fill each with a walnut half.
2. In a large skillet, cook bacon over medium heat until partially cooked but not crisp. Drain on paper towels.
3. Place cheese in a shallow bowl. Dip one side of bacon in cheese. Wrap each bacon strip around a stuffed fig, cheese side out; secure with a toothpick. Place on an ungreased 15x10x1-in. baking pan.
4. Bake until bacon is crisp, 12-15 minutes, turning once.

GREEK OLIVE TAPENADE

PARSNIP & CELERY ROOT BISQUE

With its smooth texture and earthy vegetable flavors, this simple yet elegant soup makes a tempting first course. Try chives and pomegranate seeds on top.
—Merry Graham, Newhall, CA

Prep: 25 min. • **Cook:** 45 min.
Makes: 8 servings (2 qt.)

- 2 Tbsp. olive oil
- 2 medium leeks (white portion only), chopped (about 2 cups)
- 1½ lbs. parsnips, peeled and chopped (about 4 cups)
- 1 medium celery root, peeled and cubed (about 1½ cups)
- 4 garlic cloves, minced
- 6 cups chicken stock
- 1½ tsp. salt
- ¾ tsp. coarsely ground pepper
- 1 cup heavy whipping cream
- 2 Tbsp. minced fresh parsley
- 2 tsp. lemon juice
- 2 Tbsp. minced fresh chives
  Pomegranate seeds, optional

1. In a large saucepan, heat the oil over medium-high heat; saute leeks 3 minutes. Add parsnips and celery root; cook and stir 4 minutes. Add garlic; cook and stir 1 minute. Stir in stock, salt and pepper; bring to a boil. Reduce heat; simmer, covered, until the vegetables are tender, 25-30 minutes.

2. Puree using an immersion blender. Or, cool slightly and puree in batches in a blender; return to pan. Stir in cream, parsley and lemon juice; heat through. Serve with minced chives and, if desired, pomegranate seeds.

DID YOU KNOW?

Bisque Basics

Bisque is a thick, rich soup that usually consists of pureed seafood and cream, but it may also be made with poultry, vegetables or rice. This recipe does not contain any seafood or meat, but it does contain chicken stock, so it may not be suitable for vegetarians. Bisque is quicker to make than most traditional soups because it doesn't have to simmer for hours.

LEMON ARTICHOKE ROMAINE SALAD

I created this when I was trying to duplicate a lemony Caesar salad. This version is not only delicious but healthy, too.
—Kathy Armstrong, Post Falls, ID

Takes: 15 min. • **Makes:** 8 servings

- 10 cups torn romaine
- 4 plum tomatoes, sliced
- 1 can (14 oz.) water-packed quartered artichoke hearts, rinsed and drained
- 1 can (2¼ oz.) sliced ripe olives, drained
- 3 Tbsp. water
- 3 Tbsp. lemon juice
- 3 Tbsp. olive oil
- 2 garlic cloves, minced
- 1 tsp. salt
- 1 tsp. coarsely ground pepper
- ⅓ cup shredded Parmesan cheese

1. Place first four ingredients in a large bowl. Place all remaining ingredients except cheese in a jar with a tight-fitting lid; shake well. Pour over salad; toss to coat.

2. Sprinkle salad with Parmesan cheese. Serve immediately.

GREEK OLIVE TAPENADE

Welcome to an olive lover's dream. Mix freshly minced garlic and parsley, add a few drizzles of quality olive oil, and you've got the ultimate in Mediterranean bliss.
—Lisa Sojka, Rockport, ME

Takes: 25 min.
Makes: 16 servings (2 Tbsp. each)

- 2 cups pitted Greek olives, drained
- 3 garlic cloves, minced
- 3 Tbsp. olive oil
- 1½ tsp. minced fresh parsley
  Toasted baguette slices

In a food processor, pulse olives with garlic until finely chopped. Add oil and parsley; pulse until combined. Serve with toasted baguette slices.

PARSNIP & CELERY
ROOT BISQUE

ROSEMARY GARLIC SHRIMP

Delicate shrimp take on fabulous flavor when simmered in chicken broth mixed with garlic and ripe olives.
—*Taste of Home* Test Kitchen

Takes: 20 min. • **Makes:** 8 servings

- 1¼ cups chicken or vegetable broth
- 3 Tbsp. chopped ripe olives
- 1 small cayenne or other fresh red chili pepper, finely chopped
- 2 Tbsp. lemon juice
- 1 Tbsp. minced fresh rosemary or 1 tsp. dried rosemary, crushed
- 4 garlic cloves, minced
- 2 tsp. Worcestershire sauce
- 1 tsp. paprika
- ½ tsp. salt
- ¼ to ½ tsp. pepper
- 2 lbs. uncooked shrimp (31-40 per lb.), peeled and deveined

1. In a large skillet, combine ingredients except shrimp; bring to a boil. Cook, uncovered, until liquid is reduced by half.
2. Stir in shrimp; return just to a boil. Reduce heat; simmer, uncovered, until shrimp turns pink, 3-4 minutes, stirring occasionally.

ROSEMARY GARLIC SHRIMP

DINNER ROLLS

My family loves the fragrance of these homemade rolls as they bake. We all look forward to them at every special meal.
—Anna Baker, Blaine, WA

Prep: 30 min. + rising • **Bake:** 20 min.
Makes: 2 dozen

- 2 pkg. (¼ oz. each) active dry yeast
- ½ cup warm water (110° to 115°)
- 1¼ cups warm 2% milk (110° to 115°)
- ½ cup butter, softened
- 2 large eggs
- ⅓ cup sugar
- 1½ tsp. salt
- 6 to 6½ cups all-purpose flour
  Melted butter, optional

1. In a small bowl, dissolve yeast in warm water. In a large bowl, combine the milk, softened butter, eggs, sugar, salt, yeast mixture and 3 cups flour; beat on medium speed until smooth. Stir in enough of the remaining flour to form a soft dough.
2. Turn the dough onto a floured surface; knead until smooth and elastic, about 6-8 minutes. Place in a greased bowl, turning once to grease the top. Cover with plastic wrap; let dough rise in a warm place until doubled, about 1 hour.
3. Punch down dough. Turn onto a lightly floured surface; divide in half. Divide and shape each portion into 12 balls. Place rolls in two greased 13x9-in. baking pans. Cover with clean kitchen towels; let rise in a warm place until doubled, about 30 minutes. Preheat oven to 375°.
4. Bake until golden brown, for 20-25 minutes. If desired, brush tops lightly with melted butter. Cool on wire racks. Serve rolls warm.

VEGETABLE BROWN RICE

Loaded with carrots, onions and peas, this rice makes a terrific side dish, but it can also stand on its own as a light main course. Raisins offer a slight sweetness, and pecans add a little crunch.
—Denith Hull, Bethany, OK

Prep: 10 min. • **Cook:** 30 min.
Makes: 8 servings

- 2 cups water
- 1 cup uncooked brown rice
- ½ tsp. dried basil
- 2 medium carrots, cut into matchsticks
- 1 medium onion, chopped
- 8 green onions, cut into 1-in. pieces
- ½ cup raisins
- 2 Tbsp. olive oil
- 2½ cups frozen peas (about 10 oz.)
- 1 tsp. salt
- 1 cup pecan halves, toasted

1. In a small saucepan, bring water to a boil; stir in rice and basil. Return to a boil. Reduce heat; simmer, covered, until the liquid is absorbed and rice is tender, for 30-35 minutes.
2. In a large skillet, heat oil over medium-high heat; saute carrots, onions and raisins until vegetables are lightly browned and carrots are crisp-tender, lightly browned, for 5-7 minutes. Add peas and salt; heat through. Stir in pecans and rice.
Note: To toast nuts, bake in a shallow pan in a 350° oven for 5-10 minutes or cook in a skillet over low heat until lightly browned, stirring occasionally.

GRUYERE MASHED POTATOES

GRUYERE MASHED POTATOES

Gruyere cheese and chives take mashed potatoes to a whole new level. Don't have chives? Just use extra green onion instead.
—Preci D'Silva, Dubai, United Arab Emirates

Takes: 25 min. • **Makes:** 8 servings

- 2 lbs. potatoes, peeled and cubed
- ¼ cup butter, cubed
- ½ cup sour cream
- ⅓ cup 2% milk, warmed
- 1 garlic clove, minced
- ¼ cup shredded Gruyere or Swiss cheese
- ¼ cup minced fresh chives
- 2 green onions, chopped
- ½ tsp. garlic salt
- ¼ tsp. pepper

1. Place potatoes in a 6-qt. stockpot; add water to cover. Bring to a boil. Reduce the heat; cover, uncovered, until potatoes are tender, 10-15 minutes.
2. Drain; return to pot. Mash potatoes, gradually adding sour cream, milk and garlic. Stir in remaining ingredients.

BACON-ONION GREEN BEANS

I threw together the recipe to give some color to the plate. I knew all the relatives liked green beans, so I added onion, bacon, toasted sesame seeds and a little vinegar for a nice tang.
—Karen Darrell, Wood River, IL

Takes: 25 min. • **Makes:** 8 servings

- 6 bacon strips, chopped
- 1 medium onion, chopped
- 2 Tbsp. cider vinegar
- ¼ tsp. salt
- ⅛ tsp. pepper
- 1½ lbs. fresh green beans, trimmed
- 1 Tbsp. sesame seeds, toasted

1. In a large skillet, cook chopped bacon over medium heat until crisp, stirring occasionally. Remove with slotted spoon; drain on paper towels. Pour off all but 1 Tbsp. drippings. Saute onion in drippings until tender. Stir in vinegar, salt and pepper.
2. Meanwhile, place the beans in a large saucepan; add water to cover. Bring to a boil. Cook, covered, until crisp-tender, 4-7 minutes; drain.
3. Place beans in a large bowl; toss with bacon and onion mixture. Sprinkle with sesame seeds.

BROILED LOBSTER TAIL

No matter where you live, these succulent, buttery lobster tails are just a few minutes away. Here in Wisconsin, we use frozen lobster with delicious results, but if you're near the ocean, by all means, use fresh!
—Lauren Knoelke, Milwaukee, WI

Prep: 30 min. • **Cook:** 5 min.
Makes: 4 servings

- 4 lobster tails (5 to 6 oz. each), thawed
- ¼ cup cold butter, cut into thin slices
  Salt and pepper to taste
  Lemon wedges

1. Preheat broiler. Using kitchen scissors, cut a 2-in.-wide rectangle from the top shell of each lobster tail; loosen from lobster meat and remove.
2. Pull away edges of remaining shell to release lobster meat from sides; pry meat loose from bottom shell, keeping tail end attached. Place in a foil-lined 15x10x1-in. pan. Arrange butter slices on lobster meat.
3. Broil 5-6 in. from heat until the meat is opaque, 5-8 minutes. Season with salt and pepper to taste; serve with lemon wedges.

SEASONED RIBEYE ROAST

This is an especially savory way to prepare a boneless beef roast. Gravy made from the drippings is exceptional.
—Evelyn Gebhardt, Kasilof, AK

Prep: 10 min. • **Bake:** 1¾ hours + standing
Makes: 8 servings

- 1½ tsp. lemon-pepper seasoning
- 1½ tsp. paprika
- ¾ tsp. garlic salt
- ½ tsp. dried rosemary, crushed
- ¼ tsp. cayenne pepper
- 1 beef ribeye roast (3 to 4 lbs.)

1. Preheat oven to 350°. Mix seasonings. Place roast on a rack in a roasting pan, fat side up; rub with seasonings.
2. Roast, uncovered, until meat reaches desired doneness (for medium-rare, a thermometer should read 135°; medium, 140°), 1½-2 hours. Remove from oven; tent with foil. Let stand 10 minutes before slicing roast.

SEASONED
RIBEYE ROAST

PEPPERMINT PATTY CREAM PIE

This dreamy chocolate cream pie with a touch of refreshing peppermint is the perfect way to cleanse the palate after a large meal. I first made this many years ago, not long after I got married. It was a winner then and is a winner now!
—Susan Simons, Eatonville, WA

Prep: 45 min. + chilling
Cook: 25 min. + cooling
Makes: 8 servings

Pastry for single-crust pie (9 in.), baked
2 oz. unsweetened chocolate, chopped
8 miniature chocolate-covered peppermint patties, unwrapped (about 4 oz.)
2 Tbsp. hot water
3 large eggs
¼ cup sugar
½ cup butter, softened
1 cup heavy whipping cream
Chocolate curls

1. On a lightly floured surface, roll pastry dough to a ⅛-in.-thick circle; transfer to a 9-in. pie plate. Trim pastry to ½ in. beyond rim of plate; flute edge. Refrigerate crust for 30 minutes. Preheat oven to 425°.
2. Line pastry with a double thickness of foil. Fill with pie weights, dried beans or uncooked rice. Bake on a lower oven rack until edges are golden brown, for 20-25 minutes. Remove foil and weights; bake until bottom is golden brown, 3-6 minutes. Cool completely on a wire rack.
3. In a small heavy saucepan, melt the unsweetened chocolate and peppermint patties over low heat, stirring constantly (mixture will be thick). Remove from heat; stir in hot water until smooth. Remove to a bowl; cool.
4. Meanwhile, in a clean heavy saucepan, whisk together the eggs and sugar. Cook and stir mixture gently over low heat until a thermometer reads 160°, 12-14 minutes. Do not allow to boil. Immediately transfer to a bowl; cool about 10 minutes, stirring occasionally.
5. In a large bowl, beat butter until light and fluffy. Add cooled chocolate and egg mixtures; beat on high speed until light and fluffy, about 5 minutes.
6. In a small bowl, beat cream until soft peaks form. Fold into chocolate mixture. Spoon into crust. Refrigerate, covered, until set, about 2 hours. Top with the chocolate curls.

Note: Let pie weights cool completely before storing. Beans and rice may be reused for pie weights, not cooking.

Pastry for single-crust pie (9 in.): Combine 1¼ cups all-purpose flour and ¼ tsp. salt; cut in ½ cup cold butter until crumbly. Gradually add 3-5 Tbsp. ice water, tossing with a fork until the dough holds together when pressed. Wrap in plastic and refrigerate for 1 hour.

TEST KITCHEN TIP

Secrets to Successful Pie Pastry

If you like to make your own homemade pie pastry, follow these pointers for creating a crust that bakes up flaky and golden.

- Measure ingredients accurately. Use all-purpose or pastry flour for pie crusts. Bread or cake flour will not give the desired texture.
- Combine the flour and salt thoroughly before adding the butter (or shortening) and water.
- The key to a flaky crust is not to overmix when adding the water. Overmixing causes gluten to develop, making pastry tough.
- A floured surface is essential to prevent sticking when rolling out pastry. A floured pastry cloth and rolling pin will keep the pastry from sticking and minimize the amount of flour used.
- Choose dull-finish aluminum or glass pie plates for crisp crusts. Shiny pans can produce soggy pie crusts.
- Arrange the oven racks so the pie bakes in the center of the oven.

BLACK WALNUT LAYER CAKE

BLACK WALNUT LAYER CAKE

My sister gave me the recipe for this lovely cake years ago. The thin layer of cream cheese frosting spread on the outside gives it a beautiful modern look. Garnish with additional black walnuts and orange slices if you like.
—Lynn Glaze, Warren, OH

Prep: 25 min. • **Bake:** 20 min. + cooling
Makes: 16 servings

- ½ cup butter, softened
- ½ cup shortening
- 2 cups sugar
- 2 tsp. vanilla extract
- 4 large eggs
- 3¾ cups all-purpose flour
- 2 tsp. baking soda
- ½ tsp. salt
- 1½ cups buttermilk
- 1¼ cups finely chopped black or English walnuts

FROSTING
- ½ cup butter, softened
- 1 pkg. (8 oz.) cream cheese, softened
- 1 tsp. vanilla extract
- 4½ cups confectioners' sugar
- 1 to 3 Tbsp. buttermilk
  Additional black walnuts

1. Preheat oven to 350°. Line bottoms of three greased 9-in. round baking pans with parchment paper; grease paper.
2. Cream butter, shortening and sugar until light and fluffy. Add vanilla and eggs, one at a time, beating well after each addition. In another bowl, whisk together flour, baking soda and salt; add to creamed mixture alternately with the buttermilk, beating after each addition. Fold in the chopped walnuts.
3. Transfer to prepared pans. Bake until a toothpick inserted in center comes out clean, 20-25 minutes. Cool in pans about 10 minutes before removing cakes to wire racks; remove paper. Cool completely.
4. For frosting, beat the butter and cream cheese until smooth. Beat in the vanilla. Gradually beat in confectioners' sugar and enough buttermilk to reach a spreading consistency.
5. Spread 1 cup frosting between each cake layer. Spread the top of cake with an additional 1 cup frosting. Spread remaining frosting in a thin layer over the sides of the cake. Top with additional walnuts.

Ugly Sweater Party

The ugly Christmas sweater would be nothing more than a piece of bad fashion without the ugly Christmas sweater party. Join the holiday craze by hosting an epic event that's nothing short of big, bold and tacky. This delectable assortment of appetizers and drinks will round out the hideously fun and festive merrymaking.

Apple-Gouda Pigs in a Blanket (p. 32) **Cranberry Party Punch** (p. 32) **Ugly Sweater Cookies** (p. 39)

PHILLY CHEESESTEAK WONTON CUPS

I love the versatility of wonton wrappers. You can fill them with any mix of flavors or ingredients to suit your tastes. The first batch I tried used a Mexican-inspired filling, which was delicious. These wonton cups are a spinoff on Philly cheesesteak, one of my favorite sandwiches.
—Cynthia Gerken, Naples, FL

Prep: 30 min. • **Cook:** 15 min./batch
Makes: 3 dozen

- 36 wonton wrappers
- 2 tsp. canola oil
- 1 large onion, chopped
- 1 medium green pepper, chopped
- 1 lb. sliced deli roast beef, cut into ¾-in. pieces
- ¼ cup Worcestershire sauce
- 3 tsp. Montreal steak seasoning
- ¼ tsp. pepper
- 2 cups shredded provolone cheese
  Chopped pepperoncini and steak sauce, optional

1. Preheat oven to 375°. Press wonton wrappers in greased muffin cups. Bake until golden brown, 4-5 minutes.
2. Meanwhile, in a skillet, heat oil over medium-high heat; saute onion and green pepper until tender, 3-5 minutes. Remove from pan.
3. Toss beef with Worcestershire sauce, steak seasoning and pepper. In the same pan, cook and stir the beef mixture over medium heat until heated through, about 5 minutes. Place about 2 Tbsp. of the beef mixture in each cup; sprinkle each with a scant 1 Tbsp. cheese.
4. Bake cups until heated through, 8-10 minutes. Serve immediately. If desired, top with chopped pepperoncini and serve with steak sauce.

PHILLY CHEESESTEAK WONTON CUPS

PEPPERMINT PATTY HOT COCOA

A hint of cool mint makes this rich sipper a nice change of pace from traditional hot cocoa. Add a dollop of whipped cream and crushed peppermint candies or try one of the homemade whipped creams below.
—Sue Gronholz, Beaver Dam, WI

Takes: 20 min.
Makes: 12 servings (¾ cup each)

1½ cups hot water
1 cup sugar
½ cup baking cocoa
⅛ tsp. salt
9 cups 2% milk
1 cup peppermint schnapps liqueur
   or ¾ tsp. peppermint extract
   with additional 1 cup milk
   Whipped cream and crushed
   peppermint candies

1. In a large saucepan, combine water, sugar, cocoa and salt; bring to a boil over medium heat, stirring constantly. Cook and stir 2 minutes. Add milk; heat through, stirring constantly.
2. Remove from heat; add liqueur. Cook and stir over medium heat until heated through. Top servings with whipped cream and peppermint candies.

RUBY-RED PRETZEL DIP

Plain pretzels get a pretty coating and tangy taste from this thick festive blend.
—Grace Yaskovic, Lake Hiawatha, NJ

Prep: 5 min. • **Cook:** 10 min. + chilling
Makes: 16 servings (2 Tbsp. each)

1 can (14 oz.) jellied cranberry sauce
¾ cup sugar
¼ cup vinegar
1 tsp. ground ginger
1 tsp. ground mustard
¼ tsp. ground cinnamon
⅛ tsp. pepper
1 Tbsp. all-purpose flour
1 Tbsp. cold water
   Red food coloring, optional
   Pretzels

1. Place first seven ingredients in a saucepan; heat through over medium heat, whisking until blended. In a small bowl, mix flour and cold water until smooth; stir into cranberry mixture. Bring to a boil; cook and stir 2 minutes. If desired, tint with food coloring.
2. Remove dip to a bowl; cool slightly. Refrigerate, covered, overnight. Serve with pretzels.

TEST KITCHEN TIP

Homemade Flavored Whipped Cream

What better way to chase away chills on a cold winter day than to cozy up with a steamy cup of hot cocoa? The sweet liquid indulgence gets even better when you top it with one of these flavored whipped creams.

- **Peppermint Whipped Cream**
  In a small bowl, beat ½ cup heavy whipping cream until it begins to thicken. Add 1 Tbsp. sugar and ⅛ tsp. peppermint extract; beat until stiff peaks form. Garnish with 1 Tbsp. crushed peppermint candies. Yield: 1 cup.

- **Irish Whipped Cream**
  In a small bowl, beat ½ heavy whipping cream and 1 Tbsp. Irish cream liqueur until stiff peaks form. Yield: 1 cup.

- **Chocolate Whipped Cream**
  In a small bowl, beat ½ cup heavy whipping cream until it begins to thicken. Add 2 Tbsp. chocolate syrup; beat until stiff peaks form. Garnish with grated chocolate if desired. Yield: 1 cup.

APPLE-GOUDA
PIGS IN A BLANKET

CRANBERRY PARTY PUNCH

Cranberry-filled ice cubes float atop this refreshing five-ingredient fruit punch. It is easy to stir up and serve right away.
—*Taste of Home* Test Kitchen

Prep: 20 min. + freezing • **Makes:** 20 servings (¾ cup each)

	Fresh or frozen cranberries
	Crushed ice
4	cups chilled cranberry juice
4	cups chilled pineapple juice
1½	cups sugar
1	Tbsp. almond extract
2	liters ginger ale, chilled

1. Line bottom of snowflake or other shaped molds with cranberries; top with crushed ice. Fill molds carefully with cold water; freeze until solid, about 2 hours.
2. To serve, combine juices, sugar and extract in a punch bowl; stir until sugar is dissolved. Stir in the ginger ale. Invert ice molds onto a large plate; cover with a hot damp cloth to release. Transfer to punch. Serve immediately.

APPLE-GOUDA PIGS IN A BLANKET

Beef and cheddar pigs in a blanket were my go-to New Year's Eve appetizer. I switched up the flavors to feature a fancier twist using apple slices and Gouda cheese.
—Megan Weiss, Menomonie, WI

Takes: 30 min. • **Makes:** 2 dozen

1	tube (8 oz.) refrigerated crescent rolls
1	small apple, peeled and cut into 24 thin slices
6	thin slices Gouda cheese, quartered
24	miniature smoked sausages
	Honey mustard salad dressing, optional

1. Preheat oven to 375°. Unroll crescent dough and separate into eight triangles; cut each piece lengthwise into three thin triangles. On the wide end of each triangle, place one slice apple, one folded piece cheese and one sausage; roll up tightly.
2. Place 1 in. apart on parchment paper-lined baking sheets, point side down. Bake until golden brown, 10-12 minutes. If desired, serve with dressing.

PARTY PITAS

My pita sandwiches make an appearance at every church luncheon or shower. They are easy and delicious and add a pop of color to the table.
—Janette Root, Ellensburg, WA

Takes: 15 min. • **Makes:** 16 pieces

1	pkg. (8 oz.) cream cheese, softened
½	cup mayonnaise
½	tsp. dill weed
¼	tsp. garlic salt
4	whole pita breads
1½	cups fresh baby spinach
1	lb. shaved fully cooked ham
½	lb. thinly sliced Monterey Jack cheese

1. Mix the first four ingredients. Carefully cut each pita horizontally in half; spread 2 Tbsp. mixture onto each cut surface.
2. On four pita halves, layer spinach, ham and cheese. Top with remaining halves. Cut each sandwich into four wedges; secure with toothpicks.

Pucker Up

Looking for a fun, inexpensive party favor? Create your own homemade lip balm. It makes a great stocking stuffer, too.

PEPPERMINT LIP BALM

Combine the following ingredients in a microwave-safe bowl: 1 Tbsp. shea butter, 1 Tbsp. beeswax pellets, 1 Tbsp. sweet almond oil and 4 drops food-grade peppermint essential oil. Heat in the microwave for 30 seconds or until completely melted. Using a clean dropper, fill empty lip balm tubes. Let cool completely. Adhere patterned paper to empty lip balm tubes.

CRANBERRY
PARTY PUNCH

THREE-CHEESE CRAB & ARTICHOKE DIP

This is my absolute favorite recipe for parties, potlucks and family events. Have plenty of bread and veggies for dipping or people will eat it up with a spoon.
—Jasmin Baron, Livonia, NY

Prep: 25 min. • **Bake:** 20 min.
Makes: 24 servings (¼ cup each)

- 2 cups sour cream
- 1 pkg. (8 oz.) cream cheese, softened
- ½ cup grated Parmesan cheese
- ½ cup mayonnaise
- ½ tsp. garlic powder
- ½ tsp. cayenne pepper
- ¼ tsp. pepper
- 1 can (14 oz.) water-packed artichoke hearts, rinsed, drained and coarsely chopped
- 2 cups shredded Monterey Jack cheese, divided
- 2 cups shredded sharp white cheddar cheese, divided
- 8 oz. fresh or frozen crabmeat, thawed
- 1¼ cups finely chopped green onions, divided
  Assorted fresh vegetables and toasted baguette slices

1. Preheat oven to 375°. In a large bowl, mix first seven ingredients. Stir in chopped artichokes, 1½ cups Jack cheese, 1½ cups cheddar cheese, crab and ¾ cup green onions. Transfer to a greased 13x9-in. baking dish. Sprinkle with the remaining Monterery Jack and cheddar cheeses.
2. Bake, uncovered, until edges are golden brown, 20-25 minutes. Sprinkle with the remaining green onions. Serve warm with vegetables and toasted baguette.

THREE-CHEESE CRAB & ARTICHOKE DIP

DATE-PECAN PIE BARS

I found this recipe many years ago in a magazine. The original called for walnuts, but I tweaked it to use our abundant Texas pecans. I make these for Christmas and other times throughout the year.
—Lillian Greenslade, Fort Worth, TX

Prep: 15 min. • **Bake:** 35 min. + cooling
Makes: 1½ dozen

- 1¼ cups all-purpose flour
- ⅓ cup sugar
- ½ cup cold unsalted butter, cubed

FILLING
- 2 large eggs
- ⅓ cup sugar
- ⅓ cup packed brown sugar
- 1 tsp. vanilla extract
- ½ tsp. salt
- ¼ tsp. ground nutmeg
- 2 Tbsp. all-purpose flour
- 1 tsp. baking powder
- 1 pkg. (8 oz.) pitted dates, chopped
- 1 cup chopped pecans, toasted
  Confectioners' sugar, optional

1. Preheat oven to 350°. In a large bowl, mix flour and sugar; cut in butter until crumbly. Press onto bottom of a greased 9-in. square baking pan. Bake until lightly browned, 15-20 minutes.
2. Meanwhile, in a large bowl, beat first six filling ingredients until just combined. Stir in flour and baking powder. Stir in dates and pecans. Pour over crust.
3. Bake until filling is set, 20-25 minutes. Cool completely on a wire rack. If desired, dust with confectioners' sugar. Cut into bars. Refrigerate leftovers.

SOUTHWEST ONION FRITTERS

These crispy, golden onion fritters are full of south of the border flavor. Serve with guacamole and sour cream for the perfect finishing touch.
—Jeanne Holt, Mendota Heights, MN

Prep: 15 min. • **Cook:** 5 min./batch
Makes: about 2 dozen

- ¾ cup all-purpose flour
- 2 Tbsp. yellow cornmeal
- 2 tsp. baking powder
- 2 tsp. sugar
- ¾ tsp. salt
- ½ tsp. chili powder
- ¼ tsp. ground cumin
- ¼ tsp. garlic powder
- ½ cup 2% milk
- ¼ cup sour cream
- 2 Tbsp. minced fresh cilantro
- 2 cups finely chopped onion
- 3 green onions, chopped
  Oil for deep-fat frying
  Guacamole and sour cream

1. Whisk together first eight ingredients. In another bowl, whisk together milk, sour cream and cilantro; add to flour mixture, stirring just until moistened. Fold in onions.
2. In an electric skillet or deep fryer, heat the oil to 375°. Drop batter by rounded tablespoonful into hot oil, frying a few fritters at a time. Fry until golden brown, about 1½-2 minutes per side. Drain on paper towels. Serve with guacamole and sour cream.

LOADED BAKED
POTATO ROUNDS

WHISKEY-BRANDY SLUSH

It may be cold outside, but we like to serve this icy citrus drink for Christmas gatherings at our house. It is fantastic for parties and large gatherings, and keeps well in the freezer.

—Joan Shoebottom, Lexington, MI

Prep: 10 min. + freezing
Makes: 32 servings (1 cup each)

- 7   green tea bags
- 4   cups boiling water
- 7   cups water
- 2   cups sugar
- 1   can (12 oz.) frozen orange juice concentrate
- 1   can (12 oz.) frozen lemonade concentrate
- 1   cup brandy
- 1   cup whiskey
- 2   liters lemon-lime soda, chilled Cranberries and assorted citrus slices, optional

1. Place the tea bags in a 4-cup glass measuring cup. Add boiling water; steep 3-5 minutes according to taste. Discard tea bags. Cool tea slightly.

2. In a 6-qt. stockpot, combine 7 cups water and sugar; bring to a boil, stirring to dissolve sugar. Remove from heat; cool slightly. Stir in orange juice and lemonade concentrates, brandy, whiskey and cooled tea. Transfer mixture to freezer containers, allowing headspace for expansion; freeze at least 12 hours.

3. To serve, place ½ cup slush in each glass; top each with ½ cup soda. If desired, garnish with cranberries and citrus slices.

LOADED BAKED POTATO ROUNDS

I needed an appetizer for my daughter's birthday party that would appeal to both hungry teenagers and discerning adults. These are made with simple ingredients yet yield a sophisticated result. Feel free to get creative with the flavors. Try shredded white cheddar in place of mozzarella or thyme instead of the rosemary. Take it up another notch by topping the rounds with smoked fish.

—Amanda Digges, South Windsor, CT

Prep: 35 min. • **Bake:** 15 min.
Makes: about 4 dozen

- 4   medium potatoes (about 7 oz. each), cut into ¼-in. slices
- 3   Tbsp. olive oil
- 1   Tbsp. minced fresh rosemary or 1 tsp. dried rosemary, crushed
- 1   tsp. kosher salt
- ¼   tsp. garlic powder
- ¼   tsp. coarsely ground pepper

TOPPING
- ¾   cup shredded part-skim mozzarella cheese
- ¾   cup sour cream
- 2   green onions, sliced
- ½   tsp. kosher salt
- ⅛   tsp. pepper
- 6   bacon strips, cooked and crumbled

1. Preheat oven to 425°. Toss together the first six ingredients. Place the potato slices on greased 15x10x1-in. pans. Roast until tender, 12-15 minutes.

2. Mix the first five topping ingredients; spoon onto potato slices. Top with the crumbled bacon. Transfer to serving platters. Serve immediately.

WHISKEY-BRANDY
SLUSH

UGLY SWEATER
COOKIES

Tips for an Epic Ugly Sweater Party

A party that celebrates the worst knitted sweaters around town is one that's sure to be nothing short of a good time. Here are four tips for hosting a legendary bash everyone will remember.

DECK THE HALLS

Ambiance is everything. Sure, tinsel and twinkling lights bring warmth and cheer this time of year. But too pretty is not in keeping with the ugly sweater vibe. Here's your chance to unearth those ornamental holiday monstrosities banished to basement. When it comes to decorating, opt for anything kitschy, weird, hilarious or just plain bad. The tackier, the better!

GAMES & ACTIVITIES

Have a roundup of fun games and activities to keep the party going all night long. Play a game of Christmas movie trivia or ask guests to bring a small, inexpensive gift to swap in a Secret Santa gift exchange.

MUSIC

Now we don our bad apparel, fa-la-la-la-la-la, la-la-la-la. It wouldn't be a Christmas party without Christmas music. Create a party playlist with everything from gather-round-the-fire classics to pop-star holiday hits. Guests will love a game of Name That Tune. Play a snippet of a Christmas song and see who can guess it! Or have your own No-Talent Christmas Karaoke Show and encourage party-goers to give their worst renditions of their favorite Christmas songs.

UGLIEST SWEATER AWARDS

Create people's choice awards for the best (or worst) sweaters in assorted categories. Let guests vote. Category ideas include:

• All-Around Ugliest
• Most Original
• Most Outrageous
• Funniest
• Best Couple Combo
• Most Festive
• Most Likely to Go Viral on Social Media

UGLY SWEATER COOKIES

Perhaps the most amazing thing about Ugly Sweater Cookies is how cute they are. Try these classic gingerbreads on for size.
—Christy Thelen, Kellogg, IA

Prep: 1 hour + chilling
Bake: 10 min./batch + cooling
Makes: about 5 dozen

- ¾ cup butter, softened
- 1 cup packed brown sugar
- 1 large egg
- ¾ cup molasses
- 4 cups all-purpose flour
- 1½ tsp. baking soda
- ¼ tsp. salt
- 2 tsp. ground ginger
- 1½ tsp. ground cinnamon
- ¾ tsp. ground cloves

ROYAL ICING
- 4½ cups confectioners' sugar
- ⅓ cup water
- 4 tsp. meringue powder
- ¼ tsp. cream of tartar
- ⅛ tsp. salt
- 1 to 3 Tbsp. heavy whipping cream
  Food coloring and assorted sprinkles

1. Cream butter and brown sugar until light and fluffy. Beat in egg and molasses. In another bowl, whisk together the flour, baking soda, salt and spices; gradually beat into creamed mixture. Divide the dough in half; shape each into a disk. Wrap in plastic; refrigerate, covered, until firm enough to roll, 4 hours or overnight.
2. Preheat oven to 350°. On a lightly floured surface, roll each portion of dough to ⅛-in. thickness. Cut with floured 3½-in. sweater-shaped cookie cutters. Place 2 in. apart on ungreased baking sheets.
3. Bake cookies until the edges are firm, 8-10 minutes. Remove cookies to wire racks; cool completely.
4. For icing, place first five ingredients in a bowl; beat on low speed just until blended. Beat on high until stiff peaks form, 4-5 minutes. Thin with cream to desired consistency. Tint with coloring.
5. Pipe icing onto cookies and decorate with sprinkles as desired. (Keep unused icing covered at all times with a damp cloth. If necessary, beat again on high speed to restore texture.) Let cookies stand at room temperature for several hours or until icing is dry and firm.

HOT COCOA CUPCAKES

We were snowed in one Christmas and couldn't get to the store to buy cookies for Santa. My daughter and I searched through our cupboards and found ingredients for the perfect ho-ho-homemade treats for St. Nick.
—Jennifer Gilbert, Brighton, MI

Prep: 30 min. • **Bake:** 20 min. + cooling
Makes: 2 dozen

- ½ cup butter, softened
- 1¾ cups sugar
- 2 large eggs
- 1½ tsp. vanilla extract
- 2 cups all-purpose flour
- ½ cup baking cocoa
- ¼ cup instant hot cocoa mix
- 3 tsp. baking powder
- ¼ tsp. baking soda
- 2 cups 2% milk

FROSTING
- ½ cup butter, softened
- 1 jar (7 oz.) marshmallow creme
- 1 tsp. vanilla extract
- 3¾ cups confectioners' sugar
- ¼ to ⅓ cup 2% milk
  Optional toppings: miniature marshmallows, crushed candy canes and colored sprinkles

1. Preheat oven to 350°. Line 24 muffin cups with paper or foil liners.
2. Cream butter and sugar until light and fluffy. Add eggs, one at a time, beating well after each addition. Beat in the vanilla. In another bowl, whisk together flour, baking cocoa, hot cocoa mix, baking powder and baking soda; beat into creamed mixture alternately with the milk, beating after each addition.
3. Fill prepared cups two-thirds full. Bake until a toothpick inserted in center comes out clean, 18-20 minutes. Cool in pan for 10 minutes before removing to wire racks; cool completely.
4. For frosting, beat butter until creamy. Beat in marshmallow cream and vanilla. Beat in confectioners' sugar alternately with milk. Beat on medium speed until fluffy, about 2 minutes. Spread or pipe onto cupcakes. Add toppings as desired.

Bring-a-Dish Holiday Potluck

Who doesn't love a potluck? A few hours of laughter and good cheer with loved ones and the opportunity to indulge in a lineup of sensational foods make these gatherings one of our most celebrated traditions. When it comes to bring-a-dish recipes, many cooks are left wondering just that...what should I bring? Look here for a delicious sampling of seasonal make-and-take fare so you can find a tempting dish everyone will love.

Perfect Four-Cheese Lasagna (p. 44) **Mom's Citrus Buttermilk Cake** (p. 48)

EASY ORANGE & RED ONION SALAD

Here's a unique salad that's easy to prepare when holiday preparations have you short on time. The combination of red onions and oranges may seem unusual, but it's surprisingly delightful.
—Edie DeSpain, Logan, UT

Takes: 20 min. • **Makes:** 10 servings

- 6   Tbsp. canola oil
- 2   Tbsp. white wine vinegar
- ½   tsp. grated orange zest
- 2   Tbsp. orange juice
- 1   Tbsp. sugar
- ⅛   tsp. ground cloves
       Dash salt
       Dash pepper
- 6   medium navel oranges, peeled and sliced
- 1   medium red onion, thinly sliced and separated into rings

For dressing, whisk together first eight ingredients. Place oranges and onion in a large bowl; toss gently with dressing. Refrigerate, covered, until serving.

BACON-BROCCOLI CHEESE BALL

In need of a quick appetizer, I combined a few leftovers from the refrigerator to make this easy cheese ball. For variety, shape into a log or substitute your favorite herbs for the pepper.
—Tamara Rickard, Bartlett, TN

Prep: 10 min. + chilling
Makes: 20 servings (2 Tbsp. each)

- 1   pkg. (8 oz.) cream cheese, softened
- 1   cup finely shredded cheddar cheese
- ½   tsp. pepper
- 1   cup finely chopped broccoli florets
- 6   bacon strips, cooked and crumbled
       Assorted crackers

1. Beat cream cheese, cheddar cheese and pepper until blended. Stir in broccoli. Shape into a ball; roll in bacon to coat. Wrap in plastic; refrigerate until serving.
2. Remove from refrigerator 15 minutes before serving. Serve with crackers.

EASY ORANGE & RED ONION SALAD

HONEY OATMEAL LOAVES

There's nothing like the taste and aroma of homemade bread. A friend gave me this recipe for a wedding gift. It was originally a family recipe passed down from her grandmother, and now it's a staple in our house, too. The best part? It contains lots of healthy ingredients.
—Amy Morrison, Derry, NH

Prep: 30 min. + rising
Bake: 40 min. + cooling
Makes: 2 loaves (16 slices each)

- 1¾ cups water
- 1 cup fat-free milk
- ½ cup canola oil
- ¼ cup honey
- ¼ cup molasses
- 1¼ cups quick-cooking oats
- 4 to 5 cups bread flour
- 2 pkg. (¼ oz. each) quick-rise yeast
- 2 tsp. salt
- 3 cups whole grain spelt flour or whole wheat flour

1. In a saucepan, heat water, milk, oil, honey and molasses to a simmer; stir in oats. Remove from heat; cool mixture to 120°-130°. In a large bowl, mix 4 cups bread flour, yeast and salt. Stir in cooled oat mixture. Stir in spelt flour and enough remaining bread flour to form a soft dough (dough will be sticky).
2. Turn dough onto a floured surface; knead until smooth and elastic, about 6-8 minutes. Cover with plastic wrap; let rest 10 minutes.
3. Divide dough in half. Roll each into a 12x8-in. rectangle. Roll up jelly-roll style, starting with a short side; pinch seam and ends to seal. Place in greased 9x5-in. loaf pans, seam side down.
4. Cover with kitchen towels; let rise in a warm place until almost doubled, about 1 hour. Preheat oven to 350°.
5. Bake until golden brown, 40-45 minutes. Remove from pans to wire racks; cool completely.
Freeze option: Securely wrap cooled loaves in plastic, then place in resealable plastic freezer bags to freeze. To use, thaw at room temperature.

RICH & CREAMY TWICE-BAKED POTATOES

My mom, Lynda, is a marvelous cook. I'm proud to say she taught me everything she knows, especially during my teenage years when we spent long hours together in the kitchen. She often made these twice-baked potatoes when my sister, Dina, and I were growing up. They feed a crowd and are just as good re-heated the next day.
—Cathy Gross,
Taste of Home Online Community

Prep: 25 min. • **Bake:** 1 hour 50 min.
Makes: 12 servings

- 6 large baking potatoes
- ½ cup butter, cubed
- 3 cups shredded cheddar cheese, divided
- 1 cup sour cream
- ¼ cup 2% milk
- 3 Tbsp. minced fresh parsley or 1 Tbsp. dried parsley flakes
- 1 tsp. seasoned salt
- ½ tsp. pepper

1. Preheat oven to 350°. Scrub potatoes; pierce several times with a fork. Place in a foil-lined 15x10x1-in. baking pan; bake until tender, 1½-1¾ hours. Cool slightly.
2. Cut each potato lengthwise in half. Scoop out pulp, leaving ¼-in.-thick shells; return to pan. In a large bowl, mash pulp with butter, adding 2 cups cheese and remaining ingredients. Spoon mixture into potato shells.
3. Bake until heated through, about 15-20 minutes. Sprinkle with remaining cheese; bake until the cheese is melted, about 5 minutes.

TEST KITCHEN TIP

Here's the Scoop

When making twice-baked potatoes, use a melon baller to scoop cooked potato out of the shells. It will come out quickly and neatly without tearing the skins.

PERFECT FOUR-CHEESE LASAGNA

Lasagna is one of my favorite meals, and this is the recipe I've been making since I was a teenager. It's a tantalizing combo of pasta, meat sauce, cheese and more cheese that really lives up to its name!

—Lauren Delaney-Wallace, Glen Carbon, IL

Prep: 25 min. • **Bake:** 50 min. + standing
Makes: 12 servings

- 1   lb. ground beef
- 1   medium onion, chopped
- 2   garlic cloves, minced
- 1   tsp. dried oregano
- 1   tsp. dried basil
- 2   cans (15 oz. each) tomato sauce
- 2   large eggs, lightly beaten
- 2   cups 4% cottage cheese
- ⅔   cup grated Parmesan cheese
- ¼   cup shredded cheddar cheese
- 1½ cups shredded part-skim mozzarella cheese, divided
- 12 no-cook lasagna noodles (about 7 oz.)
- 1   tsp. Italian seasoning

1. Preheat oven to 350°. In a large skillet, cook and crumble beef with onion and garlic over medium-high heat until meat is browned, 5-7 minutes; drain. Stir in herbs and tomato sauce. In a bowl, mix eggs, cottage cheese, Parmesan cheese, cheddar cheese and ½ cup mozzarella.
2. Spread 1 cup meat sauce into greased 13x9-in. baking dish; layer with four noodles, cottage cheese mixture, an additional four noodles and half of the remaining meat sauce. Repeat last two layers. Sprinkle with Italian seasoning and remaining mozzarella cheese.
3. Cover with greased foil; bake until the cheese is melted, 50-55 minutes. Let stand 10 minutes before serving.
Freeze option: Cover and freeze the unbaked lasagna. To use, partially thaw in refrigerator overnight. Remove from refrigerator 30 minutes before baking. Preheat oven to 350°. Bake lasagna, as directed, increasing time to 1-1½ hours or until heated through and a thermometer inserted in center reads 165°.

SLOW COOKER CHUCK ROAST

Nothing says comfort food like a savory, fork-tender roast bubbling in the slow cooker. This one is a welcome addition to family gatherings.

—Linnea Rein, Topeka, KS

Prep: 20 min. • **Cook:** 5 hours
Makes: 10 servings

- 1   can (8 oz.) tomato sauce
- ½   cup chopped onion
- ¼   cup water
- ¼   cup cider vinegar
- ¼   cup ketchup
- 2   tsp. Worcestershire sauce
- 1   tsp. paprika
- 1   tsp. prepared mustard
- ½   tsp. beef bouillon granules
- ¼   tsp. garlic powder
- 1   boneless beef chuck roast (4 lbs.), cut in half
- ¼   cup cornstarch
- 6   Tbsp. cold water
      Dash salt and pepper

1. Mix first 10 ingredients. Place roast in a 5-qt. slow cooker; top with sauce mixture. Cook, covered, on low until meat is tender, 5-6 hours.
2. Remove the roast from slow cooker; keep warm. Transfer cooking juices to a saucepan; skim fat. Mix cornstarch and cold water until smooth; stir into juices. Bring to a boil; cook and stir until gravy thickens, 1-2 minutes. Stir in salt and pepper. Serve with roast.

HAM & SWISS LAYERED SALAD

Takes: 30 min. • **Makes:** 12 servings

- 2   cups mayonnaise
- 1   cup sour cream
- ½   tsp. sugar
- ⅛   tsp. salt
- ⅛   tsp. pepper
- 8   cups fresh baby spinach (about 6 oz.)
- 6   hard-boiled large eggs, chopped
- ½   lb. sliced fully cooked ham, cut into strips
- 4   cups torn iceberg lettuce (about ½ head)
- 2½   cups frozen petite peas (about 10 oz.), thawed, optional
- 1   small red onion, halved and thinly sliced
- 8   oz. sliced Swiss cheese, cut into strips
- ½   lb. bacon strips, cooked and crumbled

For dressing, mix first five ingredients. In a 3-qt. or larger glass bowl, layer spinach, eggs, ham, lettuce, peas if desired, and onion. Spread with dressing. Sprinkle with cheese and bacon. Refrigerate, covered, until serving.

BRANDIED APPETIZER SAUSAGES

When our kids are home for the holidays, we serve an array of appetizers instead of a big meal. I use both wieners and smokies in this small-plate favorite.

—Sue Gronholz, Beaver Dam, WI

Takes: 30 min.
Makes: 24 servings (⅓ cup each)

- 2   cups ketchup
- ½   cup brandy
- ½   cup honey
- 1   small onion, chopped
- 4   pkg. (14 oz. each) miniature hot dogs or smoked sausages

In a 6-qt. stockpot, mix ketchup, brandy, honey and onion; stir in hot dogs. Bring to a boil. Reduce heat; simmer, covered, until hot dogs are heated through, 15-20 minutes, stirring occasionally.

"Layered salads rank among the classics in the potluck hall of fame. In this one, the combination of ham, cheese, egg and bacon is like a deconstructed sandwich, making it hearty enough for a main course."

—STACY HUGGINS, VALLEY CENTER, CA

HAM & SWISS
LAYERED SALAD

COLORFUL MINESTRONE

Butternut squash, carrots, a leek and fresh kale make my minestrone different from most others. Using whole ingredients creates a delicious blend of fresh flavors and helps keep the fat content down.
—Tiffany Anderson-Taylor, Gulfport, FL

Prep: 40 min. • **Cook:** 6½ hours
Makes: 10 servings (3¾ qt.)

- 1 Tbsp. olive oil
- 1 small onion, chopped
- 1 medium leek (white portion only), thinly sliced
- 2 oz. sliced pancetta or 2 bacon strips, chopped
- 2 garlic cloves, minced
- 1 medium butternut squash, peeled and cut into 1-in. cubes
- 2 medium carrots, coarsely chopped
- 2 celery ribs, chopped
- 1 medium potato, peeled and cut into ¾-in. pieces
- 1 Tbsp. minced fresh rosemary
- ½ tsp. salt
- ¼ tsp. pepper
- 2 cups fresh baby spinach, cut into thin strips
- 1 cup thinly sliced fresh kale
- 1 can (28 oz.) diced tomatoes, undrained
- 6 cups reduced-sodium chicken broth
- 1 can (15 oz.) cannellini beans, rinsed and drained

1. In a skillet, heat oil over medium-high heat; saute onion, leek and pancetta until onion is tender, about 2 minutes. Add garlic; cook and stir 1 minute. Transfer to a 5-qt. slow cooker. Stir in all remaining ingredients except beans.
2. Cook, covered, on low until vegetables are tender, 6-8 hours.
3. Stir in beans. Cook, covered, on low until heated through, about 30 minutes.

CHICKEN & WILD RICE BAKE

My chicken and rice bake is a wonderful lovely example of midwest cuisine. The dish is ideal for hosting because it can bake away on its own while you turn your attention to other party preparations.
—Suzanne Greenslit, Merrifield, MN

Prep: 1 hour • **Bake:** 50 min.
Makes: 10 servings

- 3 cups water
- 1 cup uncooked wild rice
- 2½ tsp. salt, divided
- ¼ cup butter, cubed
- 1 lb. sliced fresh mushrooms
- 1 medium onion, chopped
- 3 cups diced cooked chicken
- 1 jar (2 oz.) chopped pimiento, drained
- ¼ cup minced fresh parsley
- ¼ tsp. pepper
- 1 cup chicken broth
- 1 cup heavy whipping cream
- ¼ cup grated Parmesan cheese
- ¾ cup slivered almonds

1. In a large saucepan, bring water to a boil; stir in wild rice and 1 tsp. salt. Reduce heat; simmer, covered, until kernels have puffed open, 45-50 minutes. Drain any excess water.
2. Preheat oven to 350°. In a 6-qt. stockpot, heat butter over medium-high heat; saute mushrooms and chopped onion for 5 minutes. Stir in rice, chicken, pimiento, parsley, pepper, broth, cream and remaining salt.
3. Transfer to a 13x9-in. baking dish. Sprinkle casserole with the cheese and almonds. Bake, uncovered, until heated through, 50-60 minutes.

CHICKEN &
WILD RICE BAKE

String-Wrapped Cookie Cutters

Feeling crafty? Wrap string or yarn around metal cookie cutters to adorn a gift. Bakers especially will appreciate this special touch. The cookie cutters can also double as Christmas tree ornaments.

MATERIALS
Choice of 3 metal cookie cutters
Choice of string, yarn or ribbon
Tacky glue

Note: Some spools or yarn balls may be too large to pass through the hole in the cookie cutter as you wrap. To make it easier to wrap, cut a long length of string, yarn or ribbon and roll it into a small ball that will easily pass through.

DIRECTIONS
1. Use tacky glue to adhere the loose end of the string to the interior of ornament. Let the glue dry completely before beginning to wrap with string.
2. Begin wrapping string around the cookie cutter. Pull tightly to smooth out the strands. Continue wrapping until cookie cutter is covered completely. Trim excess string and use tacky glue to secure the end in place. Let dry before attaching to gift.

MOM'S CITRUS BUTTERMILK CAKE

Everyone raves over this lovely lemony cake. It's divine with fresh raspberries and a scoop of vanilla ice cream.
—Joan Hallford, North Richland Hills, TX

Prep: 25 min. • **Bake:** 45 min. + cooling
Makes: 12 servings

- 1 cup shortening
- 2 cups sugar
- 4 large eggs
- 2 tsp. lemon extract
- 3 cups all-purpose flour
- 1 tsp. baking powder
- ½ tsp. baking soda
- ½ tsp. salt
- 1 cup buttermilk

GLAZE
- 1½ cups confectioners' sugar
- 1 Tbsp. grated orange zest
- 5 Tbsp. orange juice
- 1 Tbsp. grated lemon zest
- 5 Tbsp. lemon juice
- ¼ tsp. salt

1. Preheat oven to 350°. Grease and flour a 10-in. fluted tube pan.
2. Cream shortening and sugar until light and fluffy. Add eggs, one at a time, beating well after each addition. Beat in extract. In another bowl, whisk together flour, baking powder, salt and baking soda; add to the creamed mixture alternately with the buttermilk, beating after each addition.
3. Transfer to prepared pan. Bake until a toothpick inserted in center comes out clean, 45-50 minutes.
4. Poke holes in warm cake using a fork or wooden skewer. Mix glaze ingredients; spoon slowly over cake. Cool 15 minutes before removing from pan to a wire rack; cool completely.
Note: To remove cake easily, grease the fluted tube pan with solid shortening.

EGGNOG OATMEAL COOKIES

I love eggnog, yet I somehow always end up with a surplus. These cookies help me put leftover eggnog to good use. They also have wheat and oats, so I can convince myself they're healthy!
—Kristin Weglarz, Bremerton, WA

Prep: 20 min.
Cook: 15 min./batch + cooling
Makes: about 1½ dozen

- ½ cup butter, softened
- ½ cup shortening
- 1 cup sugar
- ½ cup packed brown sugar
- 2 large eggs
- 1½ tsp. vanilla extract
- ¾ cup eggnog
- 1½ cups all-purpose flour
- 1½ cups whole wheat flour
- 1 tsp. salt
- 1 tsp. baking powder
- 1 tsp. baking soda
- 1 tsp. ground cinnamon
- ¾ tsp. ground nutmeg
- ⅛ tsp. ground cloves
- ¾ cup old-fashioned oats
- ¾ cup white baking chips

GLAZE
- 1 cup confectioners' sugar
- 3 Tbsp. eggnog
- ½ tsp. vanilla extract
- ¼ tsp. ground cinnamon
- ⅛ tsp. ground nutmeg

1. Preheat oven to 350°. Cream butter, shortening and sugars until light and fluffy. Gradually beat in eggs, vanilla and eggnog. In another bowl, whisk together the flours, salt, baking powder, baking soda and spices; gradually beat into the creamed mixture. Stir in the oats and baking chips.
2. Drop dough by scant ¼ cupfuls 2 in. apart onto greased baking sheets. Bake until bottoms are golden brown, 13-15 minutes. Cool on pans 2 minutes. Remove from pans to wire racks; cool completely.
3. Mix glaze ingredients until smooth. Drizzle over cookies.

PISTACHIO-CHERRY S'MORE BARS

Here's a fun spin on campfire treats. The graham cracker crust and golden-toasted marshmallow topping surround a rich filling of chocolate, fruit and nuts in these yummy bars. Or feel free to add ¾ cup coconut to filling if desired. I'm certain that St. Nick will give his jolly stamp of approval to these goodies.
—Jeanne Holt, Mendota Heights, MN

Prep: 15 min. • **Bake:** 30 min. + cooling
Makes: 2 dozen

- 1½ cups graham cracker crumbs
- 2 Tbsp. brown sugar
- ½ tsp. ground cinnamon
- ½ cup butter, melted

TOPPING
- ¾ cup dried tart cherries, chopped
- 1 cup white baking chips
- 1 cup dark chocolate chips
- 1 cup pistachios, coarsely chopped
- 1 cup sweetened condensed milk
- 1 tsp. grated orange zest
- 3 cups miniature marshmallows

1. Preheat oven to 350°. Line a 13x9-in. pan with foil, letting ends extend up sides; grease foil.
2. Mix cracker crumbs, brown sugar and cinnamon; stir in butter. Press mixture onto bottom of prepared pan. Sprinkle evenly with cherries, baking chips and pistachios. In a small bowl, mix milk and orange zest; drizzle over top.
3. Bake 20 minutes. Top with miniature marshmallows; bake until top is golden brown, 10-12 minutes. Cool in pan on a wire rack. Lifting with foil, remove from pan. Cut into bars.

TEST KITCHEN TIP

Sticky Marshmallows

To separate sticky marshmallows, place a spoonful of powdered sugar in the bag and shake well. A few stubborn marshmallows might still need to be separated by hand, but this generally works great.

PISTACHIO-CHERRY
S'MORE BARS

Brunch & Bubbly

Time to break out the bubbly! There's no better way to kick-off the holiday season than to gather with your favorite gal pals for an upscale brunch of sunny specialties and fabulous drinks, too. Here's a complete menu that will taste, fizz and bubble like no other. Now that's something to toast to!

Rainbow Quiche (p. 54) **Orange Juice Spritzer** (p. 53) **Layered Fresh Fruit Salad** (p. 57)

HAM & CHEESE
BREAKFAST BUNDLES

HAM & CHEESE BREAKFAST BUNDLES

My family looks forward to these rich and delicious egg bundles. They're perfect for holidays, brunches and birthdays.
—Cindy Bride, Bloomfield, IA

Prep: 35 min. • **Bake:** 15 min.
Makes: 12 servings

- 15 sheets phyllo dough (14x9 in.)
- ¾ cup butter, melted
- 4 oz. cream cheese, cut into 12 pieces
- 12 large eggs
- ½ tsp. salt
- ½ tsp. pepper
- ½ cup cubed fully cooked ham
- ½ cup shredded provolone cheese
- 2 Tbsp. seasoned bread crumbs
- 2 Tbsp. minced fresh chives

1. Preheat oven to 400°. Place one sheet of phyllo dough on a work surface; brush with butter. Layer with four additional phyllo sheets, brushing each layer. (Keep remaining phyllo covered with plastic wrap and a damp towel to keep it from drying out.) Cut layered sheets crosswise in half, then lengthwise in half. Cover stacks to keep them from drying; repeat with the remaining phyllo and butter.
2. Place each stack in a greased muffin cup. Fill each with a piece of cream cheese. Carefully break an egg into each cup. Sprinkle with salt and pepper; top with ham, cheese, bread crumbs and chives. Bring phyllo together above filling; pinch to seal and form bundles.
3. Bake until golden brown, 15-18 minutes. Serve warm.

TEST KITCHEN TIP

Phyllo Dough

Phyllo (pronounced FEE-lo) is a tissue-thin dough sold in the freezer section at most grocery stores. It's liberally basted with melted butter between each sheet, baking up crisp and flaky. Phyllo is thin and fragile, tearing easily, so always work on a smooth, dry surface. Once the dough is unwrapped and unrolled, cover it with plastic wrap, then a damp kitchen towel to keep it from drying out.

ORANGE JUICE SPRITZER

ORANGE JUICE SPRITZER

Here's a zippy twist on regular orange juice. It's not too sweet and is refreshing with any breakfast or brunch entree.
—Michelle Krzmarzick, Torrance, CA

Takes: 5 min.
Makes: 8 servings (1 cup each)

- 4 cups orange juice
- 1 liter ginger ale, chilled
- ¼ cup maraschino cherry juice
  Orange wedges and maraschino cherries, optional

In a 2-qt. pitcher, mix orange juice, ginger ale and cherry juice. Serve over ice. If desired, top servings with orange wedges and cherries.

ZIPPY PRALINE BACON

We host many overnight guests, so I'm always looking for new breakfast recipes. Bacon and eggs are a standby, but I like to take their flavor profile up a notch. My husband came home from a men's brunch raving about this bacon. Just be sure to make more than you think you might need because everybody will ask for seconds.
—Myrt Pfannkuche, Pell City, AL

Takes: 20 min. • **Makes:** about 10 servings

- 1 lb. bacon strips
- 3 Tbsp. brown sugar
- 1½ tsp. chili powder
- ¼ cup finely chopped pecans

1. Preheat oven to 425°. Arrange bacon strips in single layers on two foil-lined 15x10x1-in. pans. Bake for 10 minutes; carefully pour off drippings.
2. Mix the brown sugar and chili powder; sprinkle over bacon. Sprinkle with pecans. Bake until bacon is crisp, 5-10 minutes. Drain on paper towels.

RAINBOW
QUICHE

POMEGRANATE MACADAMIA CHEESE BALL

Cheese balls are a dime a dozen during the holidays, but this one earns points for being posh. It's creamy, sweet, spicy and studded with pecans and pomegranate seeds. We scoop it up with pita chips, but it can also be served with chutney, jam or high-quality crackers.
—Nancy Heishman, Las Vegas, NV

Prep: 25 min. + chilling • **Makes:** 4½ cups

- 2 pkg. (8 oz. each) cream cheese, softened
- 2 cups shredded smoked white cheddar cheese
- ½ cup crumbled goat cheese
- 2 garlic cloves, minced
- ½ tsp. salt
- ½ tsp. cayenne pepper
- ¼ cup dried cranberries, minced
- 2 Tbsp. white wine
- 1 can (8 oz.) crushed pineapple, drained and patted dry
- 1 cup finely chopped macadamia nuts, divided
- 4 Tbsp. minced fresh chives, divided
- 1 cup pomegranate seeds
  Baked pita chips or assorted crackers

1. Beat first six ingredients until blended. Beat in dried cranberries and wine. Stir in the pineapple, ½ cup macadamia nuts and 3 Tbsp. chives. Refrigerate, covered, 30 minutes.

2. In a shallow bowl, toss pomegranate seeds and remaining nuts. Shape cheese mixture into a ball; roll in pomegranate mixture.

3. Wrap in plastic; refrigerate 1 hour or overnight. Unwrap; roll in the remaining chives. Serve with pita chips.

TEST KITCHEN TIP

Pomegranate Seeds

The seeds and surrounding juice sacs (arils) are the only parts of the pomegranate that are edible. One medium pomegranate (about 8 oz.) yields roughly ¾ cup arils.

RAINBOW QUICHE

Boasting a bounty of veggies and a creamy egg-cheese filling, this colorful quiche is sure to impress.
—Lilith Fury, Adena, OH

Prep: 30 min. • **Bake:** 40 min. + standing
Makes: 8 servings

Pastry for single-crust pie (9 in.)
- 2 Tbsp. butter
- 1 small onion, finely chopped
- 1 cup sliced fresh mushrooms
- 1 cup small fresh broccoli florets
- ½ cup finely chopped sweet orange pepper
- ½ cup finely chopped sweet red pepper
- 3 large eggs, lightly beaten
- 1⅓ cups half-and-half cream
- ¾ tsp. salt
- ½ tsp. pepper
- 1 cup shredded Mexican cheese blend, divided
- 1 cup fresh baby spinach

1. Preheat oven to 425°. Unroll pastry sheet onto a lightly floured surface, roll to a 12-in. circle. Transfer to a 9-in. deep-dish pie plate; trim and flute edge. Refrigerate while preparing filling.

2. In a large skillet, heat the butter over medium-high heat; saute the onion, mushrooms, broccoli and peppers until mushrooms are lightly browned, 6-8 minutes. Cool slightly.

3. Whisk together eggs, cream and salt and pepper. Sprinkle ½ cup cheese over crust; top with spinach and vegetable mixture. Sprinkle with remaining cheese. Pour in egg mixture.

4. Bake on a lower oven rack 15 minutes. Reduce oven setting to 350°; bake until a knife inserted in the center comes out clean, 25-30 minutes. (Cover the edge of pie plate loosely with foil if necessary to prevent overbrowning.) Let quiche stand 10 minutes before cutting.

Pastry for single-crust pie (9 in.):
Combine 1¼ cups all-purpose flour and ¼ tsp. salt; cut in ½ cup cold butter until crumbly. Gradually add 3-5 Tbsp. ice water, tossing with a fork until the dough holds together when pressed. Wrap in plastic and refrigerate 1 hour.

POMEGRANATE
MACADAMIA
CHEESE BALL

ASPARAGUS
WRAPS

ASPARAGUS WRAPS

Asparagus makes lovely finger food, especially wrapped in pastry and tasty filling. Easily assembled, it's perfect for weeknight noshing or something a little fancier for entertaining.
—Linda Hall, Evington, VA

Prep: 20 min. • **Bake:** 15 min./batch
Makes: 2 dozen

- 3 **Tbsp. butter, softened**
- 1 **Tbsp. Mrs. Dash Onion & Herb seasoning blend**
- ¼ **tsp. garlic salt**
- 1 **pkg. (17.3 oz.) frozen puff pastry, thawed**
- 1 **cup crumbled feta cheese**
- 3 **oz. thinly sliced prosciutto or deli ham**
- 24 **thick fresh asparagus spears, trimmed**

1. Preheat oven to 425°. Mix the butter, seasoning blend and garlic salt. Unfold the puff pastry sheets onto a lightly floured surface. Spread each with 1½ Tbsp. butter mixture and sprinkle with ½ cup cheese. Top with the prosciutto, pressing lightly to adhere.
2. Using a pizza cutter or sharp knife, cut each sheet into 12 strips, about ½ in. thick. Wrap each strip, filling side in, around an asparagus spear; place on parchment paper-lined baking sheets.
3. Bake wraps until golden brown, about 15 minutes. Serve warm.

RASPBERRY CHAMPAGNE COCKTAIL

I often order fizzy, fruity beverages at restaurants. One day I decided to make one at home. This is my fresh take on raspberry champagne.
—Hillary Tedesco, Crofton, MD

Takes: 5 min. • **Makes:** 1 serving

- 1 **oz. raspberry liqueur**
- ⅔ **cup chilled champagne**
  Fresh raspberries

Pour raspberry liqueur in a champagne flute; top with champagne. Top with fresh raspberries.

CARAMEL CHIP BISCOTTI

The combination of caramel and chocolate in these delicate Italian biscuits is to die for. It is divine dunked in coffee or a sweet wine, or even enjoyed on its own. Feel free to use any flavor chocolate chips.
—Tami Kuehl, Loup City, NE

Prep: 30 min. • **Bake:** 30 min. + cooling
Makes: 2 dozen

- ½ **cup butter, softened**
- 1 **cup sugar**
- 2 **large eggs**
- 1 **tsp. vanilla extract**
- 2½ **cups all-purpose flour**
- 1½ **tsp. baking powder**
- ¼ **tsp. salt**
- 1 **cup Kraft caramel bits**
- 1 **cup (6 oz.) semisweet chocolate chips**
- 3 **oz. white candy coating, melted**

1. Preheat oven to 325°. Cream butter and sugar until light and fluffy; beat in eggs and vanilla. In another bowl, whisk together flour, baking powder and salt; gradually beat into creamed mixture (dough will be stiff). Stir in caramel bits and chocolate chips.
2. Divide the dough into three portions. On parchment-paper lined baking sheets, shape each dough portion into a 7x3-in. rectangle. Bake until a toothpick inserted in center comes out clean, 20-25 minutes. Cool on pans on wire racks 5 minutes.
3. On a cutting board, use a serrated knife to cut each rectangle crosswise into eight slices. Place slices on baking sheets, cut side down. Bake until crisp, 10-12 minutes per side. Remove from pans to wire racks; cool completely.
4. Drizzle melted candy coating over tops; let stand until set. Store between pieces of waxed paper in airtight containers.

LAYERED FRESH FRUIT SALAD

Fresh fruit flavor shines through in this medley, always welcome at potlucks. It's got a little zing from citrus zest and cinnamon—and is just sweet enough to feel like dessert.
—Page Alexander, Baldwin City, KS

Prep: 20 min. + chilling
Cook: 10 min. + cooling
Makes: 12 servings

- ½ **tsp. grated orange zest**
- ⅔ **cup orange juice**
- ½ **tsp. grated lemon zest**
- ⅓ **cup lemon juice**
- ⅓ **cup packed light brown sugar**
- 1 **cinnamon stick**

FRUIT SALAD
- 2 **cups cubed fresh pineapple**
- 2 **cups sliced fresh strawberries**
- 2 **medium kiwifruit, peeled and sliced**
- 3 **medium bananas, sliced**
- 2 **medium oranges, peeled and sectioned**
- 1 **medium red grapefruit, peeled and sectioned**
- 1 **cup seedless red grapes**

1. Place the first six ingredients in a saucepan; bring to a boil. Reduce heat; simmer, uncovered, 5 minutes. Cool completely. Remove cinnamon stick.
2. Layer the fruit in a large glass bowl. Pour juice mixture over top. Refrigerate, covered, several hours.

DANISH PUFF

My mom made this fun riff on cream puffs for special occasions. Store-bought pastry is no match for such an almond-flavored breakfast delight.
—Susan Garoutte, Georgetown, TX

Prep: 25 min. • **Bake:** 1 hour + cooling
Makes: 16 servings

- 1 cup all-purpose flour
- ½ cup cold butter, cubed
- 1 to 2 Tbsp. ice water

TOPPING
- ½ cup butter, cubed
- 1 cup water
- 1 cup all-purpose flour
- ¼ tsp. salt
- 3 large eggs
- ½ tsp. almond extract

ICING
- 1½ cups confectioners' sugar
- 2 Tbsp. butter, softened
- 2 Tbsp. water
- 1½ tsp. vanilla extract
- ½ cup sliced almonds, toasted

1. Preheat oven to 350°. Place flour in a bowl; cut in butter until crumbly. Sprinkle with water; toss with a fork until dough holds together when pressed. Divide dough in half. On greased baking sheets, press each portion into 12x3-in. rectangle.
2. For topping, in a saucepan, heat butter and water to a rolling boil. Add flour and salt all at once and beat until blended. Cook over low heat, stirring vigorously until mixture pulls away from sides of pan and forms a ball. Remove from heat; let stand 5 minutes. Add eggs, one at a time, beating well after each addition until smooth. Add extract; continue beating until mixture is smooth and shiny. Spread half of the mixture over each rectangle.
3. Bake until puffed and golden brown, about 1 hour. Cool on pans 10 minutes.
4. Mix first four icing ingredients until smooth; spread over warm pastries. Sprinkle with almonds.
Note: To toast nuts, bake in a shallow pan in a 350° oven for 5-10 minutes or cook in a skillet over low heat until lightly browned, stirring occasionally.

CHAMPAGNE COCKTAIL

This amber drink is a champagne twist on the traditional old-fashioned. Try it with extra-dry champagne.
—*Taste of Home* Test Kitchen

Takes: 5 min. • **Makes:** 1 serving

- 1 sugar cube or ½ tsp. sugar
- 6 dashes bitters
- ½ oz. brandy
- ½ cup chilled champagne
  Fresh rosemary sprig and fresh or frozen cranberries, optional

Place sugar in a champagne flute or cocktail glass; sprinkle with bitters. Add brandy; top with champagne. If desired, garnish with rosemary and cranberries.

CRANBERRY-EGGNOG DROP SCONES

Round out a festive brunch menu with a fresh-baked treat from the oven. My tender scones feature a pleasant eggnog flavor and a nice crunch from pecans.
—Linda Hickam, Healdsburg, CA

Prep: 15 min. • **Bake:** 10 min./batch
Makes: about 1½ dozen

- 2 cups all-purpose flour
- ½ cup sugar
- 1½ tsp. baking powder
- ½ tsp. baking soda
- ¼ tsp. salt
- ⅓ cup cold butter, cubed
- 1 large egg
- ½ cup eggnog
- 1½ tsp. vanilla extract
- ⅔ cup dried cranberries
- ½ cup chopped pecans

1. Preheat oven to 375°. Place first five ingredients in a food processor; pulse to blend. Add the butter; pulse until coarse crumbs form. In a bowl, whisk together egg, eggnog and vanilla. Add mixture to food processor; pulse just until blended. Remove to a bowl; stir in the cranberries and pecans.
2. Drop mixture by tablespoonfuls 2 in. apart onto greased baking sheets. Bake until golden brown, 10-13 minutes. Cool on a wire rack. Serve warm.
Note: This recipe was tested with commercially prepared eggnog.

CHAMPAGNE
COCKTAIL

How to Open a Bottle of Champagne

Curious about how to open a bottle of champagne without sending the cork flying? Popping the bubbly is easier than you think.

STEP 1: CUT AND REMOVE THE FOIL

Using the serrated knife of a wine key, cut the metal foil. After removing the foil, cover the top of the bottle with a kitchen towel and place one hand on top of the bottle, with your thumb firmly over the cork.

STEP 2: OPEN THE BOTTLE

Before opening, be certain the bottle is pointed away from bystanders (or anything fragile). Untwist the metal cage and slowly rotate the bottle, not the cork. Use the hand on top of the bottle to help ease out the cork. By controlling how quickly the cork comes out, you can gradually allow gas to escape the bottle. The result should be a gentle hiss rather than a loud bang.

STEP 3: SERVE!

Put the cork and cage off to the side and get ready to pour. Again, take it easy and pour slowly to avoid causing overflow.

Follow these simple steps to pour champagne like a pro with every pop of a cork. To your health or, as the French say, *santé!*

Kids in the Kitchen

The only thing sweeter than a Christmas cookie is making a batch with the ones you love most. Here's a fun parade of the cutest, yummiest, kid-friendliest cookies that the little ones can help with. Whether they're rolling out the dough or decorating with colored sprinkles, good times—and good cookies—are in store!

Christmas Cutouts (p. 64)

CHOCOLATE
REINDEER COOKIES

CHOCOLATE REINDEER COOKIES

Add a touch of whimsy to your holiday spread with these adorable treats. The cookies are easy to make, so little ones can join in the fun of decorating.
—*Taste of Home* Test Kitchen

Prep: 55 min.
Bake: 15 min./batch + cooling
Makes: about 5 dozen

- 2¾ cups all-purpose flour
- 1¼ tsp. baking soda
- ½ tsp. salt
- ¾ cup butter, cubed
- 1½ cups packed brown sugar
- 2 Tbsp. water
- 2 cups (12 oz.) semisweet chocolate chips
- 2 large eggs
- ½ tsp. almond extract
- 1 can (16 oz.) chocolate frosting
  DECORATIONS
  Candy eyes
  Reese's mini white peanut butter cups
  Miniature pretzels
  Peanut butter M&M's

1. Whisk together flour, baking soda and salt. Place butter, brown sugar and water in a large saucepan; cook and stir over low heat until butter is melted. Remove from heat; stir in chocolate chips until smooth. Stir in eggs and extract. Stir in the flour mixture. Let stand until firm enough to shape, about 15 minutes.
2. Shape level tablespoonfuls of dough into balls; flatten each to ¼-in. thickness. Place in a covered container, separating layers with waxed paper; freeze until firm. (May be frozen up to 3 months.)
3. To bake, preheat oven to 350°. Place the frozen dough portions 2 in. apart on greased baking sheets. Bake until set, for 12-14 minutes. Remove from pans to wire racks; cool completely.
4. Spread cookies with frosting, reserving a small amount for mouths. Decorate faces with candy eyes; add peanut butter cups for snouts, pretzels for antlers and M&M's for noses. Pipe reserved frosting to create the mouths.

CANDY CANE SNOWBALLS

Every year I bake dozens of different Christmas cookies to give to family and friends. Leftover candy canes inspired this recipe. The snowballs are dipped in a white candy coating, then into crushed peppermint candies.
—Debby Anderson, Stockbridge, GA

Prep: 30 min. + chilling
Bake: 15 min. + cooling
Makes: about 5 dozen

- 2 cups butter, softened
- 1 cup confectioners' sugar
- 1 tsp. vanilla extract
- 3½ cups all-purpose flour
- 1 cup chopped pecans
- 8 oz. white candy coating, melted
- ⅓ to ½ cup crushed peppermint candies

1. Cream butter and confectioners' sugar until light and fluffy. Beat in vanilla. Gradually beat in flour. Stir in pecans. Refrigerate, covered, until firm enough to shape, 3-4 hours.
2. Preheat oven to 350°. Shape dough into 1-in. balls. Place 2 in. apart on ungreased baking sheets.
3. Bake until lightly browned, about 15 minutes. Remove from pans to wire racks; cool completely.
4. Dip the tops of the cookies in candy coating, allowing excess to drip off; dip in peppermint candies. Let stand until set.

DIPPED VANILLAS

A touch of chocolate makes these classics stand out on holiday cookie trays. They're a tradition at our home for Christmas.
—Karen Bourne, Magrath, AB

Prep: 30 min. + chilling
Bake: 10 min./batch + chilling
Makes: about 2½ dozen

- ½ cup butter, softened
- ½ cup ground almonds
- ¼ cup sugar
- 1 tsp. vanilla extract
- 1 cup all-purpose flour
- 2 Tbsp. cornstarch
- 2 oz. semisweet chocolate, chopped
- ½ tsp. shortening
  Assorted sprinkles, optional

1. Preheat oven to 375°. Beat the first four ingredients until blended. Whisk together flour and cornstarch; gradually beat into the butter mixture.
2. Shape dough into 1-in. balls; shape into crescents. Place on greased baking sheets.
3. Bake cookies until lightly browned, for 8-10 minutes. Remove from pan to wire racks; cool completely.
4. In a microwave, melt chocolate and shortening; stir until smooth. Dip cookies partway in chocolate mixture; allow excess to drip off. Place on a waxed paper-lined baking sheet. If desired, decorate with sprinkles. Refrigerate cookies until set, about 30 minutes.

TEST KITCHEN TIP

Cookie Troubleshooting

Take some very simple precautions to make sure your cookies turn out right—and stay delicious as long as they last!

- Separate soft and crisp cookies in separate airtight containers. If you mix them, the moisture from the softer cookies will affect the texture of the crisp cookies.
- Be patient! Give cookies time to fully cool before frosting them; warm cookies will melt the frosting.

Also make sure they're cool before boxing them up; as they cool, they release moisture.
- To keep cookies from turning out tough, be careful not to overmix them. In general, the instructions will provide a clear idea of how much to mix.

CHRISTMAS CUTOUTS

(SHOWN ON P. 61)

Making and decorating these tender sugar cookies left a lasting impression on our four children. Now that they're grown, they've all asked for my recipe, baking memories with their own kids.
—Shirley Kidd, New London, MN

Prep: 25 min. + chilling
Bake: 10 min./batch + cooling
Makes: about 3½ dozen

- 1 cup butter, softened
- 1½ cups confectioners' sugar
- 1 large egg
- 1 tsp. vanilla extract
- ½ tsp. almond extract
- 2½ cups all-purpose flour
- 1 tsp. baking soda
- 1 tsp. cream of tartar

FROSTING

- 3¾ cups confectioners' sugar
- 3 Tbsp. butter, softened
- 1 tsp. vanilla extract
- 2 to 4 Tbsp. 2% milk
  Liquid or paste food coloring and assorted sprinkles, optional

1. Cream butter and confectioners' sugar until light and fluffy. Beat in the egg and extracts. In another bowl, whisk together the flour, baking soda and cream of tartar; gradually beat into the creamed mixture. Shape into a disk. Wrap and refrigerate dough until firm enough to roll, 2-3 hours.
2. Preheat oven to 375°. On a lightly floured surface, roll the dough to ⅛-in. thickness. Cut with floured 2-in. cookie cutters. Place cutouts on ungreased baking sheets.
3. Bake until the edges begin to brown, 7-8 minutes. Remove from pans to wire racks; cool completely.
4. For frosting, beat the confectioners' sugar, butter, vanilla and enough milk to reach desired consistency; tint with food coloring if desired. Spread over cookies. Decorate as desired.

NO-BAKE CHRISTMAS WREATH TREATS

Cornflakes take the place of traditional rice cereal in these sweet no-bake treats. Dressed up with green food coloring and red candies, they're a pretty addition to cookie platters and dessert buffets.
—*Taste of Home* Test Kitchen

Prep: 20 min. + standing
Cook: 5 min. • **Makes:** 8 cookies

- 20 large marshmallows
- 2 Tbsp. butter
  Green food coloring
- 3 cups cornflakes
  Red M&M's minis (about 2 Tbsp.)

1. Place marshmallows and butter in a microwave-safe bowl. Microwave, uncovered, on high until the butter is melted and the marshmallows are puffed, about 45 seconds. Tint mixture green with food coloring. Stir in cornflakes.
2. On a waxed paper-lined baking sheet, divide the mixture into eight portions. Working quickly, with buttered hands, shape each into a 3-in. wreath. Decorate immediately with M&M's, pressing gently to adhere. Let treats stand until set.

NO-BAKE CHRISTMAS
WREATH TREATS

PISTACHIO BUTTONS

Prep: 30 min. + chilling
Bake: 10 min./batch
Makes: 10 dozen

- ½ cup butter, softened
- ¾ cup sugar
- 1 large egg
- 1 tsp. almond extract
- ¼ tsp. vanilla extract
- 2 cups all-purpose flour
- 1 tsp. baking powder
- ½ tsp. salt
- 1 oz. unsweetened chocolate, melted
- ⅓ cup finely chopped pistachios
- 5 drops green food coloring, optional

1. Cream butter and sugar until light and fluffy. Beat in egg and extracts. In another bowl, whisk together the flour, baking powder and salt; gradually beat into the creamed mixture.

2. Divide the dough in half. Mix melted chocolate into one portion; mix pistachios and, if desired, food coloring into the remaining portion. Divide each half of the dough into four portions.

3. On a lightly floured surface, roll one chocolate portion into an 8x3-in. rectangle. Roll one green portion into an 8-in. log; place on the chocolate rectangle 1 in. from a long side. Roll the rectangle around the log; pinch seam to seal. Wrap in plastic; repeat with the remaining dough. Refrigerate until firm, about 1 hour.

4. Preheat oven to 350°. Unwrap dough and cut into ¼-in. slices. Place slices 2 in. apart on lightly greased baking sheets. Bake until set, 8-10 minutes. Remove from pans to wire racks to cool.

> "Big-batch cookie recipes like this one are handy during the holidays. The green centers add a festive touch."
>
> —NELLA PARKER, HERSEY, MI

SURPRISE PACKAGE COOKIES

Each of these buttery cookies has a chocolate mint candy hidden inside. They are my favorite cookie and are always part of my holiday baking.
—Lorraine Meyer, Bend, OR

Prep: 30 min. • **Bake:** 10 min./batch
Makes: about 3½ dozen

- 1 cup butter, softened
- 1 cup sugar
- ½ cup packed brown sugar
- 1 tsp. vanilla extract
- 2 large eggs
- 3 cups all-purpose flour
- 1 tsp. baking powder
- ½ tsp. salt
- 65 Andes mint candies

1. Cream butter and sugars until light and fluffy. Beat in vanilla and eggs, one at a time. In another bowl, whisk together flour, baking powder and salt; gradually beat into creamed mixture. Refrigerate, covered, until dough is firm enough to shape, about 2 hours.

2. Preheat oven to 375°. With floured hands, wrap tablespoonfuls of dough around mints (about 42) to form rectangular cookies, covering mints completely. Place 2 in. apart on greased baking sheets.

3. Bake until edges are golden brown, 10-12 minutes. Remove from pans to wire racks; cool completely.

4. In a microwave or saucepan, melt the remaining mints; drizzle over cookies.

PISTACHIO BUTTONS

Soften Butter Quickly

It happens all the time. You're in the mood to bake, you've got a great recipe and all of the ingredients are on the counter. Then you read the dreaded words: *butter, softened.* Here are two ways to soften butter in a flash. Now you're baking!

FAST With a rolling pin, roll or pound the butter flat. Whether rolling or pounding, the friction will warm the butter—and the broader surface area will encourage faster softening.

SUPER FAST Shredding creates a dirty grater, but it's the quickest method. Partially unwrap the butter (use the wrapped half as a handle to keep your hand clean) and shred it using the largest holes of a box grater. The butter will become a fluffy heap, similar in appearance to shredded mozzarella cheese.

MONSTER WHITE CHOCOLATE CRANBERRY COOKIES

White chocolate and cranberries are a classic cookie combo. These stand apart because they're extra big, soft in the middle and crisp around the edges.
—Dawn Johnson, White City, OR

Prep: 15 min.
Bake: 15 min./batch + cooling
Makes: 2½ dozen

- 1½ cups unsalted butter, melted
- 2 cups packed brown sugar
- 1 cup sugar
- 2 large eggs
- 2 large egg yolks
- 2 tsp. vanilla extract
- 4 cups all-purpose flour
- 1 tsp. baking soda
- 1 tsp. salt
- 10 oz. white baking chocolate, cut into chunks (about 2 cups)
- 1 cup macadamia nuts, chopped
- ¾ cup dried cranberries

1. Preheat oven to 325°. Beat melted butter and sugars until well blended. Beat in eggs, egg yolks and vanilla. In another bowl, whisk together flour, baking soda and salt; gradually beat into butter mixture. Stir in white chocolate, nuts and cranberries.
2. Drop dough by ¼ cupfuls 3 in. apart onto lightly greased baking sheets. Bake until edges are golden brown, 15-17 minutes. Cool on pan for 2 minutes before removing to wire racks to cool.

TEST KITCHEN TIP

Trail Mix Cookies

The egg yolks in Monster White Chocolate Cranberry Cookies add a unique richness to the dough. Turn this cookie into a trail-mix variation by swapping nuts and cranberries for semisweet chocolate chips, peanuts and raisins.

FROSTED MOLASSES SPICE COOKIES

These frosted spice cookies are always picked first at the holiday bake sale.
—Muriel Lerdal, Humboldt, IA

Prep: 35 min.
Bake: 10 min./batch + cooling
Makes: about 7½ dozen

- 1 cup butter, softened
- 1 cup packed brown sugar
- 2 large eggs
- 1 cup dark molasses
- 1 tsp. vanilla extract
- 4½ cups all-purpose flour
- 2 tsp. baking soda
- 1 tsp. salt
- 3 tsp. ground ginger
- 3 tsp. ground cinnamon
- ¼ tsp. ground allspice
- 1 cup buttermilk

FROSTING
- ¼ cup butter, softened
- ¼ cup shortening
- ¼ tsp. ground ginger
- ½ tsp. vanilla extract
- 2 cups confectioners' sugar
- 4 tsp. 2% milk
    Colored sprinkles, optional

1. Preheat oven to 375°. Cream the butter and brown sugar until light and fluffy. Beat in eggs, molasses and vanilla. In another bowl, whisk together flour, baking soda, salt and spices; add to creamed mixture alternately with buttermilk, beating well.
2. Drop dough by tablespoonfuls 2 in. apart onto greased baking sheets. Bake until set, 7-9 minutes. Remove to wire racks; cool completely.
3. For frosting, beat butter, shortening and ginger until light and fluffy; beat in vanilla. Gradually beat in confectioners' sugar and milk. Spread over cookies. If desired, decorate with sprinkles. Store in airtight containers.

PEANUT BUTTER CHRISTMAS MICE

With their black licorice tails, candy noses and peanut ears, these chewy mice were always a hit at classroom parties. My children are in their teens now but still ask me to make mouse cookies for the holidays.
—Nancy Rowse, Bella Vista, AR

Prep: 35 min. + chilling
Bake: 10 min./batch
Makes: about 5 dozen

- 1 cup creamy peanut butter
- ½ cup butter, softened
- ½ cup sugar
- ½ cup packed brown sugar
- 1 large egg
- 1 tsp. vanilla extract
- 1½ cups all-purpose flour
- ½ tsp. baking soda

DECORATIONS
    Peanuts, split in half
    Brown M&M's minis
    Miniature semisweet chocolate chips
    Black shoestring licorice, cut into 2-in. pieces

1. Beat peanut butter, butter and sugars until well blended. Beat in egg and vanilla. In another bowl, whisk together flour and baking soda; gradually beat into the peanut butter mixture (the dough will be soft). Refrigerate until firm enough to shape, about 1 hour.
2. Preheat oven to 350°. Shape dough into 1-in. balls; taper one side to resemble a mouse. Place 2 in. apart on ungreased baking sheets. Add peanuts for ears, M&M's for noses and chocolate chips for eyes.
3. Bake until set, 8-10 minutes. Remove from oven and immediately insert licorice pieces into warm cookies for tails. Remove from pans to wire racks to cool.

ALMOND
CREAM SPRITZ

ALMOND CREAM SPRITZ

Love spritz cookies at Christmastime? Try this version featuring almond-flavored dough. Sprinkle them with colored sugar for the holidays or chopped almonds for everyday cookies.
—Jo-Anne Cooper, Bonnyville, AB

Prep: 25 min. + chilling
Bake: 10 min./batch
Makes: about 3 dozen

- 1 cup butter, softened
- 3 oz. cream cheese, softened
- ½ cup sugar
- ½ tsp. almond extract
- ¼ tsp. vanilla extract
- 2 cups all-purpose flour
  Colored sugar or finely chopped almonds

1. Cream butter, cream cheese and sugar until light and fluffy. Beat in the extracts. Gradually beat in the flour. Refrigerate, covered, for 30 minutes.
2. Preheat oven to 375°. Using a cookie press fitted with a disk of your choice, press dough 2 in. apart onto ungreased baking sheets. Sprinkle with colored sugar.
3. Bake until set, 8-10 minutes. Cool on pans for 1 minute. Remove cookies to wire racks to cool completely.

Make Spritz Cookies

Spritz cookies in all flavors are holiday classics. If you've never used a cookie press, they can look intimidating. But it's really very easy!

CREAM butter and sugar until fluffy. Creaming incorporates air into the batter, giving cookies a lighter texture. Butter and cream cheese blend best when they're softened but not warm.

BEAT in the flour gradually (instead of adding it all at once). This ensures the flour is thoroughly mixed in. It also helps eliminate mess (the flour won't splatter, which saves time.

FIT a cookie press with the disk of your choice. Roll the dough into a cylinder to make it easier to insert into the press. The dough should be cool, but not too stiff.

HOLD the press against the cookie sheet—not above it—when releasing the dough. Use cool, ungreased baking sheets so the dough will stick. Never press dough onto a warm sheet.

SPRITZ SIZING is simple. Use the above images to get yours just right.

Christmas Day Leftovers

It's the day after Christmas. As the holiday fervor subsides (and after months of planning and prepping), you're finally able to catch your breath. But tummies will start to rumble all too soon, and you may find yourself staring inside a refrigerator filled with leftovers and wondering what to make. Here are fresh and tasty ideas for repurposing party remnants into fab creations that are just as good—if not better—as the original feast itself.

Beef Veggie Soup (p. 74)

BEEF VEGGIE SOUP

Brimming with chunks of beef, potatoes, carrots, green beans and mushrooms, this satisfying soup is a meal in itself. My personal preference, though, is to serve it with warm cornbread and a fruit salad.
—Ruby Williams, Bogalusa, LA

Takes: 30 min. • **Makes:** 12 servings (3 qt.)

- 1½ lbs. potatoes (about 3 medium), peeled and cut into 1-in. cubes
- 6 medium carrots, cut into ½-in. slices
- 1 Tbsp. Worcestershire sauce
- 1 tsp. ground mustard
- ½ tsp. salt
- ¼ tsp. pepper
- 2 cans (14½ oz. each) beef broth
- 3 cups cubed cooked roast beef
- 2 cups sliced fresh mushrooms
- 2 cups frozen cut green beans
- 1 cup frozen peas
- 1 can (15 oz.) tomato sauce
- 2 Tbsp. minced fresh parsley

1. Place the first seven ingredients in a 6 qt. stockpot; bring to a boil. Reduce the heat; simmer, covered, until the carrots are crisp-tender, 10-12 minutes.
2. Stir in remaining ingredients; bring to a boil. Reduce heat; simmer, uncovered, until vegetables are tender, about 5 minutes.

CURRIED POTATO PASTRIES

This is a quick and tasty recipe that makes use of leftover mashed potatoes.
—Rashmi Kapoor, Nipomo, CA

Prep: 35 min. • **Bake:** 20 min.
Makes: 1 dozen (½ cup herb oil)

- 1 Tbsp. olive oil
- 1 small onion, finely chopped
- 2 garlic cloves, minced
- 1½ tsp. grated fresh gingerroot
- 1½ tsp. cumin seeds
- 1½ tsp. minced seeded jalapeno pepper
- 3 tsp. curry powder
- ¼ tsp. cayenne pepper
- ¼ tsp. salt
- ⅛ tsp. pepper
- 1½ cups mashed potatoes (with added milk and butter)
- ¼ cup frozen peas, thawed
- 1½ tsp. lemon juice
- ½ cup shredded pepper jack cheese
- ¼ cup coarsely chopped cashews
- ¼ cup minced fresh cilantro
- 1 pkg. (17.30 oz.) frozen puff pastry, thawed

HERB OIL

- ½ cup olive oil
- ⅓ cup fresh mint leaves
- ⅓ cup fresh basil leaves
- 1½ tsp. grated lemon zest
- ⅛ tsp. salt
    Dash pepper

1. Preheat oven to 375°. In a large skillet, heat oil over medium-high heat; saute onion, garlic, ginger, cumin and jalapeno until onion is tender. Stir in seasonings until blended. Add mashed potatoes, peas and lemon juice; cook for 4 minutes, stirring occasionally. Cool slightly. Stir in cheese, cashews and cilantro.
2. Unfold puff pastry. Cut each sheet into six rectangles; moisten the edges lightly with water. Spoon about 2 Tbsp. potato mixture down the center of each rectangle. Fold a long side over filling, fold short sides toward the center, then roll up. Press seams to seal. Place 2 in. apart on a greased baking sheet, seam side down.
3. Bake until golden brown, for 18-22 minutes. Place remaining ingredients in a blender; cover and process until blended. Serve with pastries.

TURKEY & APPLE ARUGULA SALAD

Leftover cooked turkey meets fresh fruit and greens for a light meal that won't weigh you down. It's great in summer, too.
—Nancy Heishman, Las Vegas, NV

Takes: 20 min. • **Makes:** 6 servings

- ½ cup orange juice
- 3 Tbsp. red wine vinegar
- 3 Tbsp. sesame oil
- 2 Tbsp. minced fresh chives
- ¼ tsp. salt
- ¼ tsp. coarsely ground pepper

SALAD

- 4 cups cubed cooked turkey
- 4 tsp. curry powder
- ½ tsp. freshly ground pepper
- ¼ tsp. salt
- 1 large apple, chopped
- 1 cup green grapes, halved
- 3 cups fresh arugula or baby spinach
- 1 can (11 oz.) mandarin oranges, drained
- ½ cup chopped walnuts
- ½ cup pomegranate seeds

1. For dressing, whisk together the first six ingredients.
2. Place turkey in a large bowl; sprinkle with seasonings and toss to combine. Stir in apple and grapes. Add arugula and mandarin oranges. Drizzle with dressing; toss lightly to combine.
3. Sprinkle with walnuts and pomegranate seeds. Serve immediately.

TEST KITCHEN TIP

Arugula 101

Arugula is a small tender leafy green with a peppery taste. In Great Britain, it's called "rocket." While often enjoyed in salads, either on its own or in mixed greens, arugula is also delightful on pizzas, tucked into sandwiches and in pesto sauce. It pairs well with prosciutto, goat cheese, figs, sun-dried tomatoes and Parmesan cheese.

TURKEY & APPLE
ARUGULA SALAD

How to Season a Cast-Iron Skillet

1

SCRUB pan with hot water and a stiff brush to remove any rust.

2

TOWEL-DRY and apply a thin coat of vegetable oil to entire pan, including outside and handle.

3

LINE THE LOWER oven rack with aluminum foil and preheat oven to 350°. Place the skillet on the top oven rack, upside down; leave in the oven for 1 hour. Turn oven off and leave the pan inside to cool.

HAM & BROCCOLI
CORNBREAD

HAM & BROCCOLI CORNBREAD

Leftovers haunt me. Often nobody wants them, and I hate to see food go to waste. A cornbread casserole is an excellent way to leverage many combinations of leftover meat and veggies into new and exciting meals that everyone will love.
—Fay Moreland, Wichita Falls, TX

Prep: 15 min. • **Bake:** 35 min. + cooling
Makes: 12 servings

- 5 Tbsp. butter, divided
- 2 large eggs
- 1 cup 2% milk
- ½ cup sour cream
  Pinch cayenne pepper
- 2 pkg. (8½ oz. each) cornbread/muffin mix
- 2 cups chopped fresh broccoli
- 1½ cups (6 oz.) shredded sharp cheddar cheese
- 1½ cups cubed fully cooked ham
- 3 green onions, thinly sliced

1. Preheat oven to 375°. Place 3 Tbsp. butter in a 12-in. cast-iron skillet; place pan in oven until butter is melted, 3-5 minutes. Carefully tilt pan to coat bottom and sides with butter.
2. Melt remaining butter. In a large bowl, whisk together eggs, milk, sour cream, cayenne pepper and melted butter until blended. Add muffin mixes; stir just until moistened. Fold in remaining ingredients. Pour into hot pan.
3. Bake cornbread casserole until golden brown and a toothpick inserted in center comes out clean, 35-40 minutes. Let stand 15 minutes before serving.

TURKEY, BLUE CHEESE & ONION PIE

I used blue cheese and turkey to add extra appeal to a basic onion pie. Hearty and filling, it's a welcome meal on a cold day.
—Bridget Klusman, Otsego, MI

Prep: 15 min. • **Bake:** 50 min. + cooling
Makes: 8 servings

- Pastry for single-crust pie (9 in.)
- 2 Tbsp. butter
- 3 cups sliced onions
- 1½ cups finely chopped cooked turkey
- ⅔ cup crumbled blue cheese
- 4 large eggs, lightly beaten
- 1¼ cups 2% milk
- ½ tsp. salt
- ¼ tsp. dried thyme
- ¼ tsp. coarsely ground pepper
- ⅛ tsp. ground nutmeg
  Minced fresh parsley

1. Preheat oven to 425°. On a lightly floured surface, roll pastry dough into a ⅛-in.-thick circle; transfer to a 9-in. pie plate. Trim pastry to ½ in. beyond rim of plate; flute edge. Refrigerate while preparing filling.
2. In a large skillet, heat the butter over medium-low heat; cook onions until soft, 15-18 minutes, stirring occasionally. Cool slightly.
3. Layer turkey, onions and cheese in crust. In a bowl, whisk together the eggs, milk and seasonings; pour over top.
4. Bake on a lower oven rack 10 minutes. Reduce oven setting to 350°; bake until a knife inserted near the center comes out clean, 40-50 minutes. Let stand 15 minutes before cutting. Sprinkle with parsley.
Pastry for single-crust pie (9 in.):
Combine 1¼ cups all-purpose flour and ¼ tsp. salt; cut in ½ cup cold butter until crumbly. Gradually add 3-5 Tbsp. ice water, tossing with a fork until the dough holds together when pressed. Wrap in plastic and refrigerate 1 hour.

GRILLED CLUB SANDWICH WITH CARAMELIZED ONIONS

Leftover turkey slapped between two pieces of bread just won't cut it. Let the feasting continue with a post-Christmas sammy filled with caramelized onions, cranberries, hot sauce and other club-style staples, all toasted into a hot, melty panini.
—Linda Rohr, Darien, CT

Prep: 40 min. • **Cook:** 5 min./batch
Makes: 4 servings

- 2 Tbsp. olive oil
- 2 large red onions, thinly sliced
- ½ cup dried cranberries
- ¼ cup whole-berry cranberry sauce
- 2 Tbsp. minced fresh cilantro
- 2 Tbsp. mayonnaise
- 1 tsp. chipotle hot pepper sauce
- 8 slices sourdough bread
- 8 bacon strips, cooked
- ¾ lb. thinly sliced cooked turkey
- 1 cup fresh arugula or baby spinach
- ¼ lb. cheddar cheese, sliced
- ¼ lb. Stilton cheese, sliced
- ¼ cup butter, softened

1. In a large skillet, heat oil over medium heat; saute onions until softened. Reduce heat to medium-low; cook 20 minutes. Add dried cranberries; cook until onions are deep golden brown, 10-20 minutes, stirring occasionally.

2. Preheat panini maker or indoor electric grill. Mix the cranberry sauce, cilantro, mayonnaise and pepper sauce. Spread onto four bread slices; top with bacon, turkey, onion mixture, arugula, cheeses and remaining bread. Spread outsides of sandwiches with butter.

3. Cook sandwiches in panini maker until golden brown and cheese is melted, 4-5 minutes.

Note: Sandwiches can also be toasted in a skillet over medium heat until both sides are golden brown and cheese is melted. If desired, flatten the sandwiches while toasting by topping with a piece of foil and heavy skillet.

OVERNIGHT TURKEY CASSEROLE

Folks who love turkey will appreciate the flavor of this golden casserole. I love that I can make it a day ahead and just pop it from the refrigerator to the oven. Add a baked potato and a salad and you're all set!
—Monica Waletzko, Reedsburg, WI

Prep: 30 min. + chilling • **Bake:** 70 min.
Makes: 12 servings

- 2 Tbsp. butter
- ½ lb. sliced fresh mushrooms
- 6 slices white bread
- 4 cups cubed cooked turkey
- ½ cup mayonnaise
- 1 can (8 oz.) sliced water chestnuts, drained and chopped
- 6 oz. sliced Monterey Jack cheese
- 6 slices process American cheese
- 3 large eggs
- 1 can (10¾ oz.) condensed cream of chicken soup, undiluted
- 1 can (10¾ oz.) condensed cream of mushroom soup, undiluted
- 1½ cups 2% milk
- ⅔ cup dry bread crumbs
- ¼ cup butter, melted

1. In a large skillet, heat the butter over medium-high heat; saute mushrooms until tender. Cool completely. In a small bowl, mix mayonnaise and water chestnuts.

2. Place the bread in a single layer in a greased 13x9-in. baking dish; spread with the mayonnaise mixture. Top with the mushrooms. Layer with cheeses. In a bowl, whisk together eggs, soups and milk; pour over top (dish will be full). Refrigerate, covered, overnight.

3. To serve casserole, preheat oven to 350°. Remove casserole from refrigerator while oven heats.

4. Bake, uncovered, until bubbly and heated through, about 1 hour. Toss the bread crumbs with melted butter; sprinkle over top. Bake until lightly browned, for 8-10 minutes.

STUFFED MEAT LOAF SLICES

This is a family favorite requested for special occasions. It was given to us by a fellow faculty member during my husband's and my first years of teaching.
—Judy Knaupp, Rickreall, OR

Prep: 30 min. + chilling • **Bake:** 30 min.
Makes: 6 servings

- 2 cups mashed potatoes (with added milk and butter)
- 2 hard-boiled large eggs, chopped
- ½ cup Miracle Whip
- ⅓ cup grated Parmesan cheese
- ¼ cup chopped celery
- 1 green onion, chopped
- ¼ tsp. salt
- ¼ tsp. ground mustard
- ¼ tsp. pepper

MEAT LOAF
- 1 large egg, lightly beaten
- ¼ cup dry bread crumbs
- 1 tsp. salt
- 1¼ lbs. ground beef

SAUCE
- ½ cup Miracle Whip
- ¼ cup 2% milk
- 1 green onion, sliced

1. For filling, mix first nine ingredients. In a large bowl, combine beaten egg, bread crumbs and salt. Add beef; mix lightly but thoroughly. On a large piece of heavy-duty foil, pat mixture into a 14x8-in. rectangle. Spread filling over top to within 1 in. of edges. Roll up jelly-roll style, starting with a short side, removing foil as you roll. Seal seam and ends; place on a large plate. Refrigerate, covered, overnight.

2. Preheat oven to 350°. Cut roll into six slices. Place on rack in a broiler pan, cut side up. Bake until a thermometer reads 160°, for 30-35 minutes. Mix the sauce ingredients; serve with meat loaf.

STUFFED MEAT
LOAF SLICES

CRANBERRY-ORANGE
NUT COFFEE CAKE

CRANBERRY-ORANGE NUT COFFEE CAKE

Guests are delighted with this pastry's tangy cranberry sauce, crunchy pecans and sweet glaze. It's fantastic for brunch or simply enjoyed with a cup of coffee.
—Debbie Carter, Kingsburg, CA

Prep: 20 min. • **Bake:** 20 min.
Makes: 15 servings

- 1 cup chopped pecans
- ½ cup packed brown sugar
- 4 tsp. grated orange zest
- ½ tsp. ground cinnamon
- ¼ tsp. ground nutmeg
- 4 cups biscuit/baking mix
- ¼ cup sugar
- 2 large eggs
- ⅔ cup water
- ⅔ cup 2% milk
- 3 Tbsp. orange juice
- 1 cup jellied cranberry sauce

GLAZE

- 2 cups confectioners' sugar
- 1 to 2 Tbsp. orange juice
- 1 tsp. vanilla extract

1. Preheat oven to 375°. Mix the first five ingredients.
2. In a large bowl, mix biscuit mix and sugar. In another bowl, whisk together eggs, water, milk and orange juice. Add to dry ingredients; stir just until smooth.
3. Transfer to a greased 13x9-in. baking pan. Sprinkle with pecan mixture. Drop cranberry sauce by spoonfuls over top; do not spread.
4. Bake until a toothpick inserted in center comes out clean, 20-25 minutes. Mix glaze ingredients; drizzle over warm coffee cake.

TEST KITCHEN TIP

Reheating Coffee Cakes

To recapture the comforting flavor of a fresh-from-the-oven coffee cake, warm individual pieces in the microwave at 50% power, checking at 20- to 30-second intervals to see if they are warm. Let stand before tasting, as the icing may be hot. To reheat in an oven or toaster oven, wrap an unfrosted coffee cake in foil. Reheat at 350° for a few minutes or until warm to the touch.

HAM TORTILLA ROLL-UPS

Put last night's leftover ham to good use with these easy appetizers. The pinwheels are attractive and flavorful—and always popular at parties.
—Lynn Holgate, Manassas, VA

Prep: 30 min. + chilling
Makes: about 8 dozen

- 1 pkg. (8 oz.) cream cheese, softened
- 1 cup sour cream
- 1 Tbsp. dried minced onion
- ½ to ¾ tsp. garlic powder
- 1½ cups shredded cheddar cheese
- 1 cup chopped fully cooked ham
- 8 flour tortillas (8 in.), room temperature

1. Beat the first four ingredients until blended. Stir in cheddar cheese and ham. Spread the mixture over tortillas. Roll up tightly. Wrap in plastic.
2. Refrigerate at least 2 hours before serving. To serve, remove plastic wrap. Trim ends; cut into ½-in. slices.

ROASTED BANANA BREAD PUDDING

Old-fashioned banana bread pudding gets a decadent upgrade with the addition of eggnog. The velvety smooth sauce and golden brown topping are a match made in heaven. You could even add a little rum to take it up another notch.
—Devon Delaney, Westport, CT

Prep: 25 min. • **Bake:** 40 min.
Makes: 15 servings

- 2 medium bananas, unpeeled
- 4 large eggs
- 1 cup whole milk
- 1 cup eggnog or heavy whipping cream
- ⅔ cup sugar
- ¼ tsp. ground cinnamon
- ¼ tsp. salt
- 10 cups day-old cubed bread
- ⅓ cup chopped pecans, toasted
- 1 cup peanut butter chips
  Vanilla ice cream
  Additional toasted pecans, optional

1. Preheat oven to 400°. Place unpeeled bananas on a foil-lined baking sheet; roast until fragrant and skins have blackened, 12-15 minutes. Cool slightly. Reduce oven setting to 350°.
2. In a large bowl, whisk together eggs, eggnog, milk, sugar, cinnamon and salt. Peel and mash the bananas; stir into the egg mixture.
3. Spread bread cubes evenly in a greased 13x9-in. baking dish. Sprinkle with peanut butter chips and ⅓ cup pecans. Pour egg mixture over top.
4. Bake, uncovered, until puffed, golden brown and a knife inserted near the center comes out clean, 40-45 minutes. Serve warm bread pudding with ice cream and, if desired, additional pecans.
Note: This recipe was tested with commercially prepared eggnog.

HAM & CHEESE STRATA

Folks won't waste any time digging into this comforting all-in-one breakfast dish. The hearty combination of ham, cheese and mushrooms makes it a keeper.
—Ruth Castello, Raleigh, NC

Prep: 15 min. • **Bake:** 40 min.
Makes: 12 servings

- 12 slices day-old bread
- 3 Tbsp. butter, melted
- 2 cups shredded cheddar cheese
- ¾ cup cubed fully cooked ham
- ⅓ cup finely chopped green pepper
- ⅓ cup diced pimientos
- 2 cups sliced fresh mushrooms
- 5 large eggs
- 1½ cups 2% milk
- ½ tsp. salt
- ½ tsp. paprika
  Dash pepper

1. Preheat oven to 350°. Brush bread slices with the melted butter. In a greased 13x9-in. baking dish, layer half of each of the following: bread, cheese, ham, green pepper and pimientos. Top with all the mushrooms. Repeat the layers except the mushrooms. In a large bowl, whisk together the remaining ingredients; pour over the top.
2. Bake, covered, until a knife inserted near the center comes out clean, 40-45 minutes. Let strata stand 10 minutes before cutting.

Make-Ahead Holiday Desserts

The merriest month of the year can leave you feeling frenzied and frazzled...unless you plan in advance. Skip the pandemonium this year and get a jump on some of that holiday baking with these delectable make-ahead desserts. Some are casual and cute, others are elaborate and impressive...but all are delish!

Black Forest Torte (p.86)

FROSTY PEPPERMINT DESSERT

FROSTY PEPPERMINT DESSERT

I love this frozen dessert, so much like a cheesecake. With crushed peppermint candies and a homemade chocolate crust, it's decadent but delivers make-ahead convenience. I often whip up two because it disappears quickly!
—Carolyn Satterfield, Emporia, KS

Prep: 20 min. + freezing
Makes: 12 servings

- 1½ cups chocolate wafer crumbs
- ¼ cup sugar
- ¼ cup butter, melted
- 1 pkg. (8 oz.) cream cheese, softened
- 1 can (14 oz.) sweetened condensed milk
- 1 cup crushed peppermint candies (about 36 round peppermints)
- 3 drops red food coloring, optional
- 2 cups heavy whipping cream
  Additional crushed peppermints, optional

1. Mix wafer crumbs, sugar and melted butter; press onto bottom and 2 in. up sides of a greased 8-in. springform pan. Freeze while preparing filling.

2. In a large bowl, beat cream cheese until smooth; gradually beat in milk until smooth. Beat in crushed candies and, if desired, food coloring. In another bowl, beat cream until soft peaks form; fold into cream cheese mixture. Spoon into crust, spreading evenly. Freeze, covered, 8 hours or overnight.

3. Remove the dessert from the freezer 10 minutes before serving. If desired, top with additional peppermints.

TEST KITCHEN TIP

How To Crush Peppermint Candy

To easily crush peppermint candy, put candy in a heavy-duty resealable plastic bag; seal. Place on a sturdy countertop and, using a hammer or flat side of a meat mallet, pound the candy until it is thoroughly crushed.

CRANBERRY-WHITE CHOCOLATE TRIFLE

Trifles are great desserts to make when entertaining because they feed a crowd, and many recipes, like this one, can be prepared in advance. My favorite quality? On the table, they really catch the eye.
—Janet Varble, Harrisville, UT

Prep: 30 min. + chilling
Cook: 15 min. + cooling
Makes: 12 servings (¾ cup each)

- 6 Tbsp. sugar
- 3 Tbsp. cornstarch
- ⅛ tsp. salt
- 2⅔ cups whole milk
- 3 large egg yolks
- 5 oz. white baking chocolate, chopped
- 1½ tsp. vanilla extract
- 1 can (14 oz.) jellied cranberry sauce
- ⅓ cup raspberry liqueur
- 1 loaf (10¾ oz.) frozen pound cake, thawed and cut into ½-in. cubes

TOPPING
- 1½ cups heavy whipping cream
- ¼ cup confectioners' sugar
- 1 tsp. vanilla extract

1. For custard, in a large heavy saucepan, mix sugar, cornstarch and salt; stir in the milk until smooth. Cook and stir custard over medium-high heat until thickened and bubbly. Reduce the heat to low; cook and stir 2 minutes. Remove from heat.
2. In a small bowl, whisk a small amount of hot mixture into egg yolks; return all to pan, whisking constantly. Bring to a gentle boil; cook and stir 2 minutes. Remove from heat; stir in white chocolate and vanilla. Press plastic wrap onto surface of custard; cool to room temperature.
3. In a small bowl, whisk cranberry sauce and raspberry liqueur until smooth.
4. In a 3-qt. trifle or glass bowl, layer half of the cake cubes, half of the cranberry mixture and half of the custard; repeat layers. Refrigerate, covered, for at least 2 hours.
5. To serve, beat cream until it begins to thicken. Add confectioners' sugar and vanilla; beat until stiff peaks form. Pipe or spoon over top.

COCONUT LAYER CAKE

No one will be able to resist slices of this coconut cake crowned with cream cheese frosting. It's easy to bake and decorate. You can omit the pecans if you prefer.
—Marilyn Dick, Centralia, MO

Prep: 30 min. • **Bake:** 40 min. + cooling
Makes: 16 servings

- 5 large eggs, separated
- ½ cup butter, softened
- ½ cup shortening
- 2 cups sugar
- 1 tsp. vanilla extract
- 2 cups all-purpose flour
- ½ tsp. baking soda
- 1 cup buttermilk
- 2 cups sweetened shredded coconut
- ½ cup chopped pecans

FROSTING
- 1 pkg. (8 oz.) cream cheese, softened
- ¼ cup butter, softened
- 4 cups confectioners' sugar
- 1 tsp. vanilla extract
- ¼ cup sweetened shredded coconut, toasted
  Pecan halves

1. Place egg whites in a large bowl; let stand at room temperature 30 minutes. Preheat oven to 325°. Line the bottoms of two greased 9-in. round baking pans with parchment paper; grease paper.
2. Cream butter, shortening and sugar until light and fluffy. Add vanilla and egg yolks, beating well after each addition. In another bowl, whisk together flour and baking soda; beat into creamed mixture alternately with buttermilk. Stir in coconut and chopped pecans.
3. With clean beaters, beat egg whites on medium speed until stiff peaks form; fold gently into batter. Transfer the batter to prepared pans.
4. Bake until a toothpick inserted in center comes out clean, 40-45 minutes. Cool for 10 minutes before removing from pans to wire racks; remove the parchment paper. Cool cake layers completely.
5. For frosting, beat the cream cheese, butter, confectioners' sugar and vanilla until smooth and creamy. Spread between layers and over top and sides of cake. Top with coconut and pecan halves. Store in the refrigerator.

BLACK
FOREST
TORTE

BLACK FOREST TORTE

This cherry-crowned beauty, stacked layers of chocolate cake and cream filling, will have everyone talking. You can bake the cake in advance and freeze the layers until you're ready to assemble the torte.
—Doris Grotz, York, NE

Prep: 1 hour • **Bake:** 15 min. + cooling
Makes: 16 servings

- ⅔ cup butter, softened
- 1¾ cups sugar
- 4 large eggs
- 1¼ cups water
- 4 oz. unsweetened chocolate, chopped
- 1 tsp. vanilla extract
- 1¾ cups all-purpose flour
- 1 tsp. baking powder
- ¼ tsp. baking soda

CHOCOLATE FILLING
- 6 oz. German sweet chocolate, chopped
- ¾ cup butter, cubed
- ½ cup sliced almonds, toasted

WHIPPED CREAM
- 2 cups heavy whipping cream
- 1 Tbsp. sugar
- 1½ tsp. vanilla extract

TOPPING
- 1 cup cherry pie filling
- 1½ cups sliced almonds, toasted

1. Preheat oven to 350°. Line bottoms of four greased 9-in. round baking pans with parchment paper; grease paper.
2. Cream the butter and sugar until light and fluffy. Add eggs, one at a time, beating well after each addition. Beat in water just until blended.
3. In a microwave, melt unsweetened chocolate; stir until smooth. Stir in the vanilla. In a small bowl, whisk together the flour, baking powder and baking soda; add to the creamed mixture alternately with the chocolate mixture, beating after each addition. Divide batter among prepared baking pans.
4. Bake until a toothpick inserted in center comes out clean, 15-20 minutes. Cool for 10 minutes before removing from pans to wire racks; remove paper. Cool cake layers completely.
5. For chocolate filling, melt chocolate in a microwave; stir until smooth. Stir in butter until blended. Stir in almonds.
6. For whipped cream, in a small bowl, beat the cream until it begins to thicken. Add the sugar and vanilla; beat until soft peaks form.
7. To assemble, place one cake layer on a serving plate; spread with ⅓ cup chocolate filling and 1 cup whipped cream. Repeat layers twice. Top with the remaining cake and chocolate filling.
8. Spread remaining whipped cream over sides of cake. Press almonds onto sides. Spoon cherry pie filling over top of cake. Refrigerate until serving.
Note: To toast nuts, bake in a shallow pan in a 350° oven for 5-10 minutes or cook in a skillet over low heat until lightly browned, stirring occasionally.

SNOW-PUFFED MERINGUES

My family and friends enjoy a small treat after a big holiday meal. These feather-light morsels are just enough to hit the spot. To double the yield to 6 dozen, serve them as individual cookies instead of sandwiches. Skip the Nutella and dust each meringue with cocoa.
—Lorraine Caland, Shuniah, ON

Prep: 20 min.
Bake: 45 min/batch + cooling
Makes: about 3 dozen

- 4 large egg whites
- ½ tsp. vanilla extract
- ¼ tsp. salt
- ½ cup sugar
- 1 cup confectioners' sugar
- ⅓ cup Nutella

1. Place egg whites in a large bowl; let stand at room temperature 30 minutes.
2. Preheat oven to 225°. Add vanilla and salt to egg whites; beat on medium speed until foamy. Gradually add sugar, 1 Tbsp. at a time, beating on high after each addition until sugar is dissolved. Continue beating until stiff glossy peaks form. Fold in the confectioners' sugar.
3. Place meringue in a pastry bag fitted with a #1M open star tip. Pipe 1½-in. rosettes onto parchment paper-lined baking sheets.
4. Bake until firm to the touch, 45-50 minutes. Turn off oven (do not open oven door); leave meringues in oven 1½ hours. Remove from oven; cool completely on baking sheets.
5. Remove meringues from parchment paper. Pipe or spread the Nutella onto bottoms of half the cookies; cover with the remaining cookies. Store in airtight containers at room temperature.

SNOW-PUFFED
MERINGUES

CHOCOLATE ALMOND
PIZZELLES

CHOCOLATE ALMOND PIZZELLES

If you love fun baking gadets, you'll enjoy making these crispy, almond-flavored cookies, which get their unique waffle design from a pizzelle maker. They bake up golden brown in only a few minutes. Feel free to double the chocolate drizzle if you'd like to cover the cookies more generously.
—Hannah Riley, Norwalk, OH

Prep: 20 min. • **Cook:** 5 min/batch + cooling
Makes: about 4 dozen

- 3 large eggs
- ¾ cup sugar
- ½ cup butter, melted
- 2 tsp. almond extract
- 1¾ cups all-purpose flour
- 2 tsp. baking powder

TOPPING
- 1 cup semisweet chocolate chips
- ½ cup butter, cubed
- 2 Tbsp. baking cocoa
- 2 Tbsp. water
- 4 tsp. almond extract
  Chopped almonds

1. Preheat pizzelle maker. Beat first four ingredients until smooth. In another bowl, whisk together flour and baking powder; stir into egg mixture.
2. Bake in pizzelle maker according to manufacturer's directions until golden brown. Cool completely on wire racks.
3. In a microwave, melt chocolate chips and butter; stir until smooth. Stir in cocoa, water and extract until blended. Drizzle over pizzelles. Sprinkle with almonds; let stand until set. Store in airtight containers.

TEST KITCHEN TIP

Pizzelle Pizzazz

There are so many ways to enjoy these classic Italian cookies. Serve them plain; dust with confectioners' sugar; dip one half of each cookie in melted chocolate; or roll them into cones and fill them with a cream cheese filling similar to a cannoli.

RASPBERRY SANDWICH SPRITZ

I started baking these Christmas classics when I was in high school, and I still make them for my children and grandkids. The jam, buttery shortbread, chocolate and sprinkles add up to an irresistible treat.
—Joan O'Brien, Punta Gorda, FL

Prep: 30 min.
Bake: 10 min/batch + standing
Makes: about 2 dozen

- 1 cup butter, softened
- ¾ cup sugar
- 1 large egg
- 1 tsp. vanilla extract
- 2¼ cups all-purpose flour
- ½ tsp. salt
- ¼ tsp. baking powder
- 1 cup seedless raspberry jam
- 1 cup (6 oz.) semisweet chocolate chips, melted
  Chocolate sprinkles

1. Preheat oven to 375°. Cream butter and sugar until light and fluffy. Beat in the egg and vanilla. In another bowl, whisk together flour, salt and baking powder; gradually beat into creamed mixture.
2. Using a cookie press fitted with a ribbon disk, press long strips onto ungreased baking sheets; cut ends to release from disk. Cut each strip into 2-in. lengths (no need to separate them).
3. Bake until edges are golden brown, 12-15 minutes. Re-cut cookies if necessary. Remove from pans to wire racks; cool completely.
4. Spread jam on bottoms of half of the cookies; top with remaining cookies. Dip each end of cookies in melted chocolate; allow excess to drip. Dip in sprinkles. Place on waxed paper; let stand until set.

APRICOT ALMOND BARS

I often bring these treats to Christmas potlucks and parties. A tin of the yummy bars makes a great gift, too.
—Lynne Danley, Gresham, OR

Prep: 20 min. • **Bake:** 25 min.
Makes: 5 dozen

- 1 cup butter, softened
- 1 cup packed light brown sugar
- ½ tsp. salt
- 3 tsp. vanilla extract
- 3 cups all-purpose flour
- 1 jar (12 oz.) apricot preserves, warmed

ALMOND LAYER

- 2 cans (8 oz. each) almond paste, crumbled into small pieces
- 1 cup sugar
- 2 tsp. vanilla extract
- 4 large eggs

FROSTING

- 2 oz. unsweetened chocolate, chopped
- ½ cup half-and-half cream
- 3 cups confectioners' sugar
- ¼ cup butter, softened
- 2 tsp. vanilla extract

1. Preheat oven to 350°. Cream butter, brown sugar and salt until light and fluffy. Beat in vanilla. Gradually beat in the flour. Press dough onto the bottom of a greased 15x10x1-in. baking pan. Spread with the apricot preserves.
2. In another bowl, beat almond paste and sugar on low speed until blended. Beat in vanilla and eggs, one at a time. Pour over the preserves.
3. Bake 20-25 minutes or until a toothpick inserted in almond layer comes out clean. Cool slightly on a wire rack.
4. Meanwhile, place chocolate in a large bowl. In a small saucepan, bring cream just to a boil; pour over chocolate. Stir with a whisk until smooth. Add confectioners' sugar, butter and vanilla; beat the mixture until smooth.
5. Spread over warm bars. Cool the bars completely before cutting.

CARAMEL GINGERBREAD CUPCAKES

One night, my niece and I put our heads together and came up a with a fabulous cupcake. We combined a gingerbread cookie recipe with our favorite cupcake recipe, then enhanced the cupcakes with a luscious caramel frosting and a drizzle of caramel ice cream topping. Guests asked for seconds and thirds until nothing was left but a delicious memory and a stellar recipe to share. Make cupcakes in advance and frost the day you serve them.
—Delaine Smith, Barrie, ON

Prep: 25 min. • **Bake:** 15 min. + cooling
Makes: 10 cupcakes

- 1½ cups all-purpose flour
- ¾ cup granulated sugar
- ¼ cup packed brown sugar
- 2 tsp. baking powder
- 1 tsp. ground ginger
- ½ tsp. ground cinnamon
- ½ tsp. ground nutmeg
- ¼ tsp. ground cloves
- ¼ tsp. salt
- 1 large egg
- ½ cup 2% milk
- ⅓ cup canola oil
- ¼ cup molasses
- 1 tsp. vanilla extract
- ½ tsp. caramel extract

FROSTING

- 2 cups confectioners' sugar
- ¼ cup butter, softened
- 1 tsp. caramel extract
- 2 to 3 Tbsp. 2% milk
  Caramel sundae syrup

1. Preheat oven to 350°. Line 10 muffin cups with paper liners.
2. Whisk together first nine ingredients. In another bowl, whisk together egg, milk, oil, molasses and extracts. Add to the flour mixture; stir just until moistened.
3. Fill prepared cups two-thirds full. Bake until a toothpick inserted in center comes out clean, 15-18 minutes. Cool cupcakes in pans 10 minutes before removing to wire racks; cool completely.
4. For frosting, beat confectioners' sugar, butter, extract and enough milk to reach desired consistency. Spread frosting over the cupcakes. Drizzle with caramel syrup before serving.

CHOCOLATE-CARAMEL MACCHIATO PIE

This pie was one of my first entries in the National Pie Championship. It features a unique crust made from biscotti. The coffee flavor and chocolate curls on top make it extra impressive.
—Amy Freeze, Avon Park, FL

Prep: 30 min. + freezing
Makes: 10 servings

- 8 undipped biscotti (about 6 oz.)
- ¼ cup butter, melted

FILLING AND TOPPING

- 1 pkg. (8 oz.) softened cream cheese, divided
- 4 oz. dark chocolate candy bar, melted
- ¼ cup strong brewed coffee, cooled
- 1 carton (12 oz.) frozen whipped topping, thawed, divided
- 4 oz. milk chocolate, melted
- ¼ cup caramel sundae syrup
  Shaved chocolate
  Additional caramel syrup, optional

1. Preheat oven to 350°. Pulse biscotti in a food processor until fine crumbs form (about 1¼ cups). Add butter; pulse until blended. Press onto bottom and up sides of a greased 9-in. pie plate. Bake until lightly browned, 8-10 minutes. Cool on a wire rack.
2. Beat 4 oz. cream cheese until creamy. Gradually beat in melted dark chocolate and coffee until blended. Fold in ¾ cup whipped topping. Spread in the crust. Freeze until set, about 30 minutes.
3. Beat remaining cream cheese until creamy. Gradually beat in melted milk chocolate until blended. Fold in ¾ cup whipped topping. Spread over first layer. Freeze until set, about 30 minutes.
4. Place remaining whipped topping in a large bowl; fold in ¼ cup caramel syrup. Spread over the pie; top with shaved chocolate. Refrigerate until serving. If desired, drizzle with additional caramel syrup before serving.

CHOCOLATE-CARAMEL
MACCHIATO PIE

GIVING THANKS

Few things warm hearts more than the cozy goodness found at a Thanksgiving table. Celebrate this special time with a menu featuring all of the delicious classics everyone anticipates. Be sure to impress guests with new favorites, too, that promise to become much-loved staples on your table for years to come.

Gather & Feast

The invigorating chill of November is always a shock to the senses. The air is cool and crisp, and the days are shorter and darker. As we endure the elements, we also take time to revel in our deepest joy: gathering with those we love most to share a bountiful meal. With a tender, juicy turkey, homespun sides, a warm pie and other cozy staples, this menu will have everyone counting their blessings.

Roasted Citrus & Herb Turkey (p. 102) **Pearl Onion Broccoli Bake** (p. 99)

Thanksgiving Countdown

Planning a feast from start to finish can be daunting, but we've got **all the right ingredients** to help you streamline your stress-free celebration. Armed with **the best bird and delicious accompaniments**, your Turkey Day is bound to be a smashing success. Use this timeline as your guide to the main event.

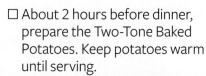

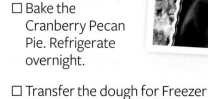

A FEW WEEKS BEFORE

☐ Prepare two grocery lists—one for nonperishable items to buy now and one for perishable items to buy a few days before Thanksgiving.

☐ Prepare dough for the Freezer Crescent Rolls. Store in airtight containers in the freezer.

TWO DAYS BEFORE

☐ Buy remaining grocery items.

☐ Wash china, stemware and table linens.

THE DAY BEFORE

☐ Bake the Butternut Squash Cake Roll. Cover and refrigerate until serving.

☐ Prepare the Cranberry-Apple Chutney but do not add the walnuts. Store in the refrigerator.

☐ Bake the Glazed Apple Turnovers. Store in an airtight container until ready to serve.

☐ Bake the Cranberry Pecan Pie. Refrigerate overnight.

☐ Transfer the dough for Freezer Crescent Rolls from the freezer to the refrigerator to thaw overnight.

☐ Set the table.

THANKSGIVING DAY

☐ Bake the Freezer Crescent Rolls. Keep covered until serving.

☐ About 4-5 hours before dinner, put the ingredients for the Slow-Cooked Sage Dressing in the slow cooker.

☐ About 4-5 hours before dinner, stuff and prepare the Roasted Citrus & Herb Turkey. Bake for 3½-4 hours. Prepare gravy. Let turkey stand for 20 minutes before carving.

☐ About 3-4 hours before dinner, place ingredients for the Hot Holiday Cider in the slow cooker.

☐ About 2-3 hours before dinner, mix together the ingredients for the Crunchy Vegetable Dip. Chill in the refrigerator.

☐ About 2 hours before dinner, prepare the Two-Tone Baked Potatoes. Keep potatoes warm until serving.

☐ About 45 minutes before dinner, prepare and bake the Pearl Onion Broccoli Bake. Keep warm until serving.

☐ About 35 minutes before dinner, prepare and bake the Cordon Bleu Appetizers.

RIGHT BEFORE DINNER

☐ Warm Freezer Crescent Rolls in the oven.

☐ As guests arrive, remove the Crunchy Vegetable Dip from the refrigerator and serve with crackers and vegetables.

☐ After dinner, but before dessert, warm the Glazed Apple Turnovers in the oven.

☐ After dinner, but before dessert, dust Butternut Squash Cake Roll with confectioners' sugar if desired.

FREEZER CRESCENT ROLLS

Bake up sweet convenience with this freezer-friendly dough. This recipe was handed down to me from my aunt. I love having homemade rolls available anytime I want, especially during the holidays.
—Kristine Buck, Payson, UT

Prep: 30 min. + freezing • **Bake:** 15 min.
Makes: 32 rolls

- 2 pkg. (¼ oz. each) active dry yeast
- 2 cups warm water (110° to 115°)
- ½ cup butter, softened
- ⅔ cup nonfat dry milk powder
- ½ cup sugar
- ½ cup mashed potato flakes
- 2 large eggs
- 1½ tsp. salt
- 6 to 6½ cups all-purpose flour

1. In a large bowl, dissolve yeast in warm water. Add butter, milk powder, sugar, potato flakes, eggs, salt and 3 cups flour; beat until smooth. Stir in just enough remaining flour to form a soft dough.
2. Turn the dough onto a well-floured surface; knead until smooth and elastic, 6-8 minutes. Place in a greased bowl, turning once to grease the top. Cover; let rise in a warm place until doubled, about 1 hour.
3. Punch down dough. Turn onto a lightly floured surface; divide in half. Roll each portion into a 12-in. circle; cut each into 16 wedges. Roll up wedges from the wide ends. Place on wax paper-lined baking sheets, point side down; curve to form crescents. Freeze until firm. Transfer to airtight freezer containers; freeze up to 4 weeks.

To use frozen rolls: Arrange frozen rolls 2 in. apart on greased baking sheets. Cover with lightly greased plastic wrap; thaw in the refrigerator overnight. To bake, preheat oven to 350°. Let rolls rise in a warm place until doubled, about 1 hour. Bake until golden brown, 15-17 minutes. Serve warm.

To bake rolls without freezing: Prepare and shape rolls as directed; arrange 2 in. apart on greased baking sheets. Cover with lightly greased plastic wrap; let rise in a warm place until doubled, about 45 minutes. Preheat oven to 350°. Bake until golden brown, 15-17 minutes.

CRUNCHY VEGETABLE DIP

CRUNCHY VEGETABLE DIP

This new recipe was a big hit with my family. Dig into it as an appetizer or for a light lunch.
—Dottie Miller, Jonesborough, TN

Prep: 15 min. + chilling
Makes: 16 servings (2 Tbsp. each)

- 1 pkg. (8 oz.) cream cheese, softened
- 1 Tbsp. mayonnaise
- 1 Tbsp. lemon juice
- ½ tsp. salt
- ⅛ tsp. pepper
- ¾ cup grated carrots
- ½ cup diced celery
- ½ cup diced green pepper
- ⅓ cup chopped green onions
  Assorted crackers and fresh vegetables

In a bowl, beat first five ingredients until smooth. Stir in vegetables. Refrigerate, covered, 2-3 hours. Serve with crackers and vegetables.

CORDON BLEU APPETIZERS

Looking for a cheesy snack with mass appeal? Adults and kids alike will crave these most satisfying appetizers!
—Susan Mello, Jackson Heights, NY

Prep: 20 min. • **Bake:** 15 min.
Makes: 1½ dozen

- 4 oz. cream cheese, softened
- 1 tsp. Dijon mustard
- 1 cup shredded Swiss cheese
- ¾ cup diced fully cooked ham
- ½ cup minced fresh chives, divided
- 18 slices French bread (½ in. thick)

1. Preheat oven to 350°. Beat cream cheese and mustard until smooth. Stir in Swiss cheese, ham and ¼ cup chives. Spread about 1 Tbsp. mixture over each bread slice; place in a 15x10x1-in. pan.
2. Bake until lightly browned, 12-15 minutes. Sprinkle with remaining chives.

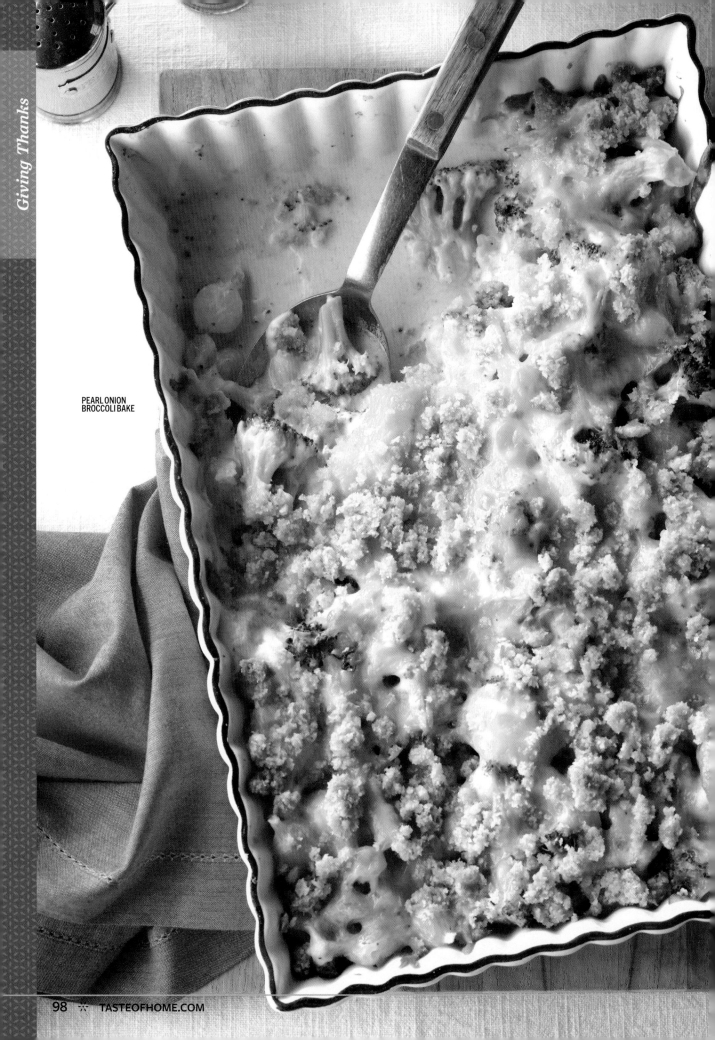

PEARL ONION
BROCCOLI BAKE

PEARL ONION BROCCOLI BAKE

With its creamy white cheese sauce and buttery crumb topping, this dish is pure comfort food. If you're looking for a mild way to dress up broccoli, this is the recipe.
—Charles Keating, Manchester, MD

Prep: 20 min. • **Bake:** 25 min.
Makes: 12 servings (¾ cup each)

- 2 pkg. (16 oz. each) frozen broccoli florets
- 1 pkg. (14.4 oz.) pearl onions
- ½ cup butter, divided
- ¼ cup all-purpose flour
- ¾ tsp. salt
- ⅛ tsp. pepper
- 2 cups 2% milk
- 6 oz. cream cheese, cubed
- 1 cup shredded cheddar cheese
- 2 cups soft bread crumbs

1. Preheat oven to 350°. Cook broccoli in 1 in. of water until almost tender; drain. Cook pearl onions in 1 in. of water until almost tender; drain. Transfer both to a greased 13x9-in. baking dish.
2. In a large saucepan, melt ¼ cup butter; whisk in the flour, salt and pepper until smooth. Gradually whisk in milk. Bring to a boil; cook and stir until thickened, 1-2 minutes. Reduce heat; stir in cream cheese until blended. Add to vegetables; stir gently to coat. Sprinkle with shredded cheddar cheese.
3. Melt remaining butter; toss with bread crumbs. Sprinkle over casserole. Bake, uncovered, until topping is golden brown, 25-30 minutes.
Note: To make soft bread crumbs, tear the bread into pieces and place in a food processor or blender. Cover and pulse until crumbs form. One slice of bread yields ½-¾ cup crumbs.

HOT HOLIDAY CIDER

Warming, slightly tart cider is perfect for a holiday open house—and fills the house with its wonderful aroma.
—Cindy Tobin, West Bend, WI

Prep: 10 min. • **Cook:** 3 hours
Makes: 16 servings (about ¾ cup each)

- 8 cups apple cider or juice
- 4 cups cranberry juice
- 2 cups orange juice
- ½ cup sugar
- 3 cinnamon sticks (3 in.)
- 1 tsp. whole allspice
- 1 tsp. whole cloves

1. Place first four ingredients in a 5- or 6-qt. slow cooker. Place spices on a double thickness of cheesecloth. Gather corners of cloth to enclose spices; tie securely with string. Add to slow cooker.
2. Cook, covered, on low until heated through, 3-4 hours. Discard spice bag. Serve warm.

SLOW-COOKED SAGE DRESSING

When oven space is at a premium, slow cooker dressing comes to the rescue. This recipe is rich with butter and sage, and because it doesn't need the oven, very cook-friendly.
—Ellen Benninger, Greenville, PA

Prep: 15 min. • **Cook:** 4 hours
Makes: 12 servings (about ¾ cup each)

- 1¼ cups butter, cubed
- 1½ tsp. rubbed sage
- 1 tsp. salt
- ½ tsp. pepper
- 14 to 15 cups day-old cubed bread
- 3 cups chopped celery
- 1½ cups chopped onion

1. In a microwave, melt the butter with seasonings. Place bread, celery and onion in a large bowl; toss with butter mixture. Transfer to a 5-qt. slow cooker.
2. Cook, covered, on low until heated through, 4-5 hours, stirring once.

BUTTERNUT SQUASH CAKE ROLL

I'm sweet on squash! Roll up this pretty dessert for any autumn special occasion, and you will be, too.
—Elizabeth Nelson, Manning, ND

Prep: 40 min. • **Bake:** 15 min. + chilling
Makes: 10 servings

- 3 large eggs
- 1 cup sugar
- ⅔ cup mashed cooked butternut squash
- ¾ cup all-purpose flour
- 1 tsp. baking soda
- ½ tsp. ground cinnamon
- 1 cup finely chopped walnuts
  Confectioners' sugar
FILLING
- 1 pkg. (8 oz.) cream cheese, softened
- 2 Tbsp. butter, softened
- 1 cup confectioners' sugar
- ¾ tsp. vanilla extract
  Additional confectioners' sugar, optional

1. Preheat oven to 375°. Line bottom of a 15x10x1-in. pan with parchment paper.
2. In a large bowl, beat eggs on high speed for 3 minutes. Gradually add 1 cup sugar, beating until thick and lemon colored, for 2 minutes. Stir in squash. In another bowl, whisk together the flour, baking soda and cinnamon; fold into the squash mixture. Transfer to prepared pan, spreading the batter evenly. Sprinkle with walnuts.
3. Bake until a toothpick inserted in center comes out clean, 13-15 minutes. Cool on a wire rack 10 minutes.
4. Invert cake onto a tea towel dusted with confectioners' sugar. Gently peel off paper. Roll up cake in the towel jelly-roll style, starting with a short side. Cool completely on a wire rack.
5. In a bowl, beat the first four filling ingredients until smooth. Unroll cake; spread filling over cake to within 1 in. of edges. Roll up again, without towel; trim ends. Place on a platter; seam side down. Refrigerate, covered, 1 hour. If desired, dust with additional confectioners' sugar before serving.

CRANBERRY-APPLE CHUTNEY

In our house, this chutney is a must-have for Thanksgiving. Use it to garnish turkey slices, or spoon it over cream cheese on Melba rounds for an appetizer.
—Mary Ellen Gilbert, Franconia, NH

Prep: 15 min. • **Cook:** 35 min. + chilling
Makes: 16 servings (¼ cup each)

- 1¼ cups sugar
- ½ cup water
- 1 pkg. (12 oz.) fresh or frozen cranberries
- 2 large tart apples, peeled and finely chopped
- 1 medium onion, chopped
- ½ cup golden raisins
- ½ cup packed brown sugar
- ¼ cup cider vinegar
- 1 tsp. ground cinnamon
- ¼ tsp. salt
- ⅛ tsp. ground allspice
- ⅛ tsp. ground cloves
- ½ cup chopped walnuts, toasted

1. In a large saucepan, bring sugar and water to a boil over medium heat, stirring to dissolve sugar. Reduce heat; simmer, uncovered, 3 minutes. Carefully stir in all the remaining ingredients except walnuts; return to a boil. Reduce the heat; simmer, uncovered, until cranberry-apple mixture reaches desired thickness, 20-25 minutes, stirring occasionally.

2. Serve warm or cold. Stir in the walnuts before serving.

TEST KITCHEN TIP

Ways to Make Your Meal a Success!

- When grocery shopping, don't forget about any garnishes that you plan on adding to recipes for a finished look.
- Stock up on various sizes of disposable containers so you can send guests home with leftovers.
- If you plan to make soup or stock with the turkey carcass, save celery leaves, leftover chopped onion and carrot sticks. Add them to the stock for extra flavor.

GLAZED APPLE TURNOVERS

I first tasted these as tarts at a get-together with friends. I tweaked the recipe to turn it a fun hand-held treat for breakfast, dessert or a snack.
—Kami Horch, Calais, ME

Prep: 35 min. • **Bake:** 20 min.
Makes: 16 servings

- ⅔ cup sugar
- 1 cup unsweetened apple cider or juice
- 2 Tbsp. cider vinegar
- 7 medium apples, peeled and chopped (about 7 cups)
- 3 tsp. apple pie spice
- 2 tsp. ground cinnamon
- 2 pkg. (17.3 oz. each) frozen puff pastry, thawed
- 4 cups confectioners' sugar
- 2 Tbsp. butter, softened
- 2 tsp. vanilla extract
- 1 to 2 tsp. half-and-half cream

1. In a large heavy saucepan, spread sugar; cook, without stirring, over medium-low heat until it begins to melt. Cook until the melted sugar turns a medium amber color, stirring occasionally. Mix cider and vinegar; pour slowly into melted sugar (mixture will harden). Reduce heat; cook and stir until mixture returns to a liquid. Add apples and spices; toss to coat. Remove from heat; let stand, covered, until cooled.

2. Preheat oven to 400°. Drain apples, reserving juices. On a lightly floured surface, roll each sheet of puff pastry sheet into a 12-in. square. Cut each into four squares. Top each square with 3 Tbsp. drained apple. Fold pastry over the filling to form a triangle; press edges with a fork to seal. Place on greased baking sheets.

3. Bake until golden brown, for 18-20 minutes. For glaze, mix confectioners' sugar, butter, vanilla and reserved apple juices. Stir in enough cream to reach a thick drizzling consistency. Spoon over turnovers. Serve warm.

TWO-TONE BAKED POTATOES

TWO-TONE BAKED POTATOES

One potato...two potato...This recipe is twice as nice as far as spud lovers are concerned. I have a reputation for trying out new recipes. Everyone is glad I took a chance on this one!
—Sherree Stahn, Central City, NE

Prep: 30 min. • **Bake:** 1¼ hours
Makes: 12 servings

- 6 medium russet potatoes (about 8 oz. each)
- 6 medium sweet potatoes (about 8 oz. each)
- ⅔ cup sour cream, divided
- ⅓ cup 2% milk
- ¾ cup shredded cheddar cheese
- 4 Tbsp. minced fresh chives, divided
- 1½ tsp. salt, divided

1. Preheat oven to 400°. Scrub russet and sweet potatoes; pierce several times with a fork. Place in foil-lined 15x10x1-in. pans; bake until tender, 60-70 minutes. Reduce oven setting to 350°.
2. When cool enough to handle, cut a third off the top of each russet potato (discard top or save for another use). Scoop out pulp, leaving ½-in.-thick shells. In a bowl, mash pulp, adding ⅓ cup sour cream, milk, cheese, 2 Tbsp. chives and ¾ tsp. salt.
3. Cut a thin slice off the top of each sweet potato; discard slice. Scoop out the pulp, leaving ½-in. thick shells. Mash pulp with remaining sour cream, chives and salt.
4. Spoon russet potato mixture into half of each russet and sweet potato skin. Spoon sweet potato mixture into other half. Return to pans. Bake until heated through, 15-20 minutes.

ROASTED CITRUS & HERB TURKEY

Thanksgiving has never been the same since I tried this recipe. I have made it for the past few years, and it never fails to impress both in presentation and taste. This is a true showstopper!
—Nancy Niemerg, Dieterich, IL

Prep: 30 min. • **Bake:** 3½ hours + standing
Makes: 16 servings (2 cups gravy)

- ¼ cup butter, softened
- 2 Tbsp. Italian seasoning
- 1 turkey (14 to 16 lbs.)
- 2 tsp. salt
- 2 tsp. pepper
- 1 large onion, quartered
- 1 medium orange, quartered
- 1 medium lemon, quartered
- 3 fresh rosemary sprigs
- 3 fresh sage sprigs
- 3 cups chicken broth, divided
- 3 to 4 Tbsp. all-purpose flour
- ⅛ tsp. browning sauce, optional

1. Preheat oven to 325°. Mix butter and Italian seasoning.

2. Place turkey on a rack in a roasting pan, breast side up; pat dry. Using your fingers, carefully loosen skin from turkey breast; rub half of the butter mixture under the skin. Secure skin to underside of breast with toothpicks. Rub cavity with salt and pepper; fill with onion, orange, lemon and herbs. Tuck wings under turkey; tie the drumsticks together.

3. Melt remaining butter mixture; brush over outside of turkey. Add 2 cups broth to roasting pan.

4. Roast turkey, uncovered, until a thermometer inserted in thickest part of thigh reads 170°-175°, 3½-4 hours, basting turkey occasionally with pan drippings. (Cover loosely with foil if it browns too quickly.)

5. Remove turkey from oven; tent with foil. Let stand 20 minutes before carving.

6. Pour the pan drippings into a small saucepan; skim fat. Mix flour, remaining broth and, if desired, browning sauce until smooth; whisk into pan. Bring to a boil; cook and stir gravy until thickened, 1-2 minutes. Serve with turkey.

ROASTED CITRUS & HERB TURKEY

Carve a Turkey

1

2

PLACE bird on a carving board and remove any stuffing. Holding the end of the drumstick, pull the leg away from the body and cut between the thigh joint and body to remove the entire leg. Repeat with other leg.

TO SEPARATE the drumstick and thigh, cut through the connecting joint.

3

4

HOLDING the drumstick by the end, slice meat into ¼-in. slices. Cut thigh meat parallel to the bone into ¼-in. slices.

HOLD the bird with a meat fork and make a deep cut into the breast meat just above the wing area.

5

6

SLICE down from the top of the breast into the cut made in Step 4. Slice meat ¼-in. thick. Repeat Steps 4 and 5 on other side of bird.

TO REMOVE wings, cut through the connecting joints by the wing bones and backbone.

Sticks and Cones

Do-it-yourself scented pinecones make a dramatic centerpiece for your Thanksgiving table. They make your house smell wonderful, too!

MATERIALS:
Pinecones
Birch or other branches
Wide-mouthed glass jar
Ribbon
Essential oils for scented spray
(recipes below)
Unscented witch hazel
Distilled water
Plastic spray bottle
Plastic funnel (do not reuse for food)

DIRECTIONS

1. Start by making one of the all-natural scented sprays from the recipes below. Insert funnel into top of open spray bottle. Pour in 2 Tbsp. unscented witch hazel and 6 Tbsp. distilled water. Add drops of essential oils according to the chosen recipe. Place spray cap on bottle. Shake gently until mixed well.

2. Gather pinecones and cut branches from outdoors or purchase these items from a craft store. Lay the pinecones on a flat, cleanable surface. Mist pinecones all over with scented spray and let dry. Place scented pinecones in glass jar, filling to brim.

3. Arrange the cut ends of branches among the pinecones. Wrap a length of ribbon around center of jar, knot in place and trim ends.

SCENTED SPRAY RECIPES

- **Apple Pie Spice**
  10 drops cinnamon essential oil and 5 drops clove essential oil.
- **Orange Spice**
  10 drops orange essential oil and 5 drops cinnamon essential oil.
- **Winter Essence**
  10 drops pine essential oil and 5 drops peppermint essential oil.

CRANBERRY PECAN PIE

CRANBERRY PECAN PIE

I prepared this pie for the first time around Thanksgiving. I brought it to work to share with my co-workers, and it was a success. Now I freeze cranberries when they're in season, so I can make it year-round.
—Dawn Liet Hartman, Mifflinburg, PA

Prep: 25 min. + chilling
Bake: 45 min. + chilling • **Makes:** 8 servings

6	Tbsp. shortening
1½	tsp. buttermilk
2	Tbsp. hot water
1	cup all-purpose flour
½	tsp. salt

FILLING

3	large eggs
1	cup light or dark corn syrup
⅔	cup sugar
¼	cup butter, melted
1	tsp. vanilla extract
2	cups fresh or frozen cranberries, thawed
1	cup chopped pecans
	Sweetened whipped cream, optional

1. Beat the shortening and buttermilk until blended. Gradually add the water, beating until light and fluffy. Beat in the flour and salt. Shape dough into a disk. Wrap; refrigerate 4 hours or overnight.

2. Preheat oven to 425°. On a lightly floured surface, roll dough to a ⅛-in.-thick circle; transfer to a 9-in. pie plate. Trim the pastry to ½ in. beyond the edge of plate; flute edge.

3. In a large bowl, whisk first five filling ingredients until blended. Stir in the cranberries and pecans. Pour into crust.

4. Bake on a lower oven rack 10 minutes. Reduce oven setting to 350°; bake until filling is almost set, 35-40 minutes. Cool completely on a wire rack. Refrigerate, covered, overnight before serving. If desired, serve with whipped cream.

Friendsgiving

Low-stress and low-key are the hallmarks of a Thanksgiving dinner spent with friends. Bring your favorite group of people together and make them part of the action with a casual potluck party. Delicious food, wine, laughter and fellowship—with everyone pitching in—will make the occasion one to remember. A little planning and a selection of amazing dishes, and your Friendsgiving party is one they'll all be grateful for.

Bourbon Sweet Potato Pie (p. 114) **Autumn Surprise Pie** (p. 115)

ROASTED RED PEPPER CHEESE PUFFS

I came up with this recipe one day when I was planning on making lasagna. Instead, I used some of the ingredients to create these tasty bites. They're as pretty as they are delicious!
—Kelly Williams, Forked River, NJ

Prep: 35 min. • **Bake:** 20 min./batch
Makes: 32 appetizers

- ¾ cup part-skim ricotta cheese
- ½ cup chopped roasted sweet red pepper, patted dry
- ¼ cup shredded provolone cheese
- 2 Tbsp. chopped ripe olives
- 1 Tbsp. minced fresh parsley
- 1 tsp. dried oregano
- ¼ tsp. pepper
- 3 Tbsp. grated Romano cheese, divided
- 1 pkg. (17.3 oz.) frozen puff pastry, thawed
- 1 tsp. 2% milk

1. Preheat oven to 375°. For filling, mix the first seven ingredients and 2 Tbsp. Romano cheese. Unfold one pastry sheet; cut into 16 squares. Place 2 Tbsp. filling on one half of each square. Brush the edges of the pastry with milk; fold over to form a rectangle. Seal the edges with a fork; place 1 in. apart on a parchment paper-lined baking sheet. Repeat with second pastry sheet and remaining filling.
2. Cut a slit in the top of each puff. Brush with milk; sprinkle with the remaining Romano cheese. Bake until golden brown, 20-22 minutes. Remove from pans to wire racks to cool slightly. Serve warm.

TEST KITCHEN TIP

Ricotta Only, Please!

Many cooks use cottage cheese in place of ricotta for lasagna. Although this recipe is based on lasagna, the higher liquid content in cottage cheese would make the pastry soggy—so stick with ricotta.

SWEET POTATO
PANZANELLA

SWEET POTATO PANZANELLA

This a cherished fall lunch dish, and it makes a terrific side for a larger meal. It is filled with flavor and texture but isn't too high in calories.
—Mary Leverette, Columbia, SC

Takes: 30 min. • **Makes:** 8 servings

- 2 cups cubed peeled sweet potatoes
- 4 cups cubed French bread
- 4 Tbsp. olive oil, divided
- ⅛ tsp. salt
- ⅛ tsp. pepper
- 4 cups fresh baby spinach
- ½ small red onion, thinly sliced
- ¼ cup minced fresh basil
- ¼ cup minced fresh cilantro
- ⅓ cup red wine vinegar

1. Preheat oven to 450°. Place sweet potatoes in a large saucepan with enough water to cover them; bring to a boil. Reduce heat; cook, covered, just until tender, 8-12 minutes. Drain; cool slightly.
2. Meanwhile, toss bread cubes with 2 Tbsp. oil, salt and pepper. Spread evenly in an ungreased 15x10x1-in. pan. Bake until golden brown, about 5 minutes. Transfer to a large bowl; cool slightly.
3. Add spinach, onion, herbs and potatoes to the toasted bread. In a small bowl, whisk together vinegar and the remaining oil. Drizzle over salad; toss gently to combine.

PUMPKIN-COCONUT SOUP

Thai food lovers will go crazy for this soup. It has a deep flavor from the combination of onion, coconut milk and spices.
—Susan Hein, Burlington, WI

Prep: 20 min. • **Cook:** 25 min.
Makes: 12 servings (3½ qt.)

- 2 Tbsp. butter
- 1 large onion, chopped
- 2 Tbsp. minced fresh gingerroot
- 2 cartons (32 oz. each) chicken stock
- 2 cans (15 oz. each) pumpkin
- 1 tsp. salt
- ¾ tsp. ground cinnamon
- ½ tsp. ground nutmeg
- ½ tsp. pepper
- 2 cups light coconut milk
  Optional toppings: sour cream, pepitas and minced fresh parsley

1. In a large saucepan, heat butter over medium-high heat; saute onion and ginger until tender. Add stock, pumpkin and seasonings; whisk until blended. Bring to a boil. Reduce heat; simmer, covered, until flavors are blended, about 15 minutes.
2. Puree soup using an immersion blender. Or cool slightly and puree in batches in a blender; return to pan. Stir in the coconut milk; heat through. Serve with toppings as desired.

GREEN BEANS WITH SMOKED TURKEY BACON

I like cooking with curry, and this is a wonderful slow cooker favorite of mine with loads of flavor. It can be a main dish or a side dish. If you're cooking for vegetarians, just leave out the bacon.
—Nancy Heishman, Las Vegas, NV

Prep: 25 min. • **Cook:** 5 hours
Makes: 10 servings

- 2 lbs. fresh green beans, trimmed
- 1 can (15 oz.) garbanzo beans or chickpeas, rinsed and drained
- 1 large red onion, chopped
- 1 large sweet red pepper, chopped
- 8 turkey bacon strips, chopped
- 1 can (15 oz.) crushed tomatoes
- ¼ cup lemon juice
- 2 Tbsp. minced fresh parsley
- 3 garlic cloves, minced
- 3 tsp. curry powder
- 1 tsp. freshly ground pepper
- ¾ tsp. salt
- ¼ cup minced fresh basil
- 1½ cups crumbled feta cheese

1. Place the first four ingredients in a 6-qt. slow cooker. In a large nonstick skillet, cook the bacon over medium heat until crisp, stirring occasionally. Add to the slow cooker.
2. In a small bowl, mix tomatoes, lemon juice, parsley, garlic and dry seasonings. Pour over the bean mixture.
3. Cook, covered, on low until the green beans are tender, 5-6 hours. Stir in basil. Top with cheese before serving.

PARMESAN-PRETZEL
CRISPS

PARMESAN-PRETZEL CRISPS

I usually have the ingredients on hand for these tasty snacks. They're so easy to make, but guests think you have really gone the extra mile!
—Pauline Porterfield, Roxboro, NC

Prep: 10 min. • **Bake:** 10 min./batch
Makes: about 3 dozen

- 1½ cups shredded Parmesan cheese
- ¼ cup finely crushed pretzels
- ⅛ tsp. crushed red pepper flakes
  Pizza sauce and sliced fresh basil, optional

1. Preheat oven to 350°. Toss together cheese, pretzels and red pepper flakes. Place 2 tsp. of the mixture in each cup of a greased nonstick mini-muffin tin.
2. Bake until golden brown, 10-15 minutes. If desired, serve with pizza sauce and sliced fresh basil.

APPLE PROSCIUTTO BRUSCHETTA

This is a simple but delicious holiday appetizer. I use Honeycrisp apples, but you can use whatever apples you prefer. For adult parties, I add a splash of cream sherry wine for an extra-special flavor.
—Nancy Heishman, Las Vegas, NV

Prep: 20 min. • **Bake:** 10 min./batch
Makes: 3 dozen

- 1 cup finely chopped peeled apple
- 1 cup grated Asiago cheese
- 2 oz. finely chopped prosciutto
- 1 tsp. minced fresh oregano
- 1 tsp. minced fresh thyme
- ¼ tsp. ground cinnamon
- ⅛ tsp. coarsely ground pepper
- 1 tsp. cream sherry or apple juice, optional
- 36 slices French bread baguette (¼ in. thick)

1. Preheat oven to 375°. For topping, combine first seven ingredients and, if desired, sherry.
2. Place baguette slices on foil-lined baking sheets. Top each with 1 rounded Tbsp. of topping. Bake until lightly browned and cheese is melted, 8-10 minutes.

APPLE QUINOA SPOON BREAD

APPLE QUINOA SPOON BREAD

My cousin is a strict vegetarian, so creating satisfying veggie dishes is my holiday challenge. I added hearty, healthy quinoa and vegetables to spoonbread to make a well-rounded casserole. Serve it as a Thanksgiving side or pair it with a seasonal salad for a great vegetarian main course.
—Christine Wendland, Browns Mills, NJ

Prep: 25 min. • **Bake:** 25 min.
Makes: 9 servings

- ⅔ cup water
- ⅓ cup quinoa, rinsed
- 1 Tbsp. canola oil
- 1 small apple, peeled and diced
- 1 small onion, finely chopped
- 1 small parsnip, peeled and diced
- ½ tsp. celery seed
- 1¼ tsp. salt, divided
- 1 Tbsp. minced fresh sage
- ¾ cup yellow cornmeal
- ¼ cup all-purpose flour
- 1 Tbsp. sugar
- 1 tsp. baking powder
- 1 large egg
- 1½ cups 2% milk, divided

1. Preheat oven to 375°. In a small saucepan, bring water to a boil. Add quinoa. Reduce heat; simmer, covered, until liquid is absorbed, 12-15 minutes. Fluff with a fork; cool slightly.
2. Meanwhile, in a large skillet, heat oil over medium heat; saute apple, onion and parsnip with celery seed and ½ tsp. salt until softened, 4-5 minutes. Remove from heat; stir in sage.
3. In a large bowl, whisk together the cornmeal, flour, sugar, baking powder and the remaining ¾ tsp. salt. In another bowl, whisk together egg and 1 cup milk. Add to the cornmeal mixture, stirring just until moistened. Fold in quinoa and the apple mixture.
4. Transfer to a greased 8-in. square baking dish. Pour the remaining milk over top.
5. Bake, uncovered, until edges are golden brown, 25-30 minutes. Let stand 5 minutes before serving.

WHITE GRAPE JUICE BRINED TURKEY BREAST

Why not brine your turkey in white grape juice cocktail this year? I found this fantastic recipe many years ago in a holiday menu magazine. It has just the right amount of spices and seasonings.
—Edie DeSpain, Logan, UT

Prep: 25 min. + chilling
Bake: 2 hours + standing
Makes: 12 servings

- 4 fresh rosemary sprigs
- 1 bottle (46 oz.) white grape juice
- ¼ cup kosher salt
- 6 bay leaves
- 4 garlic cloves, sliced
- 2 large oven roasting bags
- 1 bone-in turkey breast (5 to 6 lbs.)
- 1 Tbsp. butter, melted
- 2 garlic cloves, minced
- 1 tsp. paprika
- 1 tsp. dried thyme
- ½ tsp. rubbed sage
- ½ tsp. onion powder
- ¼ tsp. pepper

1. In a large saucepan, combine the first five ingredients; bring to a boil. Cook and stir until salt is dissolved. Cool completely.
2. Place one oven roasting bag inside the other. Place turkey breast inside the inner bag; pour in the cooled brine. Seal each bag, pressing out as much air as possible; turn to coat turkey. Place in a large dish. Refrigerate for 8-24 hours, turning occasionally.
3. Preheat oven to 325°. Place a rack in a foil-lined roasting pan. Mix the remaining ingredients. Remove turkey from brine; rinse and pat dry. Place in prepared pan; rub with the butter mixture.
4. Roast turkey until a thermometer reads 170°, 2-2½ hours. (If the turkey browns too quickly, cover loosely with foil.) Remove from oven; tent with foil. Let stand for 15 minutes before carving.

MULLED WINE

This mulled wine is soothing and satisfying with a delightful blend of spices warmed to perfection. Refrigerating the wine mixture overnight allows the flavors to blend, so don't omit this essential step.
—*Taste of Home* Test Kitchen

Prep: 15 min. • **Cook:** 30 min. + chilling
Makes: 5 servings

- 1 bottle (750 ml) fruity red wine
- 1 cup brandy
- 1 cup sugar
- 1 medium orange, sliced
- 1 medium lemon, sliced
- ⅛ tsp. ground nutmeg
- 2 cinnamon sticks (3 in.)
- ½ tsp. whole allspice
- ½ tsp. aniseed
- ½ tsp. whole peppercorns
- 3 whole cloves
  Optional garnishes: orange slices, star anise and additional cinnamon sticks

1. In a large saucepan, combine the first six ingredients. Place the remaining spices on a double thickness of cheesecloth. Gather the corners of the cloth to enclose spices; tie securely with string. Place in pan.
2. Bring to a boil, stirring occasionally. Reduce heat; simmer gently, covered, for 20 minutes. Transfer to a covered container and let cool slightly. Refrigerate, covered, overnight.
3. Strain the wine mixture into a large saucepan, discarding fruit and spice bag; reheat. Serve warm. Garnish as desired.

HARVEST BOW TIES

Spaghetti squash and bow tie pasta make this meatless dish hearty and filling. Add a can of black beans if you'd like more protein. For added spice, switch up the tomatoes for Italian diced tomatoes or diced tomatoes with mild green chilies.
—Anne Lynch, Beacon, NY

Prep: 25 min. • **Cook:** 15 min.
Makes: 8 servings

1	small spaghetti squash (about 1½ lbs.)
12	oz. uncooked bow tie pasta (about 4½ cups)
2	Tbsp. olive oil
1	lb. sliced fresh mushrooms
1	cup chopped sweet onion
2	garlic cloves, minced
1	can (14½ oz.) diced tomatoes, undrained
6	oz. fresh baby spinach (about 8 cups)
¾	tsp. salt
½	tsp. pepper
2	Tbsp. butter
2	Tbsp. sour cream
	Grated Parmesan cheese, optional

1. Halve squash lengthwise; discard seeds. Place squash on a microwave-safe plate, cut side down. Microwave, uncovered, on high until tender, 9-11 minutes. Cool slightly.
2. Meanwhile, in a 6-qt. stockpot, cook pasta according to package directions. Drain; return to pot.
3. In a large skillet, heat oil over medium-high heat; saute mushrooms and onion until tender. Add garlic; cook and stir for 1 minute. Separate strands of squash with a fork; add to the skillet. Stir in tomatoes, spinach, salt and pepper; cook until the spinach is wilted, stirring occasionally. Stir in butter and sour cream until blended.
4. Add to pasta. Heat through, tossing to coat. If desired, top with grated Parmesan cheese.

HARVEST BOW TIES

BOURBON
SWEET POTATO PIE

SWEET CORN CUPCAKES

I love corn, and I try to sneak it into just about everything I make. Other fans of corn will also enjoy these delightful treats.
—Carol Wit, Tinley Park, IL

Prep: 40 min. • **Bake:** 15 min. + cooling
Makes: 1 dozen

- ⅓ cup reduced-fat plain yogurt
- 1¼ cups fresh or frozen corn, thawed, divided
- ¼ cup unsalted butter, softened
- ¼ cup sugar
- ¼ cup packed brown sugar
- 1 large egg
- 1¼ cups cake flour
- ½ tsp. baking powder
- ¼ tsp. baking soda
- ¼ tsp. salt

FROSTING
- ⅔ cup unsalted butter, cubed
- 1 cup confectioners' sugar
- 1 tsp. molasses
- ½ tsp. vanilla extract
- ⅛ tsp. salt

1. Preheat oven to 350°. Line 12 muffin cups with paper liners. Place yogurt and ¾ cup corn in a food processor; process until blended.

2. In a large bowl, beat butter and sugars until blended. Beat in egg. In another bowl, whisk together flour, baking powder, baking soda and salt. Add to the butter mixture alternately with the yogurt mixture, beating after each addition. Fold in the remaining ½ cup corn.

3. Fill the prepared cups half full. Bake until a toothpick inserted in center comes out clean, 15-18 minutes. Cool for 10 minutes before removing from pan to a wire rack; cool completely.

4. For frosting, in a small heavy saucepan, melt butter over medium heat. Heat until golden brown, 5-7 minutes, stirring constantly. Transfer to a large bowl; cool slightly. Beat in the remaining ingredients until smooth. Spread over cupcakes. Store in a covered container.

BOURBON SWEET POTATO PIE

There is nothing I don't love about this pie! I adore the flavors, and I like that I can sneak some healthy whole grains into the crust. It belongs on every holiday dessert buffet.
—Mary Leverette, Columbia, SC

Prep: 25 min. • **Bake:** 40 min.
Makes: 8 servings

- 1 cup quick-cooking oats
- ¾ cup packed dark brown sugar
- ¾ cup self-rising flour
- ½ cup butter, melted
- ⅔ cup chopped walnuts

FILLING
- 2 medium sweet potatoes (about 8 oz. each)
- 2 large eggs, lightly beaten
- ½ cup packed dark brown sugar
- ½ cup butter, melted
- ¼ cup self-rising flour
- 2 Tbsp. bourbon
  Sweetened whipped cream

1. Preheat oven to 325°. Mix the first four ingredients. Firmly press 1⅔ cups of the mixture onto the bottom and up the sides of a well-greased 9-in. pie plate. Bake until light golden brown, 6-8 minutes. Cool on a wire rack.

2. Stir walnuts into the remaining oat mixture. Reserve for topping.

3. For filling, pierce potatoes with a fork; microwave on high until very tender, 10-13 minutes, turning once halfway. Let cool slightly. Peel and place in a large bowl; mash until smooth. Beat in eggs, brown sugar, melted butter, flour and bourbon until well blended. Pour the filling into the crust.

4. Sprinkle with reserved topping. Bake until golden brown and the filling is set, 30-35 minutes. Cool on a wire rack; serve or refrigerate within 2 hours. Serve with whipped cream.

Note: As a substitute for 1 cup of self-rising flour, place 1½ tsp. baking powder and ½ tsp. salt in a measuring cup. Add all-purpose flour to measure 1 cup.

AUTUMN SURPRISE PIE

AUTUMN SURPRISE PIE

What better way to welcome fall than with a homemade apple pie? This version calls for apples, pears and raisins flavored with rum extract.

—Karen Gauvreau, Clearwater, FL

Prep: 40 min. + chilling • **Bake:** 45 min.
Makes: 8 servings

- 1½ cups all-purpose flour
- 3 Tbsp. sugar
- ¼ tsp. plus ⅛ tsp. salt
- ¼ tsp. plus ⅛ tsp. baking powder
- 6 Tbsp. cold butter, cubed
- ⅓ cup fat-free milk
- 1½ tsp. cider vinegar

FILLING
- ½ cup sugar
- ¼ cup all-purpose flour
- 1 tsp. ground cinnamon
- ¼ tsp. ground nutmeg
- ¼ tsp. ground cloves
- 5 cups sliced peeled apples
- 2 cups sliced peeled ripe pears
- ⅓ cup raisins
- ¾ tsp. rum extract

TOPPING
- 1 large egg, lightly beaten
- 1 tsp. coarse sugar

1. Mix first four ingredients; cut in butter until crumbly. Mix milk and vinegar; add gradually to the crumb mixture, tossing with a fork until the dough holds together when pressed. Divide dough into two portions, one slightly larger than the other. Shape each portion into a disk; cover and refrigerate for 1 hour or overnight.

2. Preheat oven to 425°. On a lightly floured surface, roll the larger portion of dough to a ⅛-in.-thick circle; transfer to a greased 9-in. pie plate. Trim the crust even with the rim of the pie plate. Refrigerate while preparing filling.

3. Mix the first five filling ingredients. Place apples, pears and raisins in a large bowl. Add the sugar mixture and extract; toss to combine. Spoon filling into crust.

4. Roll out the remaining dough to a ⅛-in.-thick circle; cut into ¾-in.-wide strips. Arrange strips over the filling in a lattice pattern. Trim and seal the strips to the edge of the bottom crust; flute edge. Brush lattice with beaten egg. Sprinkle with coarse sugar.

5. Bake on a lower oven rack 15 minutes. Reduce oven setting to 350°. Bake until crust is golden brown and filling is bubbly, 30-35 minutes. Cool on a wire rack.

Top Tips for a Fabulous Friendsgiving Party

A holiday potluck party is the low-stress alternative to a fancy feast, so keep things simple, and don't be afraid to ask for help. From setup to serving to cleanup, this party is about sharing, and everyone has something to bring to the table. Keep these tips in mind:

• The host makes the turkey and the gravy. The main course doesn't *have* to be turkey, but whatever it is, you should provide it.

• Make a plan for general food categories and the number of dishes, and include it with your invitations. Ask guests to RSVP with what they're bringing, so you don't end up with all desserts. If necessary, make specific requests (see suggestions below).

• Assign appetizers to your most reliable friend, and ask him or her to arrive early. (Having a backup appetizer is not a bad idea, either.)

• Ask that dishes are ready to go, or need only minimal reheating. You don't want a fight over kitchen space.

• Music helps set the mood. Have a party playlist, or ask a friend (who you know has good taste in music) to act as DJ.

• Wine and a non-alcohol option are easy, crowd-pleasing drink choices; a single specialty cocktail makes the occasion stand out.

• Keep the decor simple, casual and pretty. This party is about relaxation, so you want people to feel at ease.

• Let your guests help. Have a list of simple tasks they can do. Serving drinks, taking coats, stacking dishes —it all helps.

• Stock up on takeout cartons, and send guests home with leftovers. They (and your not-overloaded refrigerator) will love it!

Giving
Back Party

Thanksgiving is a time of open hearts and helping hands. Across the country, families are giving back. Whether it's working at a local food bank, shelter or other charitable organization, people are showing gratitude for their own abundance by helping others. After a day spent volunteering, celebrate with a casual, low-key potluck party that's all about comfort and goodwill.

Italian Grilled Steak Sandwich (p. 122) **Pineapple Coleslaw** (p. 122) **Orange Gelatin Pretzel Salad** (p. 125)

HAM & CHEESE
CRESCENT BUNDLES

HAM & CHEESE CRESCENT BUNDLES

This savory Danish is fluffy in the middle and crispy on the outside. It's a nice quick meal for either breakfast or lunch. The fun design is a hit with kids and adults alike.
—Marisa Raponi, Vaughan, ON

Prep: 20 min. • **Bake:** 15 min.
Makes: 1 dozen

- 1 pkg. (8 oz.) refrigerated crescent rolls
- ½ cup spinach dip
- 4 slices Black Forest ham (about 4 oz.)
- 1 cup shredded cheddar cheese

1. Preheat oven to 350°. Unroll crescent dough and separate into four rectangles; press perforations to seal.
2. Spread each rectangle with 2 Tbsp. dip to within ½ in. of edges. Top with ham and cheese. Roll up jelly-roll style, starting with a short side; pinch seam to seal. Cut each roll crosswise into thirds; place in greased muffin cups, cut sides down.
3. Bake until golden brown, 12-15 minutes. Run a knife around the edges to remove from pan.

HONEY APPLE SALAD

All of my favorite recipes are quick, simple and tasty. I came across this salad while looking for something to make with honey. Substituting several of the ingredients, I served it to my husband and two teenage daughters. It was a hit!
—Mary Lou Hawkins, Brook Park, OH

Takes: 15 min. • **Makes:** 8 servings

- ½ cup mayonnaise
- ¼ cup honey
- 2 Tbsp. sour cream
- ½ tsp. salt
- 3½ cups diced red apples
- 2 Tbsp. lemon juice
- 2 cups green grapes
- 1 cup thinly sliced celery
- ½ cup chopped dates
- ½ cup chopped walnuts

For dressing, mix first four ingredients. In a large bowl, toss apples with lemon juice. Add grapes, celery and dates. Add the dressing; toss to coat. Stir in walnuts.

PUMPKIN HUSH PUPPY MEATBALLS

PUMPKIN HUSH PUPPY MEATBALLS

My Italian husband loves meatballs. I adore pumpkin, so I decided to combine our favorites and make sausage and pumpkin meatballs!
—Paula Marchesi, Lenhartsville, PA

Prep: 30 min. • **Cook:** 40 min.
Makes: about 4 dozen

- 1½ cups yellow cornmeal
- 1½ cups all-purpose flour
- 2¼ tsp. baking powder
- 1½ tsp. salt
- ¼ tsp. cayenne pepper
- 1 can (15 oz.) pumpkin
- 2 green onions, sliced
- 1 Tbsp. seeded jalapeno pepper, minced
- 1½ lbs. bulk Italian sausage
- 2 cups shredded Monterey Jack cheese
- 1 pkg. (8 oz.) cream cheese, cubed and softened
  Jalapeno pepper jelly

1. Preheat oven to 375°. Whisk together first five ingredients. Stir in the pumpkin, green onions and jalapeno. Add sausage, Jack cheese and cream cheese; mix lightly but thoroughly.
2. With wet hands, shape mixture into 1½-in. balls. Place on parchment paper-lined 15x10x1-in. pans.
3. Bake meatballs until cooked through, 40-45 minutes, rotating pans halfway. Serve with pepper jelly.

TEST KITCHEN TIP

Make It, Freeze It

These meatballs can be made up to six weeks before you plan on serving them. Freeze the unbaked meatballs on pans until solid, then transfer to airtight containers and freeze. Either thaw before baking, or increase your baking time to cook them frozen.

HERBED TURKEY & CRANBERRY SLOPPY JOES

These deliciously different joes pile on the flavor with herbs, spices, cranberries and more. Keep the meat mixture warm in a slow cooker and let guests assemble their own sandwiches.
—Jamie Miller, Maple Grove, MN

Prep: 15 min. • **Cook:** 20 min.
Makes: 10 servings

- 2 lbs. ground turkey
- 1 cup chopped sweet onion
- 1 celery rib, finely chopped
- 2 garlic cloves, minced
- 1 can (14½ oz.) petite diced tomatoes, undrained
- ½ cup dried cranberries
- ¼ cup chili sauce
- 1 tsp. dried sage leaves
- 1 tsp. dried thyme
- 1 tsp. dried rosemary, crushed
- ¾ tsp. salt
- ½ tsp. pepper
- ⅔ cup jellied cranberry sauce
- ⅓ cup mayonnaise
- 2 tsp. Dijon mustard
- 10 hamburger buns, split

1. In a large skillet, cook and crumble turkey with onion, celery and garlic over medium-high heat until the turkey is no longer pink, 6-8 minutes; drain.
2. Stir in the tomatoes, dried cranberries, chili sauce and seasonings; bring to a boil. Reduce heat; simmer, covered, until flavors are blended, 6-8 minutes. Stir in cranberry sauce; heat through.
3. Mix mayonnaise and mustard; spread on buns. Fill with turkey mixture.

PEAR CUSTARD BARS

Every time I take this crowd-pleasing treat to a potluck, I come home with an empty pan. Cooking and baking come naturally for me—as a farm girl, I helped my mother feed my 10 siblings.
—Jeannette Nord, San Juan Capistrano, CA

Prep: 20 min. + chilling
Bake: 50 min. + cooling • **Makes:** 16 bars

- ½ cup butter, softened
- ⅓ cup sugar
- ¼ tsp. vanilla extract
- ¾ cup all-purpose flour
- ⅔ cup chopped macadamia nuts

TOPPING

- 1 can (15¼ oz.) pear halves, drained
- 1 pkg. (8 oz.) cream cheese, softened
- ½ cup sugar plus ½ tsp. sugar, divided
- ½ tsp. vanilla extract
- 1 large egg
- ½ tsp. ground cinnamon

1. Preheat oven to 350°. Grease an 8-in. square baking pan; set aside. Cream butter and ⅓ cup sugar until light and fluffy; beat in vanilla. Gradually beat in flour. Stir in the macadamia nuts.
2. Press into prepared pan. Bake until light brown, about 20 minutes. Cool on a wire rack. Increase oven setting to 375°.
3. Cut pears into ⅛-in. slices; blot dry. Beat cream cheese until smooth; beat in ½ cup sugar and vanilla. Beat in egg just until blended. Spread over crust. Arrange pears in a single layer over top. Mix the ½ tsp. sugar and cinnamon; sprinkle over pears.
4. Bake until the center is almost set, 28-30 minutes (filling will firm upon cooling). Cool for 45 minutes on a wire rack. Refrigerate, covered, for at least 2 hours before cutting.

The Grateful Pumpkin

A white pumpkin is the canvas for thankful thoughts from all your guests. It's a happy display of the good things in life that lasts until the leftovers head home.

ARTICHOKE & SPINACH
CHICKEN CASSEROLE

ARTICHOKE & SPINACH CHICKEN CASSEROLE

Try this homey and comforting casserole for an alternative entree at Thanksgiving. The spinach adds nice color and the red pepper flakes add a pleasant, mild heat.
—Janice Christofferson, Eagle River, WI

Prep: 30 min. • **Bake:** 45 min.
Makes: 8 servings

- 3 cups uncooked bow tie pasta
- 2 Tbsp. butter
- ½ lb. sliced fresh mushrooms
- 1 medium onion, chopped
- 2 large eggs
- 1½ cups 2% milk
- 1 tsp. Italian seasoning
- ½ tsp. salt
- ¼ tsp. pepper
- ¼ to ½ tsp. crushed red pepper flakes
- 3 cups cubed cooked chicken
- 1 can (14 oz.) water-packed quartered artichoke hearts, rinsed and drained
- 1 pkg. (10 oz.) frozen chopped spinach, thawed and squeezed dry
- 2 cups shredded Monterey Jack cheese
- 2 Tbsp. grated Parmesan cheese

TOPPING
- ⅓ cup seasoned bread crumbs
- 2 Tbsp. grated Parmesan cheese
- 1 Tbsp. butter, melted
- ½ tsp. paprika

1. Preheat oven to 350°. Cook pasta according to package directions; drain.
2. In a large skillet, heat butter over medium-high heat; saute mushrooms and onion until tender. Remove from heat.
3. In a large bowl, whisk together eggs, milk and seasonings. Stir in chicken, artichoke hearts, spinach, cheeses and the mushroom mixture. Stir in the pasta.
4. Transfer to a greased 13x9-in. baking dish. Bake, covered, for 40 minutes.
5. Mix topping ingredients; sprinkle over the casserole. Bake, uncovered, until bubbly and topping is golden brown, 5-10 minutes.

PINEAPPLE
COLESLAW

ITALIAN GRILLED STEAK SANDWICH

If you need to feed a hungry crowd, you can't go wrong with steak sandwiches. They're easy to make and everyone loves them.
—Gilda Lester, Millsboro, DE

Prep: 35 min. + marinating
Grill: 15 min. + cooling • **Makes:** 8 servings

- ½ cup reduced-sodium teriyaki sauce
- 2 Tbsp. lemon juice
- 2 Tbsp. olive oil
- 2 Tbsp. Worcestershire sauce
- 1 beef flank steak (1 lb.)
- 1 round loaf Italian bread (about 2 lbs.), unsliced
- 4 plum tomatoes, chopped
- 4 green onions, thinly sliced
- ¼ cup Greek olives, coarsely chopped
- ¼ cup sliced pepperoni
- 1 Tbsp. thinly sliced fresh basil leaves
- 2 Tbsp. plus ¼ cup prepared Italian salad dressing, divided
- 2 cups fresh arugula

1. Place the first four ingredients in a large bowl or shallow dish. Add the steak and turn to coat. Refrigerate, covered, for 8 hours or overnight.
2. Remove steak, discarding marinade. Grill steak, covered, over medium heat or broil 4 in. from heat until meat reaches desired doneness (for medium-rare, a thermometer should read 135°; medium, 140°), 6-8 minutes per side. Cool completely.
3. Cut bread loaf horizontally in half. Hollow out both halves, leaving a ½-in. shell (save the removed bread for another use). Cut steak across the grain into thin slices. In a bowl, toss tomatoes with green onions, olives, pepperoni, basil and 2 Tbsp. of dressing. In another bowl, toss arugula with the remaining dressing.
4. Place half of the arugula in the bread bottom. Layer with steak, tomato mixture and the remaining arugula; replace bread top. Wrap in foil; refrigerate at least 1 hour. Cut into wedges to serve.

PINEAPPLE COLESLAW

When I was a child, my mother often served this salad with multicolored miniature marshmallows on top, much to my delight. The added sweetness really complemented the salad's tangy flavor.
—Betty Follas, Morgan Hill, CA

Prep: 15 min. • **Makes:** 8 servings

- ¾ cup mayonnaise
- 2 Tbsp. sugar
- 2 Tbsp. cider vinegar
- 1 to 2 Tbsp. 2% milk
- 4 cups shredded cabbage
- ¾ cup pineapple tidbits
  Paprika, optional

1. For dressing, mix first four ingredients. Place cabbage and pineapple in a large bowl. Add dressing; toss to coat.
2. Refrigerate until serving. If desired, sprinkle with paprika.

SMOKY CHICKEN SPREAD

The unique smoky flavor in this spread comes from smoked almonds. It makes a hearty snack on your favorite crackers. Don't expect many leftovers!
—Mary Beth Wagner, Rio, WI

Prep: 15 min. + chilling
Makes: 32 servings (2 Tbsp. each)

- ¾ cup mayonnaise
- ¼ cup finely chopped onion
- 1 Tbsp. honey
- ½ tsp. seasoned salt
- ⅛ tsp. pepper
- 3 cups finely chopped cooked chicken
- ½ cup finely chopped celery
- ½ cup coarsely chopped smoked almonds
  Assorted crackers

1. In a large bowl, mix first five ingredients. Stir in chicken, celery and almonds. Refrigerate, covered, at least 2 hours.
2. Serve with crackers.

ITALIAN GRILLED
STEAK SANDWICH

ORANGE GELATIN
PRETZEL SALAD

ORANGE GELATIN PRETZEL SALAD

Salty pretzels pair nicely with sweet oranges in this refreshing layered salad. It's a family favorite that's a slam dunk at potlucks.
—Peggy Boyd, Northport, AL

Prep: 20 min. + chilling
Bake: 10 min. + cooling
Makes: 12 servings

- ¾ cup butter, melted
- 1 Tbsp. plus ¾ cup sugar, divided
- 2 cups finely crushed pretzels
- 2 cups boiling water
- 2 pkg. (3 oz. each) orange gelatin
- 2 cans (8 oz. each) crushed pineapple, drained
- 1 can (11 oz.) mandarin oranges, drained
- 1 pkg. (8 oz.) cream cheese, softened
- 2 cups whipped topping
  Additional whipped topping and mandarin oranges, optional

1. Preheat oven to 350°. Mix melted butter and 1 Tbsp. sugar; stir in pretzels. Press onto the bottom of an ungreased 13x9-in. baking dish. Bake 10 minutes. Cool completely on a wire rack.
2. In a large bowl, add boiling water to gelatin; stir for 2 minutes to completely dissolve. Stir in fruit. Refrigerate until partially set, about 30 minutes.
3. Meanwhile, in a bowl, beat cream cheese and the remaining sugar until smooth. Fold in whipped topping. Spread over crust. Gently spoon gelatin mixture over top.
4. Refrigerate, covered, until firm, 2-4 hours. To serve, cut into squares. If desired, top with additional whipped topping and oranges.

Single-Serving Size!

To make individual servings of Orange Gelatin Pretzel Salad for your guests, prepare the layers as directed. In each of twelve 9-oz. cups or ½-pint canning jars, layer about 2 Tbsp. of the pretzel mixture, 2 Tbsp. of the cream cheese mixture and ⅓ cup of the gelatin mixture. Refrigerate and serve as directed.

CARAMEL SURPRISE CHOCOLATE CHIP COOKIES

This has been my go-to cookie recipe for more than 20 years. I love the responses I get from people who try to guess what the surprise center is. I always double or even triple this recipe when taking it to potlucks.
—Becky McClaflin, Blanchard, OK

Prep: 30 min. • **Bake:** 10 min/batch
Makes: about 3 dozen

- ½ cup butter, softened
- ½ cup butter-flavored shortening
- ¾ cup sugar
- ¾ cup packed brown sugar
- 1 large egg
- 2 tsp. vanilla extract
- 2½ cups all-purpose flour
- 1½ tsp. baking soda
- ½ tsp. salt
- 1 cup (6 oz.) semisweet chocolate chips
- 1 cup coarsely chopped walnuts
- 1 pkg. (5 oz.) Milk Duds

1. Preheat oven to 350°. Cream first four ingredients until light and fluffy; beat in egg and vanilla. In another bowl, whisk together flour, baking soda and salt; gradually beat into creamed mixture. Stir in chocolate chips and walnuts.
2. Shape tablespoonfuls of dough into balls. Wrap each ball of dough around a Milk Dud; place 2 in. apart on ungreased baking sheets.
3. Bake until golden brown, 10-12 minutes. Remove from pans to wire racks to cool.

CHAI-SPICED BREAD PUDDING

Nothing says the holidays to me more than the warming spices of chai. This comforting bread pudding incorporates those flavors to make a dessert everyone raves about.
—Jessie Apfe, Berkeley, CA

Prep: 25 min. + standing • **Bake:** 35 min.
Makes: 9 servings

- 4 large eggs, lightly beaten
- 2 cups 2% milk
- ½ cup packed brown sugar
- 1 tsp. ground cinnamon
- 1 tsp. vanilla extract
- ¾ tsp. ground ginger
- ½ tsp. ground cardamom
- ¼ tsp. salt
- ⅛ tsp. ground cloves
- 2 Tbsp. rum, optional
- 6 slices day-old French bread (1 in. thick), cubed
- ⅓ cup slivered almonds
  Vanilla ice cream or sweetened whipped cream

1. Preheat oven to 350°. Grease an 8-in. square baking dish; set aside. In a large bowl, whisk together first nine ingredients and, if desired, rum. Gently stir in bread; let stand for 15 minutes or until bread is softened.
2. Transfer to prepared baking dish. Sprinkle with almonds.
3. Bake, uncovered, until puffed, golden and a knife inserted near the center comes out clean, 35-40 minutes. Serve warm with ice cream.

Pumpkin Spice Delight

The kids are back in school, the leaves are changing colors and suddenly pumpkin spice is flavoring our favorite foods and beverages. It can only mean one thing—fall is here! See how easy it is to infuse your own homemade treats with the warm, cozy notes of nutmeg, ginger, cinnamon and cloves.

Pumpkin Waffles with Orange Walnut Butter (p. 132)
Pumpkin Doughnut Drops (p. 129) **Pumpkin Spice Latte** (p. 129)

PUMPKIN DOUGHNUT DROPS

PUMPKIN DOUGHNUT DROPS

I always have a few special treats on hand when my grandchildren come to visit. These cake doughnuts dusted in sugar are one of our favorites.
—Beva Staum, Muscoda, WI

Prep: 10 min. • **Cook:** 5 min./batch
Makes: about 7 dozen

- 2 large eggs
- 1¼ cups sugar
- 2 Tbsp. shortening
- 1 cup canned pumpkin
- 2 tsp. white vinegar
- 1 tsp. vanilla extract
- 3 cups all-purpose flour
- ½ cup nonfat dry milk powder
- 3 tsp. baking powder
- ½ tsp. salt
- ½ tsp. ground cinnamon
- ½ tsp. ground nutmeg
- ½ cup lemon-lime soda
  Oil for deep-fat frying
  Additional sugar

1. In a large bowl, beat eggs, sugar and shortening until blended. Beat in pumpkin, vinegar and vanilla. In another bowl, whisk together the flour, milk powder, baking powder, salt and spices. Add to the egg mixture alternately with soda, beating after each addition.

2. In an electric skillet or deep fryer, heat oil to 375°. Drop teaspoonfuls of batter, a few at a time, into hot oil. Fry until golden brown, about 1 minute per side. Drain on paper towels. Roll doughnuts in additional sugar while warm.

TEST KITCHEN TIP

Frying Doughnuts

When making doughnuts, fry them in batches for about one minute on each side; let the oil reheat to 365° before starting the next round. Use heatproof tongs for flipping and transferring piping-hot doughnuts from oil to paper towels.

PUMPKIN SPICE LATTE

PUMPKIN SPICE LATTE

Skip the long lines at the coffeehouse. Each sip of this spiced-just-right beverage tastes like a piece of pumpkin pie.
—*Taste of Home* Test Kitchen

Takes: 20 min. • **Makes:** 6 servings

- 3 cups 2% milk
- ¾ cup canned pumpkin
- ⅓ cup packed brown sugar
- ½ tsp. ground cinnamon
- ¼ tsp. ground ginger
- ⅛ tsp. ground nutmeg
- 1½ cups hot brewed espresso or strong-brewed dark roast coffee
  Whipped cream and additional nutmeg, optional

Place first six ingredients in a large saucepan. Cook and stir over medium heat until heated through. Stir in hot espresso. Pour into warm mugs. If desired, top with whipped cream and additional nutmeg.

PUMPKIN PIE SMOOTHIE

I wanted pumpkin pie for breakfast but without the effort. This smoothie delivers that wonderful pumpkin-cinnamon combo. Dress it up with a little whipped cream and a sprinkle of granola on top.
—Alisa Christensen,
Rancho Santa Margarita, CA

Takes: 10 min. • **Makes:** 2 servings

- 1 carton (5.3 oz.) fat-free plain Greek yogurt
- ½ cup 2% milk
- 2 Tbsp. maple syrup
- ¼ tsp. ground cinnamon or pumpkin pie spice
- 2 tsp. almond butter or peanut butter
- ⅔ cup canned pumpkin
- 1 cup ice cubes
- 1 Tbsp. granola

Place first seven ingredients in a blender; process until blended. Pour into glasses; top with granola.

PUMPKIN CHIP COOKIES

These golden cake-like cookies are one of my favorites, especially in fall. The subtle pumpkin and cinnamon flavors pair well with chocolate chips.
—Tami Burroughs, Salem, OR

Prep: 10 min. • **Bake:** 10 min./batch
Makes: about 10 dozen

- 1½ cups butter, softened
- 2 cups packed brown sugar
- 1 cup sugar
- 1 large egg
- 1 tsp. vanilla extract
- 1 can (15 oz.) pumpkin
- 4 cups all-purpose flour
- 2 tsp. baking soda
- 2 tsp. ground cinnamon
- 1 tsp. salt
- 2 cups quick-cooking oats
- 2 cups (12 oz.) semisweet chocolate chips

1. Preheat oven to 350°. Cream butter and sugars until light and fluffy. Beat in egg and vanilla. Beat in the pumpkin. In another bowl, whisk together flour, baking soda, cinnamon and salt; gradually beat into creamed mixture. Stir in oats and chocolate chips.

2. Drop by tablespoonfuls 2 in. apart onto ungreased baking sheets. Bake until lightly browned, 10-12 minutes. Remove from pans to wire racks to cool.

TEST KITCHEN TIP

Making Same-Size Drop Cookies

An ice cream scoop is perfect for making uniformly sized drop cookies. (A tablespoon-size scoop makes standard 2-in. cookies.) Just scoop the dough, even off the top with a flat-edge metal spatula and release onto a baking sheet.

PUMPKIN
CHIP COOKIES

AUTUMN HARVEST PUMPKIN PIE

This is the best holiday pie I've ever tasted. Use canned pumpkin if you don't have fresh pumpkins or to save time.
—Stan Strom, Gilbert, AZ

Prep: 30 min. + chilling
Bake: 55 min. + cooling
Makes: 8 servings

- 2 cups all-purpose flour
- 1 cup cake flour
- 2 Tbsp. sugar
- ½ tsp. salt
- ½ cup cold unsalted butter, cubed
- ½ cup butter-flavored shortening
- 1 large egg
- ⅓ cup cold water
- 1 Tbsp. cider vinegar

FILLING

- 2½ cups canned pumpkin (about 19 oz.)
- 1¼ cups packed light brown sugar
- ¾ cup half-and-half cream
- 2 large eggs
- ¼ cup apple butter
- 2 Tbsp. orange juice
- 2 Tbsp. maple syrup
- 2 tsp. ground cinnamon
- 2 tsp. pumpkin pie spice
- ¼ tsp. salt

1. In a large bowl, mix the first four ingredients; cut in butter and shortening until crumbly. Whisk together egg, water and vinegar; gradually add to flour mixture, tossing with a fork until the dough holds together when pressed. Divide dough in half so that one portion is slightly larger than the other; shape each into a disk. Wrap in plastic; refrigerate dough 1 hour or overnight.

2. Preheat oven to 425°. On a lightly floured surface, roll larger portion to a ⅛-in.-thick circle; transfer to a 9-in. deep-dish pie plate. Trim pastry to ½ in. beyond edge of pie plate; flute edge. Refrigerate until ready to fill.

3. Roll smaller portion of dough to ⅛-in. thickness. Cut with a floured leaf-shaped cookie cutter; place 1 in. apart on a baking sheet. Bake cutouts until golden brown, 8-10 minutes.

4. Meanwhile, in a large bowl, beat filling ingredients until blended; transfer to crust. Bake on a lower oven rack 10 minutes. Cover the edge loosely with foil. Reduce oven setting to 350°. Bake until a knife inserted near the center comes out clean, 45-50 minutes.

5. Cool on a wire rack; serve or refrigerate pie within 2 hours. Top with leaf cutouts before serving.

Note: This recipe was tested with commercially prepared apple butter.

CREAM CHEESE FILLED PUMPKIN MUFFINS

You'll love these moist muffins. They're studded with cranberries, and the cream cheese filling is a nice surprise.
—Jessie Apfel, Berkeley, CA

Prep: 25 min. • **Bake:** 20 min.
Makes: 1 dozen

- 3 oz. cream cheese, softened
- ¼ cup sugar
- 1 Tbsp. maple syrup

MUFFINS

- 1½ cups all-purpose flour
- 1 cup packed brown sugar
- 2 tsp. pumpkin pie spice
- 1 tsp. ground cinnamon
- ½ tsp. baking powder
- ½ tsp. baking soda
- ¼ tsp. salt
- 2 large eggs
- 1 cup canned pumpkin
- ⅓ cup canola oil
- ½ cup dried cranberries

1. Preheat oven to 350°. For filling, beat cream cheese, sugar and maple syrup until smooth.

2. In a large bowl, whisk together the first seven muffin ingredients. In another bowl, whisk together eggs, pumpkin and oil. Add to dry ingredients, stirring just until moistened. Fold in cranberries.

3. Fill 12 paper-lined or greased muffin cups one-third full. Drop cream cheese filling by tablespoonfuls into center of each muffin; cover with remaining batter.

4. Bake until a toothpick inserted in muffin portion comes out clean, 20-25 minutes. Cool 5 minutes before removing from pan to a wire rack. Serve warm. Refrigerate leftover muffins.

PUMPKIN WAFFLES WITH ORANGE WALNUT BUTTER

This is so delicious! Bring a flourish to the breakfast table with these fragrant waffles topped with nutty orange butter.
—Brandi Davis, Pullman, WA

Takes: 30 min. • **Makes:** 4 servings

- ½   cup butter, softened
- 1   Tbsp. grated orange zest
- ¼   cup chopped walnuts
  WAFFLES
- 1   cup plus 2 Tbsp. all-purpose flour
- 2   Tbsp. brown sugar
- 1   tsp. ground cinnamon
- ½   tsp. salt
- ½   tsp. baking powder
- ¼   tsp. baking soda
- 2   large eggs
- 1   cup 2% milk
- ½   cup canned pumpkin
- 2   Tbsp. butter, melted
  Maple syrup

1. Preheat waffle maker. Mix softened butter and orange zest; stir in walnuts.
2. Whisk together the first six waffle ingredients. In another bowl, whisk together eggs, milk, pumpkin and melted butter; add to dry ingredients. Stir just until moistened.
3. Bake the waffles according to the manufacturer's directions until golden brown. Serve waffles with butter mixture and syrup.

PUMPKIN ICEBOX CAKE

This tube cake is a fun, simple way to make a quick dessert. Pumpkin, chocolate and spice are very nice.
—Juli Meyers, Hinesville, GA

Prep: 1 hour+ chilling
Cook: 20 min. + chilling
Makes: 12 servings

- 1   envelope unflavored gelatin
- ⅔   cup cold 2% milk
- 1   can (15 oz.) pumpkin
- 1   cup packed brown sugar
- 1   tsp. pumpkin pie spice
- ½   tsp. salt
- 4   large egg yolks
- 1   cup heavy whipping cream
- 1   Tbsp. sugar
- 1   pkg. (9 oz.) chocolate wafers

1. In a large saucepan, sprinkle the gelatin over milk; let stand 1 minute. Heat and stir over low heat until gelatin is completely dissolved. Whisk in the pumpkin, brown sugar, pie spice and salt; cook and stir over medium heat until thickened and bubbly. Reduce heat to low; cook and stir for 2 minutes. Remove from heat.
2. In a small bowl, whisk a small amount of hot mixture into the egg yolks; return all to pan, whisking constantly. Bring to a gentle boil; cook and stir 2 minutes. Immediately transfer to a clean bowl; cool 30 minutes. Press plastic wrap onto surface of mixture; refrigerate 30 minutes.
3. In a small bowl, beat the cream until it begins to thicken. Add sugar; beat until soft peaks form. Fold into the pumpkin mixture. Refrigerate, covered, until cold.
4. Spread scant tablespoonfuls of the pumpkin mixture over wafers; arrange on a serving plate to form a 10-in. ring of closely overlapping wafers. Spread remaining pumpkin mixture over entire ring. Refrigerate 8 hours or overnight.

PUMPKIN PIE DIP

Takes: 10 min. • **Makes:** 4 cups

- 1   pkg. (8 oz.) cream cheese, softened
- 2   cups confectioners' sugar
- 1   cup canned pumpkin
- ½   cup sour cream
- 1   tsp. ground cinnamon
- 1   tsp. pumpkin pie spice
- ½   tsp. ground ginger
  Gingersnap cookies

Beat the cream cheese and confectioners' sugar until smooth. Beat in pumpkin, sour cream and spices until blended. Transfer to a bowl; serve with gingersnaps. Refrigerate leftovers.

PUMPKIN ICE CREAM

Ice cream lovers can't get enough of this creamy, rich ice cream that boasts lots of delish pumpkin flavor.
—Molly Badger, Provo, UT

Prep: 15 min. + chilling
Process: 20 min. + freezing • **Makes:** 1½ qt.

- 1   cup whole milk
- ½   cup packed brown sugar
- ¼   tsp. ground ginger
- ¼   tsp. ground cinnamon
- ⅛   tsp. ground nutmeg
- ½   cup maple syrup
- 1   can (15 oz.) pumpkin
- 2   cups heavy whipping cream

1. In a large saucepan, heat milk to 180°; stir in brown sugar until dissolved. Remove from heat; whisk in the spices, maple syrup and pumpkin.
2. Transfer to a large bowl; place bowl in a pan of ice water. Stir mixture gently and occasionally 2 minutes. Stir in cream. Press plastic wrap onto surface of milk mixture; refrigerate several hours or overnight.
3. Fill cylinder of ice cream maker no more than two-thirds full; freeze according to manufacturer's directions. (Refrigerate any remaining mixture until ready to freeze.) Transfer ice cream to freezer containers, allowing headspace for expansion. Freeze until firm, 2-4 hours.

"Try my rich, creamy pumpkin pie dip with gingersnap cookies or sliced pears or apples. It's also great spread on zucchini bread or any nut bread."

—LAURIE LACLAIR, NORTH RICHLAND HILLS, TX

PUMPKIN-WALNUT SQUARES

The buttery crust and crumb topping plus the creamy pumpkin filling make this a popular dessert at potlucks. Try it with whipped cream, ice cream or all by its yummy self.
—Ruth Beller, Sun City, CA

Prep: 25 min. • **Bake:** 50 min.
Makes: 2 dozen

- 1¾ cups all-purpose flour
- ⅓ cup sugar
- ⅓ cup packed brown sugar
- 1 cup cold butter, cubed
- 1 cup chopped walnuts
- 2 large eggs, lightly beaten
- 1 can (15 oz.) pumpkin
- 1 can (14 oz.) sweetened condensed milk
- 1 tsp. ground cinnamon
- ½ tsp. salt
- ½ tsp. ground allspice
  Confectioners' sugar, optional

1. Preheat oven to 350°. Mix the flour, sugar and brown sugar; cut in butter until crumbly. Stir in walnuts. Reserve 1 cup mixture for topping; press the remaining mixture onto bottom and halfway up sides of a 13x9-in. baking dish.
2. In a large bowl, beat all remaining ingredients just until smooth. Pour into crust; sprinkle with reserved topping.
3. Bake until golden brown, 50-55 minutes. Cool slightly on a wire rack. Serve warm or refrigerate and serve cold. If desired, dust with confectioners' sugar. Refrigerate leftovers.

PUMPKIN-WALNUT SQUARES

Homemade Pumpkin Pie Spice

Homemade pumpkin pie spice may be used as a substitute in any recipe that calls for store-bought pumpkin pie spice. Mix 4 tsp. ground cinnamon, 2 tsp. ground ginger, 1 tsp. ground cloves and ½ tsp. ground nutmeg. Store in an airtight container in a cool, dry place up to 6 months.

NO-KNEAD PUMPKIN CINNAMON ROLLS

My cousin gave this recipe to my mother many years ago. My mother shared it with me, and I have been making it ever since. The rolls are amazingly moist and tender, especially right out of the oven.
—Kathleen Gill, Miles City, MT

Prep: 35 min. + rising • **Bake:** 20 min.
Makes: 1 dozen

- 1 pkg. (¼ oz.) active dry yeast
- ⅔ cup warm water (110° to 115°)
- ½ cup canned pumpkin
- 1 large egg
- ¼ cup butter, softened
- ¼ cup sugar
- 1 tsp. salt
- ½ tsp. pumpkin pie spice
- 2¼ to 2½ cups all-purpose flour

FILLING
- ½ cup packed brown sugar
- 1 tsp. ground cinnamon
- 2 Tbsp. butter, melted

FROSTING
- 1¼ cups confectioners' sugar
- 2 Tbsp. 2% milk
- ⅛ tsp. pumpkin pie spice

1. Dissolve yeast in warm water. In a large bowl, combine the pumpkin, egg, butter, sugar, salt, pie spice, yeast mixture and 1 cup flour; beat on medium speed for 3 minutes until smooth. Stir in enough remaining flour to form a soft dough (dough will be sticky).

2. Do not knead. Place in a greased bowl, turning once to grease the top. Cover with plastic wrap and let rise in a warm place until doubled, about 1 hour.

3. For filling, mix the brown sugar and cinnamon. Stir down dough, beating about 25 times; turn dough onto a well-floured surface (dough will be sticky). Roll into a 12x10-in. rectangle. Brush with melted butter to within ½ in. of edges; sprinkle with brown sugar mixture. Roll up jelly-roll style, starting with a long side; pinch seam to seal. Cut into 12 slices.

4. Place in a greased 9-in. round pan, cut side down. Cover with a kitchen towel; let rise in a warm place until doubled, about 45 minutes. Preheat oven to 375°.

5. Bake pumpkin rolls until golden brown, for 20-25 minutes. Place on a wire rack to cool slightly. In a small bowl, mix frosting ingredients; spread over warm rolls.

EASTER GATHERINGS

Take a breath of fresh air and cherish all the beautiful, colorful and tasty delights spring has to offer. Loaded with garden-fresh appeal, mouthwatering goodness and a touch of whimsy, the delightful dishes in this charming section are guaranteed to put a spring in everyone's step!

Easter Dinner: Three Takes

When it comes to food, every holiday has its must-haves. If your typical Easter dinner includes ham, carrots, potatoes, bread or a luscious lemon dessert, try one of these three delicious takes on each one to design your best menu ever. The creative possibilities are limited only by your pantry and your imagination. Mixing and matching has never been so much fun!

Baked Ham with Honey-Chipotle Glaze (p. 146) **Baked Ham with Cherry Sauce** (p. 146)
Slow-Cooked Ham with Pineapple Sauce (p. 146)

SKILLET POTATOES
WITH RED PEPPER &
WHOLE GARLIC CLOVES

SKILLET POTATOES WITH RED PEPPER & WHOLE GARLIC CLOVES

You'll be surprised that a skillet potato recipe this simple has so much flavor. I love how the whole garlic cloves turn sweet after being caramelized. Yum!
—Anita Osborne, Thomasburg, ON

Prep: 10 min. • **Cook:** 35 min.
Makes: 8 servings

- 2 Tbsp. olive oil
- 12 garlic cloves, peeled
- 2 lbs. potatoes, cut into ¼- to ½-in. cubes (about 7 cups)
- 1 tsp. salt
- ½ tsp. pepper
- 1 large sweet red pepper, cut into ½-in. pieces

1. In a large skillet, heat oil over medium-low heat. Add the garlic cloves; cook garlic, uncovered, until almost tender, for about 10 minutes, stirring occasionally.
2. Increase heat to medium. Stir in the potatoes, salt and pepper. Cook the potatoes, uncovered, for 15 minutes, stirring occasionally. Add red pepper; cook and stir until potatoes are tender, about 10 minutes.

CARAMELIZED ONION POTATO SALAD

I turn to this recipe on days when I have a little extra time and I'm craving comfort food. The tarragon vinegar and the caramelized onions in this salad will leave you smacking your lips. You can serve it immediately, but it will taste much better after being refrigerated for several hours. Double or triple the recipe if you are making it for a large event.
—Colleen Delawder, Herndon, VA

Prep: 20 min. • **Cook:** 25 min. + chilling
Makes: 10 servings

- 2 Tbsp. olive oil
- 2 medium onions, quartered and sliced
- 4 lbs. medium red potatoes, peeled and cubed (about 8 cups)
- 1 Tbsp. salt

DRESSING
- ⅔ cup mayonnaise
- ⅓ cup tarragon vinegar or white wine vinegar
- ¼ cup minced fresh parsley or 4 tsp. dried parsley flakes
- ¼ cup whole-grain Dijon mustard
- ½ tsp. salt
- ½ tsp. pepper

1. In a large skillet, heat oil over medium-high heat; saute the onions until softened, 2-4 minutes. Reduce heat to medium-low; cook onions until deep golden brown, 20-30 minutes, stirring occasionally.
2. Meanwhile, place potatoes, salt and enough water to cover in a 6-qt. stockpot; bring to a boil. Reduce heat and cook, uncovered, until tender, 10-15 minutes. Drain; place in a large bowl. Add the caramelized onions. Cool slightly.
3. Mix dressing ingredients; stir gently into potato mixture. Refrigerate, covered, until cold, about 8 hours.

ROASTED POTATOES & ONIONS WITH WILTED GREENS

I'm usually not a fan of side dishes because I find them boring and bland. But this is one of best sides I have ever made. It's an adaptation of one of my mother-in-law's recipes. If I want a meal with protein, I throw in some sauteed diced pancetta.
—Elizabeth Hartman, Salt Lake City, UT

Prep: 15 min. • **Bake:** 25 min.
Makes: 8 servings

- 2 lbs. small red potatoes (about 16), halved
- 2 medium red onions, cut into thin wedges
- 2 Tbsp. olive oil
- 1½ tsp. salt, divided
- 1¼ tsp. pepper, divided
- 5 oz. fresh arugula (about 6 cups)
- 3 Tbsp. cider vinegar

1. Preheat oven to 425°. Toss potatoes and onions with oil, 1 tsp. salt and 1 tsp. pepper. Spread in a greased 15x10x1-in. pan. Roast until the potatoes are tender, 25-30 minutes, stirring occasionally.
2. Transfer to a large bowl. Add arugula, vinegar and the remaining salt and pepper; toss to combine. Serve immediately.

FLUFFY BISCUITS

If you're looking for a flaky basic biscuit, you'll think this recipe is the best. These golden brown rolls bake up tall, light and tender. Their mild flavor tastes even better when the warm biscuits are spread with butter or your favorite flavor of jam.
—Nancy Horsburgh, Everett, ON

Takes: 30 min. • **Makes:** about 1 dozen

- 2 cups all-purpose flour
- 4 tsp. baking powder
- 1 Tbsp. sugar
- ½ tsp. salt
- ½ cup shortening
- 1 large egg
- ⅔ cup 2% milk

1. Preheat oven to 450°. In a bowl, whisk together first four ingredients. Cut in shortening until the mixture resembles coarse crumbs. Whisk together the egg and milk. Add to dry ingredients; stir just until moistened.
2. On a well-floured surface, knead dough gently 8-10 times. Roll to ¾-in. thickness; cut with a floured 2½-in. biscuit cutter. Place on a lightly greased baking sheet.
3. Bake until golden brown, 8-10 minutes. Serve warm.

TEST KITCHEN TIP

Baking Biscuits

For biscuits to bake properly, arrange your oven rack so that the baking sheet is in the center of the oven. Be sure to use a hot oven (425°-450°) and a baking time of 10-12 minutes for standard-size biscuits. Insulated baking sheets will not allow the bottom of biscuits to brown regular baking sheets do.

HEARTY HONEY-OATMEAL ROLLS

Roll call! Friends and family request this recipe more than any other I make. The rolls are soft and chewy and go with any meal. They're good for sandwiches, too.
—Callie Palen-Lowrie, Louisville, CO

Prep: 40 min. + standing • **Bake:** 25 min.
Makes: 1½ dozen (plus honey butter)

- 1 cup old-fashioned oats
- 1 cup water
- 4 to 4½ cups all-purpose flour
- 1 pkg. (¼ oz.) active dry yeast
- ¾ tsp. salt
- 1 cup 2% milk
- ⅓ cup butter, cubed
- 3 Tbsp. honey
- 1 large egg

TOPPING
- 1 large egg
- 1 Tbsp. water
- 2 Tbsp. old-fashioned oats

HONEY BUTTER
- ½ cup butter, softened
- ¼ cup honey
- Dash salt

1. In a small bowl, combine oats and water; let stand, covered, 2 hours. Drain.
2. In a large bowl, mix 2 cups flour, yeast and salt. In a small saucepan, heat milk, butter and honey to 120°-130°. Add to dry ingredients; beat on medium speed 2 minutes. Add the egg and drained oats; beat on high for 2 minutes. Stir in enough remaining flour to form a soft dough (dough will be sticky).
3. On a floured surface, knead dough until smooth and elastic, 6-8 minutes. Place in a greased bowl, turning once to grease the top. Cover and let rise in a warm place until doubled, about 1 hour.
4. Punch down dough. Turn onto a lightly floured surface; divide dough and shape into 18 balls. Place 2 in. apart on a greased baking sheet. Cover with a kitchen towel; let rise in a warm place until doubled, about 30 minutes. Preheat oven to 375°.
5. Whisk egg with water. Brush over rolls; sprinkle with oats. Bake until golden brown, about 20 minutes. Remove from pan to a wire rack.
6. Meanwhile, in a small bowl, beat honey butter ingredients until smooth. Serve with warm rolls.

CELEBRATION BRAID

During the holidays I sometimes make a couple of these golden loaves a day to give as gifts. Everyone in our family loves them any time of year.
—Marcia Vermaire, Fruitport, MI

Prep: 35 min. + rising
Bake: 20 min. + cooling
Makes: 1 loaf (32 servings)

- 2 pkg. (¼ oz. each) active dry yeast
- 1 cup warm water (110° to 115°)
- 2 large eggs
- ⅓ cup butter, softened
- ¼ cup sugar
- 1 tsp. salt
- 4½ to 5 cups all-purpose flour
- 1 large egg yolk
- 1 Tbsp. water

1. In a small bowl, dissolve yeast in warm water. In a large bowl, combine eggs, butter, sugar, salt, yeast mixture and 3 cups flour; beat on medium speed 3 minutes. Stir in enough remaining flour to form a soft dough.
2. On a floured surface, knead dough until smooth and elastic, 6-8 minutes. Place in a greased bowl, turning once to grease the top. Cover and let rise in a warm place until doubled, about 1 hour.
3. Punch down dough. Turn onto a lightly floured surface; divide into four portions. Shape each into an 18-in. rope. Place ropes side by side on a greased baking sheet. Beginning at one end, braid dough by placing the first rope over the second rope, under the third and over the fourth. Repeat three or four times, beginning each time from the same end. Pinch ends to seal; tuck under.
4. Cover with a kitchen towel; let rise in a warm place until doubled, about 45 minutes. Preheat oven to 350°.
5. Whisk egg yolk with water and brush over braid. Bake until golden brown, 20-25 minutes. Remove from pan to a wire rack to cool.

CELEBRATION
BRAID

CITRUS RAINBOW CARROTS

I grow lots of carrots in my garden, and I'm always experimenting with new ways to prepare them. I serve these on Easter. The recipe is easy to make and can easily be doubled for a large group. I sometimes slice the carrots several days in advance to save time on the day of the party.
—Sue Gronholz, Beaver Dam, WI

Takes: 25 min. • **Makes:** 6 servings

- 2 lbs. medium rainbow or regular carrots, diagonally sliced
- 3 Tbsp. butter
- 2 Tbsp. sugar
- 1½ tsp. grated orange zest
- 2 Tbsp. orange juice
- ¾ tsp. salt
- ¼ tsp. pepper
- ⅛ tsp. ground cloves

1. Place carrots and enough water to cover in a large saucepan; bring to a boil. Reduce heat; cook, uncovered, until tender, 8-10 minutes. Drain; return to pan.
2. Add remaining ingredients. Cook over medium-high heat until carrots are glazed, 2-3 minutes, stirring occasionally.
Note: Rainbow carrots can be deep burgundy, golden yellow, jeweled orange or creamy white in color.

CITRUS RAINBOW CARROTS

CREAMY CARROT PARSNIP SOUP

We live on a farm, so we like anything made from scratch. My family would eat soup every day as long as it didn't come from a can. This creamy concoction tastes as if it's fresh from the garden. Subtle hints of horseradish and ginger spark every steaming spoonful.
—Phyllis Clinehens, Maplewood, OH

Prep: 25 min. • **Cook:** 40 min.
Makes: 12 servings (3 qt.)

- 8 cups chopped carrots
- 6 cups chopped peeled parsnips
- 4 cups chicken broth
- 3 cups water
- 2 tsp. sugar
- 1 tsp. salt
- 3 Tbsp. butter
- 1 medium onion, chopped
- 4 garlic cloves, minced
- 1 tsp. peeled grated horseradish
- 1 tsp. minced fresh gingerroot
- 2 cups buttermilk
  Sour cream
  Fresh dill sprigs, optional

1. Place first six ingredients in a 6-qt. stockpot; bring to a boil. Reduce heat; simmer, covered, until vegetables are very tender, 25-30 minutes.
2. In a small skillet, heat the butter over medium-high heat; saute onion, garlic, horseradish and ginger until the onion is tender. Add to carrot mixture. Puree soup using an immersion blender, or cool slightly and puree soup in batches in a blender. Stir in buttermilk; heat through (do not boil). Serve with sour cream and, if desired, dill.

CARROT RAISIN SALAD

This colorful salad is one of my mother-in-law's favorites. Its crunchy texture makes it fun to eat, and the raisins give it a slightly sweet flavor. Best of all, it's easy to prepare.
—Denise Baumert, Dalhart, TX

Takes: 10 min. • **Makes:** 8 servings

- 4 cups shredded carrots
- ¾ to 1½ cups raisins
- ¼ cup mayonnaise
- 2 Tbsp. sugar
- 2 to 3 Tbsp. 2% milk

In a bowl, mix first four ingredients. Stir in enough milk to reach desired consistency. Refrigerate until serving.

TEST KITCHEN TIP

Flavor Boosters

Carrot raisin salad is a classic potluck pleaser. This traditional recipe is divine, but if you want to add a little extra flavor or texture, add one or more of the following ingredients. Include whatever amount suits your tastes.

- Dried cranberries
- Chopped walnuts or pecans
- Chopped dates
- Crushed pineapple
- Diced apple
- Mini marshmallows
- Chopped maraschino cherries

BAKED HAM WITH CHERRY SAUCE

There's nothing I'd rather serve for Easter dinner or another springtime occasion than succulent baked ham. My recipe features a flavorful rub plus a delicious cherry sauce with a hint of almond.
—Lavonn Bormuth, Westerville, OH

Prep: 10 min. • **Bake:** 1¾ hours
Makes: 12 servings

- 1 fully cooked bone-in ham (6 to 8 lbs.)
- 1 cup packed brown sugar
- 3 Tbsp. maple syrup
- 1 tsp. ground mustard
- 3 Tbsp. cornstarch
- ½ cup sugar
- 1 cup cold water
- 1 can (15 oz.) pitted dark sweet cherries, undrained
- 2 Tbsp. lemon juice
- 1 tsp. almond extract

1. Preheat oven to 325°. Place ham on a rack in a roasting pan. Using a sharp knife, score surface of ham with ¼-in.-deep cuts in a diamond pattern. Mix brown sugar, syrup and mustard; rub over ham and press into cuts. Bake, covered, until a thermometer reads 140°, 1¾-2 hours.
2. In a small saucepan, mix cornstarch, sugar and water until smooth. Add the cherries; bring to a boil. Cook and stir until thickened, 1-2 minutes. Remove from heat; stir in lemon juice and almond extract. Serve warm with ham.

BAKED HAM WITH HONEY-CHIPOTLE GLAZE

Your Easter celebration will be so simple to orchestrate with this sweet, smoky ham recipe at your fingertips. It feeds a crowd and tastes fantastic.
—*Taste of Home* Test Kitchen

Prep: 10 min. • **Bake:** 2 hours
Makes: 16 servings

- 1 fully cooked bone-in ham (8 to 10 lbs.)
- 1 cup packed brown sugar
- 3 Tbsp. honey
- 2 Tbsp. cider vinegar
- 2¼ cups ginger ale
- 4 chipotle peppers in adobo sauce, minced
- 3 garlic cloves, minced
- 1½ tsp. Dijon mustard
- ¾ tsp. ground cinnamon
- ¾ tsp. ground cumin

1. Preheat oven to 325°. Place ham on a rack in a roasting pan. Using a sharp knife, score surface of ham with ½-in.-deep cuts in a diamond pattern. Bake, uncovered, 1½ hours.
2. Meanwhile, for the glaze, in a small saucepan, mix brown sugar, honey, vinegar and ginger ale. Bring to a boil; cook until the mixture is reduced by half, about 15 minutes. Stir in remaining ingredients. Reduce heat and simmer, uncovered, 5 minutes. Remove from heat. Reserve 1 cup mixture for sauce; keep warm.
3. Brush ham with some of the remaining glaze. Bake the ham, uncovered, until a thermometer reads 140°, about 30 minutes, brushing twice with additional glaze. Serve with reserved sauce.

SLOW-COOKED HAM WITH PINEAPPLE SAUCE

We serve this dish during the holidays because everyone is crazy about it. But it makes it to the table year-round because it's super simple to prepare.
—Terry Roberts, Yorktown, VA

Prep: 10 min. • **Cook:** 6 hours
Makes: 12 servings

- 1 fully cooked boneless ham (4 to 5 lbs.)
- 1 Tbsp. cornstarch
- 2 Tbsp. lemon juice
- 1 cup packed brown sugar
- 1 Tbsp. yellow mustard
- ¼ tsp. salt
- 1 can (20 oz.) unsweetened crushed pineapple, undrained

1. Place ham in a 5-qt. slow cooker. In a small saucepan, mix the cornstarch and lemon juice until smooth. Stir in remaining ingredients; bring to a boil, stirring occasionally. Pour sauce over the ham, covering completely.
2. Cook, covered, on low 6-8 hours (a thermometer inserted in ham should read at least 140°).
Note: This recipe is not recommended for spiral-sliced ham.

BAKED HAM WITH
HONEY-CHIPOTLE GLAZE

BAKED HAM
WITH CHERRY SAUCE

SLOW-COOKED HAM
WITH PINEAPPLE SAUCE

LEMON CURD
CHEESECAKE

LEMON CURD CHEESECAKE

This creamy lemon cheesecake has a lovely soft texture and cuts nicely. The curd adds a fresh, tangy flavor.
—Becky West, Statesboro, GA

Prep: 40 min. • **Bake:** 70 min. + chilling
Makes: 12 servings

- 1¾ cups crushed vanilla wafers (about 55 wafers)
- ¼ cup butter, melted
- 3 pkg. (8 oz. each) cream cheese, softened
- 1 cup sour cream
- 2 cups sugar
- 2 tsp. grated lemon zest
- 2 Tbsp. lemon juice
- 3 large eggs, lightly beaten

LEMON CURD
- ½ cup sugar
- 1½ tsp. grated lemon zest
- 6 Tbsp. lemon juice
- 1 large egg
- 1 large egg yolk
- 2 Tbsp. butter, cubed
  Lemon peel strips, optional

1. Preheat oven to 325°. Place a greased 9-in. springform pan on a double thickness of heavy-duty foil (about 18 in. square). Wrap securely around pan.
2. In a small bowl, mix crushed wafers and melted butter. Press onto the bottom and ¾ in. up sides of prepared springform pan. Bake 8 minutes. Cool on a wire rack.
3. In a large bowl, beat cream cheese, sour cream and sugar until smooth. Beat in lemon zest and juice. Add eggs; beat on low just until blended. Pour into crust. Place springform pan in a larger baking pan; add 1 in. of hot water to larger pan.
4. Bake until center is just set and top appears dull, 1-1¼ hours. Remove springform pan from water bath. Cool cheesecake on a wire rack 10 minutes. Loosen sides from pan with a knife; remove foil. Cool 1 hour longer.

5. Meanwhile, in a small heavy saucepan, whisk together first five curd ingredients. Add the butter; cook over medium heat, whisking constantly, until mixture is just thick enough to coat a metal spoon and a thermometer reads at least 170°. Do not allow to boil. Remove immediately to a small bowl; cool completely.
6. Gently spread curd over cheesecake. Refrigerate overnight, covering when completely cooled. Remove rim from pan. If desired, top with fresh lemon peel.

EASY LEMON TARTS

Convenient refrigerated cookie dough makes these small tarts quick and easy. Add a sprinkle of fresh lemon zest on top for an extra garnish.
—Dawn Higgins, Manassas, VA

Prep: 25 min. • **Bake:** 20 min. + cooling
Makes: 3 dozen

- 1 tube (16½ oz.) refrigerated sugar cookie dough
- 4 oz. cream cheese, softened
- 6 Tbsp. thawed lemonade concentrate
- ⅓ cup instant lemon pudding mix
- 1½ cups whipped topping
- ⅓ cup crushed lemon-drop candies, optional

1. Preheat oven to 350°. Divide and shape dough into 36 balls (about 2 tsp. each). Using floured hands, press each dough ball onto the bottom and sides of a greased mini-muffin cup.
2. Bake until golden, 18-22 minutes. Reshape cups if necessary. Cool in pans 5 minutes. Remove to wire racks to cool completely.
3. For filling, place the cream cheese, lemonade concentrate and pudding mix in a large bowl; beat for 2 minutes. Beat in ½ cup whipped topping. Fold in remaining whipped topping.
4. Spoon scant 1 Tbsp. filling into each cup. If desired, sprinkle with crushed candies. Refrigerate leftovers.

LEMON MERINGUE LADYFINGER PIE

Adding a little bit of orange liqueur gives this pie a nice zing, but it's delightful with simply the lemon syrup, too.
—Karen Bowlden, Boise, ID

Prep: 40 min. + chilling
Bake: 30 min. + chilling
Makes: 10 servings

- 3 cups crushed Lorna Doone shortbread cookies (about 60 cookies)
- 6 Tbsp. butter, melted
- 3 medium lemons
- ¾ cup plus ⅔ cup sugar, divided
- 1 pkg. (8 oz.) cream cheese, softened
- 1 cup heavy whipping cream
- 6 soft ladyfingers, split
- 2 Tbsp. orange liqueur, optional

MERINGUE
- 3 large egg whites
- ½ cup sugar

1. Preheat oven to 350°. Mix crushed cookies and melted butter; press onto bottom and sides of a greased 9-in. deep-dish pie plate. Bake until lightly browned, 10 minutes. Cool on a wire rack.
2. Finely grate 2 tsp. zest from lemons. Cut all lemons in half; squeeze juice. For lemon syrup, in a small saucepan, mix ¾ cup sugar and lemon juice; bring to a boil. Reduce heat; simmer, uncovered, until sugar is dissolved, 3-5 minutes, stirring occasionally. Remove to a bowl; cool completely.
3. For cream filling, in a large bowl, beat cream cheese, lemon zest and remaining ⅔ cup sugar until smooth. Gradually add cream and ½ cup lemon syrup, beating until thickened. Transfer 1 cup mixture to crust; layer with half of the ladyfingers. If desired, stir orange liqueur into remaining lemon syrup; brush over ladyfingers. Repeat layers. Spread remaining cream filling over top.
4. For meringue, in a bowl, beat the egg whites on medium speed until foamy. Add ½ cup sugar, 1 Tbsp. at a time, beating on high after each addition until sugar is dissolved. Continue beating until stiff, glossy peaks form. Spread over pie.
5. Bake in a 350° oven until meringue is golden brown, 20-25 minutes. Cool on a wire rack 1 hour. Refrigerate until filling is set, about 4 hours.

TEST KITCHEN TIP

A Lesson in Lemons

Look for lemons that are bright yellow, firm and feel heavy for their size. Store at room temperature for 3 days. For longer storage, place in the crisper drawer of your refrigerator for 2 to 3 weeks. Juice or grated peel can be frozen up to 1 year. One medium lemon yields 3 tablespoons juice and 2 teaspoons grated zest.

Easter Treats to Share

Every year, we wait in sweet anticipation for that happy Sunday in spring when we wake to find a pretty woven basket filled with goodies. Help the Easter Bunny by making special treats right in the comfort of your kitchen. Kids will delight in pretty Peeps atop confectionery nests and the one-of-a-kind taste of homemade marshmallows, while friends and neighbors will appreciate carrot cake jam, biscotti bars or scones.

Bird Nests (p. 159)

HOMEMADE
HONEY
GRAHAMS

HOMEMADE HONEY GRAHAMS

The way that my boys gobble up graham crackers, it's a good thing I don't buy them at the store. My homemade version is less expensive, with the added bonus of using minimally processed ingredients. These are fantastic, but they don't last long!
—Crystal Jo Bruns, Iliff, CO

Prep: 15 min. + chilling
Bake: 10 min./batch
Makes: 32 cookies

- 1 cup whole wheat flour
- ¾ cup all-purpose flour
- ½ cup toasted wheat germ
- 2 Tbsp. dark brown sugar
- 1 tsp. baking powder
- 1 tsp. ground cinnamon
- ½ tsp. salt
- ½ tsp. baking soda
- 6 Tbsp. cold butter, cubed
- ¼ cup honey
- 4 Tbsp. ice water

1. Whisk together first eight ingredients; cut in butter until crumbly. In another bowl, whisk together honey and water; gradually add to dry ingredients, tossing with a fork until dough holds together when pressed.
2. Divide dough in half. Shape each half into a disk; wrap and refrigerate until firm enough to roll, about 30 minutes.
3. Preheat oven to 350°. On a lightly floured surface, roll each portion of dough into an 8-in. square. Using a knife or fluted pastry wheel, cut each into sixteen 2-in. squares. If desired, prick holes with a fork. Place 1 in. apart on parchment paper-lined baking sheets.
4. Bake until edges are light brown, 10-12 minutes. Remove from pans to wire racks to cool. Store in an airtight container.

SOFT ALMOND BISCOTTI BARS

These bars are a variation on the fabulous cinnamon almond biscotti that my mom and grandmother always made for the holidays. Instead of crisp, crumbly cookies that are difficult to shape, these bars are chewy and satisfying with cinnamon flavor and toasted almonds inside and out.
—Jannine Fisk, Malden, MA

Prep: 20 min. • **Bake:** 20 min.
Makes: 4 dozen

- 1 cup sugar
- 1 cup packed brown sugar
- ⅓ cup canola oil
- 2 large eggs
- 4 Tbsp. water, divided
- 2½ cups all-purpose flour
- 2 tsp. baking powder
- 1 tsp. ground cinnamon
- 2 cups coarsely chopped almonds, toasted
- 1 large egg yolk
- 1 cup sliced almonds

1. Preheat oven to 375°. Line a 15x10x1-in. baking pan with parchment paper, letting ends extend up sides; grease paper.
2. In a large bowl, beat sugars and oil until blended. Beat in eggs, then 3 Tbsp. water. In another bowl, whisk the flour, baking powder and cinnamon; gradually beat into sugar mixture. Stir in chopped almonds (dough will be sticky).
3. Press into prepared pan, lightly flouring top as needed. Mix egg yolk and remaining water; brush over dough. Top with sliced almonds, gently pressing into dough. Bake 20-25 minutes or until golden brown.
4. Cool in pan on a wire rack. Lifting with parchment paper, remove from pan. Cut into 24 squares; cut each square into two biscotti triangles.
Note: To toast nuts, bake in a shallow pan in a 350° oven for 5-10 minutes or cook in a skillet over low heat until lightly browned, stirring occasionally.

HOMEMADE VANILLA MARSHMALLOWS

My husband Dale's grandmother fixed these fluffy marshmallows for special occasions. She didn't have an electric mixer, so beating the ingredients by hand for 30 minutes was a labor of love. Now, Dale makes them. They're delicious!
—Nancy Shields, Hillsdale, MI

Prep: 25 min. + cooling • **Cook:** 20 min.
Makes: about 8 dozen

  Confectioners' sugar
- 2 cups cold water, divided
- 4 envelopes unflavored gelatin
- 4 cups sugar
- ⅛ tsp. salt
- 2 tsp. vanilla extract
  Toasted sweetened shredded coconut and ground pecans, optional

1. Generously dust a 13x9-in. pan with confectioners' sugar. In a large bowl, sprinkle gelatin over ¾ cup cold water.
2. In a large heavy saucepan, combine the sugar, salt and remaining water. Bring the mixture to a boil over medium heat, stirring occasionally. Cook, covered, for 3 minutes. Uncover; cook, without stirring, over medium-high heat until a candy thermometer reads 248° (firm-ball stage). Slowly add to gelatin mixture, beating on low speed until incorporated. Add vanilla; beat on medium until thick and doubled in volume, 10 minutes.
3. Spread into prepared pan. Let stand, covered, at room temperature 6 hours or overnight.
4. Using a knife coated with cooking spray, cut into 1-in. squares. Roll in coconut, pecans or additional confectioners' sugar. Store marshmallows in airtight containers in a cool, dry place.

LEMONY
SNACK MIX

CARROT CAKE JAM

Try this unique jam for a change of pace. Spread on a bagel with cream cheese, it tastes almost as good as real carrot cake.
—Rachelle Stratton, Rock Springs, WY

Prep: 45 min. • **Process:** 5 min.
Makes: 8 half-pints

- 1 can (20 oz.) unsweetened crushed pineapple, undrained
- 1½ cups shredded carrots
- 1½ cups chopped peeled ripe pears
- 3 Tbsp. lemon juice
- 1 tsp. ground cinnamon
- ¼ tsp. ground cloves
- ¼ tsp. ground nutmeg
- 1 pkg. (1¾ oz.) powdered fruit pectin
- 6½ cups sugar

1. Place first seven ingredients in a large saucepan; bring to a boil. Reduce heat; simmer, covered, until pears are tender, 15-20 minutes, stirring occasionally. Stir in pectin. Bring to a full rolling boil over high heat, stirring constantly. Stir in the sugar; return to a full rolling boil. Boil and stir 1 minute.
2. Remove from heat; skim off foam. Ladle hot mixture into eight hot sterilized half-pint jars, leaving ¼-in. headspace. Remove air bubbles and adjust headspace, if necessary, by adding hot mixture. Wipe rims. Center lids on jars; screw on bands until fingertip tight.
3. Place jars into canner with simmering water, ensuring that they are completely covered with water. Bring to a boil; process for 5 minutes. Remove jars and cool.
Note: The processing time listed is for altitudes of 1,000 feet or less. Add 1 minute to the processing time for each 1,000 feet of additional altitude.

LEMONY SNACK MIX

I'm on a gluten-restricted diet. I came up with this snack mix one day when I wanted something fast and easy that tasted like lemon bars. It makes a great gift, and folks love the light and fresh citrus flavor.
—Patricia Sensenich, Olathe, KS

Takes: 15 min. • **Makes:** 2¾ qt.

- 5 cups Rice Chex
- 4 cups Corn Chex
- 1½ cups white baking chips
- 4 tsp. grated lemon zest
- 2 Tbsp. lemon juice
- ¼ cup butter, softened
- 1½ cups confectioners' sugar
- ¼ cup yellow coarse sugar, optional

1. Place cereals in a large bowl. In top of a double boiler or a metal bowl over hot water, melt baking chips with lemon zest and juice; stir until smooth. Stir in butter until blended.
2. Pour over cereal; toss to coat. Add the confectioners' sugar and, if desired, coarse sugar; toss to coat. Spread mix onto waxed paper to cool. Store in airtight containers.

HOMEMADE STRAWBERRY RHUBARB SAUCE

There's nothing quite like the magical pairing of sweet strawberries with tart rhubarb. This sauce is divine poured over ice cream, pancakes or French toast.
—Mia Werner, Waukegan, IL

Takes: 15 min. • **Makes:** 1¾ cups

- 2 cups halved fresh strawberries
- 1 cup sliced fresh or frozen rhubarb
- ⅔ cup sugar
- 1 Tbsp. cornstarch
- 2 Tbsp. cold water

In a small saucepan, combine the fresh strawberries, rhubarb and sugar; bring to a boil over medium heat, stirring to dissolve sugar. In a small bowl, mix the cornstarch and water until smooth; stir into fruit mixture. Cook and stir until thickened, 1-2 minutes. Serve warm or refrigerate, covered, and serve cold.
Note: If using frozen rhubarb, measure rhubarb while still frozen, then thaw it completely. Drain in a colander, but do not press liquid out.

CARROT
CAKE JAM

Carrot Cake
Jam

COCONUT ALMOND CANDY

The secret ingredient in this homemade candy is a true surprise—no one tasting these delicious morsels will guess what's in the sweet, creamy filling!
—Katrina Smith, Lawrence, KS

Prep: 45 min. + chilling • **Makes:** 2 dozen

2	cups sweetened shredded coconut
½	cup mashed potatoes (with added milk and butter)
¼	tsp. vanilla extract
⅛	tsp. salt, optional
2	cups confectioners' sugar
24	unblanched almonds, toasted
1	pkg. (11½ oz.) milk chocolate chips
1	Tbsp. butter

1. In a large bowl, mix coconut, potatoes, vanilla and, if desired, salt. Gradually beat in the confectioners' sugar. Refrigerate, covered, until firm enough to shape, about 1 hour.

2. Dust hands with confectioners' sugar. Shape mixture into twenty-four 1-in. ovals. Flatten slightly, then wrap each around an almond. Place on waxed paper-lined baking sheets; freeze candies until firm, at least 30 minutes.

3. In a microwave, melt chocolate chips and butter; stir until smooth. Using a fork, dip candies in the chocolate mixture; allow excess to drip off. Return to baking sheets; refrigerate until set. Store between layers of waxed paper in an airtight container in the refrigerator.

TEST KITCHEN TIP

Refreshed Coconut

If flaked coconut has been frozen or becomes dried out, make it fresh again by placing the amount needed in a bowl and sprinkling with a few drops of water. Cover and microwave until warm.

COCONUT
ALMOND CANDY

SPICY CINNAMON POPCORN

Plain popcorn never made movie night history. Try this cinnamon-spiced version with a little kick in every bite.
—Mary Relyea, Canastota, NY

Prep: 25 min. • **Bake:** 45 min. • **Makes:** 3 qt.

10	cups popped popcorn
1½	cups coarsely chopped pecans
¾	cup sugar
¾	cup packed brown sugar
½	cup light corn syrup
2	to 3 Tbsp. Louisiana-style hot sauce
2	Tbsp. honey
6	Tbsp. butter, cubed
3	tsp. ground cinnamon

1. Preheat oven to 250°. Place popcorn and pecans in a large bowl.
2. In a large heavy saucepan, combine the two sugars, corn syrup, pepper sauce and honey; bring to a boil, stirring constantly to dissolve sugar. Using a pastry brush dipped in water, wash down the sides of the pan to eliminate sugar crystals. Cook, without stirring, over medium heat until a candy thermometer reads 290° (soft-crack stage), about 10 minutes. Remove from heat; gradually stir in butter and cinnamon. Pour carefully over popcorn mixture; toss to coat.
3. Transfer to a greased 15x10x1-in. baking pan. Bake 45 minutes, stirring occasionally. Cool completely.
4. Break into pieces. Store popcorn in an airtight container.

Note: We recommend testing your candy thermometer before each use by bringing water to a boil; the thermometer should read 212°. Adjust your recipe temperature up or down based on your test.

BLUEBERRY STREUSEL SCONES

These rich scones make a perfect Easter treat to share. They are a bit sweeter than typical scones and have a delectably tender crumb topping.
—Teresa Ralston, New Albany, OH

Prep: 25 min. • **Bake:** 15 min.
Makes: 1 dozen

2	cups all-purpose flour
⅓	cup sugar
2	tsp. baking powder
¼	tsp. salt
⅓	cup cold butter, cubed
1	large egg
½	cup plus 2 Tbsp. heavy whipping cream
1	tsp. vanilla extract
1	cup fresh or frozen blueberries

STREUSEL

¼	cup all-purpose flour
¼	cup packed brown sugar
½	tsp. ground cinnamon
⅛	tsp. salt
2	Tbsp. cold butter

1. Preheat oven to 400°. In a large bowl, whisk together first four ingredients. Cut in butter until mixture resembles coarse crumbs. Whisk together egg, cream and vanilla; add to the crumb mixture, stirring just until moistened. Stir in the blueberries. Drop by ¼ cupfuls 2 in. apart onto greased baking sheets.
2. For streusel, in a small bowl, mix brown sugar, cinnamon and salt; cut in the butter until crumbly. Press gently onto scones.
3. Bake until golden brown, 12-16 minutes. Serve warm.

Note: If using frozen blueberries, use without thawing to avoid discoloring the scones.

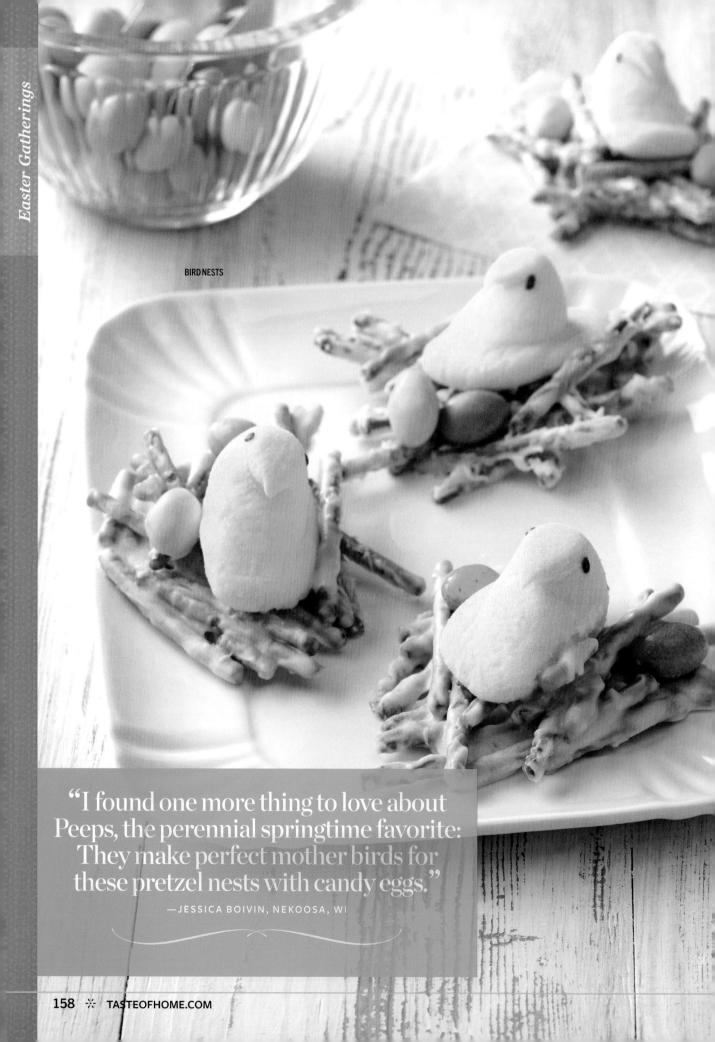

BIRD NESTS

"I found one more thing to love about Peeps, the perennial springtime favorite: They make perfect mother birds for these pretzel nests with candy eggs."

—JESSICA BOIVIN, NEKOOSA, WI

Hand-Stamped Spring

Transform a basic kitchen towel into an Easter gift some-bunny is sure to love.

Craft by Diane Toyos,
Bellefonte, Pennsylvania

Put those uneaten Easter basket Peeps to good use. The bunny-shaped version makes a clever DIY stamp in a project perfect for giving to someone special or keeping for yourself.

Wash and iron a plain white flour sack towel to create a smooth work surface. Coat a few Peeps marshmallow bunnies with Mod Podge and dry thoroughly. Dip one side of one marshmallow bunny into fabric paint and stamp on the towel to create your pattern of choice. Repeat with a fresh Peep and additional paint colors, if desired. When the paint is dry, use a hot glue gun to attach craft pompoms for bunny tails.

BIRD NESTS

Prep: 40 min. • **Makes:** 2 dozen

- 2 pkg. (10 to 12 oz. each) white baking chips
- 1 pkg. (10 oz.) pretzel sticks
- 24 yellow chicks Peeps candy
- 1 pkg. (12 oz.) M&M's eggs or other egg-shaped candy

1. In a large metal bowl over simmering water, melt white baking chips; stir until smooth. Reserve ½ cup melted chips for decorations; keep warm.
2. Add pretzel sticks to remaining chips; stir to coat evenly. Drop pretzel mixture into 24 mounds on waxed paper; shape into bird nests using two forks.
3. Dip bottoms of Peeps in reserved chips; place in nests. Attach eggs with remaining chips. Let stand until set.

JELLY BEAN BRITTLE

Here's a fun version of brittle that's made just for Easter. The jelly beans add both color and flavor.
—K. Kittell, Lenexa, KS

Prep: 10 min. • **Cook:** 20 min. + cooling
Makes: 2½ lbs.

- 4 Tbsp. butter, divided
- 2½ cups small jelly beans
- 3 cups sugar
- 1 cup light corn syrup
- ½ cup water
- ½ tsp. salt
- 2 tsp. baking soda

1. Line two 15x10x1-in. pans with foil. Melt 1 Tbsp. butter; brush over foil. Sprinkle the pans evenly with jelly beans.
2. In a large heavy saucepan, combine the sugar, corn syrup and water. Bring to a boil over medium heat, stirring constantly to dissolve sugar. Using a pastry brush dipped in water, wash down the sides of the pan to eliminate sugar crystals. Cook, without stirring, over medium heat until a candy thermometer reads 240° (soft-ball stage). Stir in remaining butter and salt; cook until a thermometer reads 300° (hard-crack stage), stirring frequently.
3. Remove from heat; stir in baking soda (mixture will foam). Immediately pour over jelly beans. Spread with a buttered metal spatula. Cool completely.
4. Break brittle into pieces. Store candy pieces between layers of waxed paper in an airtight container.
Note: We recommend testing your candy thermometer before each use by bringing water to a boil; the thermometer should read 212°. Adjust your recipe temperature up or down based on your test.

Spring Sides

There's nothing like garden-fresh pickin's once the weather turns warm. Revel in the sweet taste of spring with fresh takes on asparagus, spinach, peas, strawberries and other nutrient-rich fruits and veggies. Whether you're hitting the produce aisle, your local farmers market or your own backyard bounty, these timeless potluck sidekicks are sure to get top billing.

STRAWBERRY SALAD
WITH POPPY SEED
DRESSING

STRAWBERRY SALAD WITH POPPY SEED DRESSING

My family is always happy to see this fruit and veggie salad. If strawberries aren't available, substitute mandarin oranges and dried cranberries.
—Irene Keller, Kalamazoo, MI

Takes: 30 min. • **Makes:** 10 servings

- ¼ cup sugar
- ⅓ cup slivered almonds
- 1 bunch romaine, torn (about 8 cups)
- 1 small onion, halved and thinly sliced
- 2 cups halved fresh strawberries

DRESSING
- ¼ cup mayonnaise
- 2 Tbsp. sugar
- 1 Tbsp. sour cream
- 1 Tbsp. 2% milk
- 2¼ tsp. cider vinegar
- 1½ tsp. poppy seeds

1. Place sugar in a small heavy skillet; cook and stir over medium-low heat until melted and caramel colored, about 10 minutes. Stir in almonds until coated. Spread on foil to cool.
2. Place romaine, onion and strawberries in a large bowl. Whisk together dressing ingredients; toss with salad. Break candied almonds into pieces; sprinkle over salad. Serve immediately.

OVEN-ROASTED ASPARAGUS

Asparagus never tasted so good! Simply seasoned with butter and green onions, roasted asparagus spears keep their bright green color, too. They're so good, in fact, that you might want to make extra.
—Jody Fisher, Stewartstown, PA

Takes: 20 min. • **Makes:** 6 servings

- 2 lbs. fresh asparagus, trimmed
- ¼ cup butter, melted
- 2 to 4 green onions, chopped
- ½ tsp. salt

1. Preheat oven to 425°. Place asparagus in a 15x10x1-in. pan. Toss with melted butter and green onions; spread evenly. Sprinkle with salt.
2. Roast until crisp-tender, 10-15 minutes.

SHRIMP PASTA SALAD

SHRIMP PASTA SALAD

I adore shrimp, so discovering how well it works in pasta salad was a treat for me. The light lemon-dill sauce pulls it all together.
—Traci Wynne, Denver, PA

Prep: 15 min. + chilling
Cook: 15 min. • **Makes:** 10 servings

- 8 oz. uncooked small pasta shells (about 2⅔ cups)
- 1 lb. peeled and deveined cooked shrimp, chopped
- 1 cup frozen peas
- 4 green onions, chopped
- ¼ cup minced fresh parsley
- 1 cup mayonnaise
- 1 cup plain yogurt
- ¼ cup lemon juice
- 2 Tbsp. snipped fresh dill
- ½ tsp. salt
- ¼ tsp. white pepper

1. Cook pasta according to the package directions. Drain; rinse with cold water and drain again.
2. In a large bowl, combine the pasta, shrimp, peas, green onions and parsley. Mix remaining ingredients; stir into pasta mixture. Refrigerate, covered, at least 2 hours.

DID YOU KNOW?

Fresh Dill

Dill is available as fresh leaves, dried and crushed, or seeds. Its fresh, sweet, grassy flavor complements sour cream, cream cheese, cottage cheese, dips and spreads, meats, eggs, potato salad and pasta salad.

12-HOUR SALAD

VEGGIE MACARONI
& CHEESE

VEGGIE MACARONI & CHEESE

This creamy mac and cheese definitely doesn't come from a box. The fresh veggies add so much texture and color, everyone will be saying, "More, please!"
—Marsha Morril, Harrisburg, OR

Prep: 30 min. • **Bake:** 15 min.
Makes: 12 servings

    1½ cups uncooked elbow macaroni
     3 cups fresh broccoli florets
     2 cups fresh cauliflowerets
     3 large carrots, halved
        lengthwise and thinly sliced
     2 celery ribs, sliced
     1 Tbsp. butter
     1 medium onion, chopped
     ¼ cup all-purpose flour
     1 cup 2% milk
     1 cup chicken broth
     3 cups shredded sharp
        cheddar cheese
     1 Tbsp. Dijon mustard
     ¼ tsp. salt
     ⅛ tsp. pepper
     ¼ tsp. paprika

1. Preheat oven to 350°. In a 6-qt. stockpot, cook macaroni according to package directions, adding the broccoli, cauliflower, carrots and celery during the last 6 minutes of cooking. Drain; transfer to a greased 13x9-in. baking dish.
2. Meanwhile, in a large saucepan, heat the butter over medium-high heat; saute the onion until tender. Stir in flour until blended. Gradually stir in the milk and broth; bring to a boil. Cook and stir until thickened, about 2 minutes; stir in cheese, mustard, salt and pepper.
3. Add to macaroni mixture, stirring to coat; sprinkle with paprika. Bake macaroni and cheese casserole, uncovered, until heated through, 15-20 minutes.

12-HOUR SALAD

Talk about deliciously devious. This salad was all part of our mom's scrumptious scheme to get her kids to eat vegetables. The bonus round was making it a day in advance, giving her more time for other preparations on party days.
—Dorothy Bowen, Thomasville, NC

Prep: 20 min. + chilling • **Makes:** 12 servings

    8   cups torn mixed salad greens
    1½   cups chopped celery
    2   medium green peppers, chopped
    1   medium red onion, chopped
    2½   cups frozen peas (about
         10 oz.), thawed
    1   cup mayonnaise
    1   cup sour cream
    3   Tbsp. sugar
    1   cup shredded cheddar cheese
    ½   lb. bacon strips, cooked
         and crumbled

1. Place salad greens in a 3-qt. bowl or 13x9-in. dish. Layer with celery, peppers, onion and peas.
2. Mix the mayonnaise, sour cream and sugar; spread over top. Sprinkle with the cheddar cheese and bacon. Refrigerate salad, covered, for 12 hours or overnight.

QUICK CREAM OF MUSHROOM SOUP

My daughter-in-law, a gourmet cook, served this soup as the first course for a holiday dinner. She received the recipe from her mom and graciously shared it with me. Now I'm happy to share it with my own friends and family.
—Anne Kulick, Phillipsburg, NJ

Takes: 30 min. • **Makes:** 6 servings

    2   Tbsp. butter
    ½   lb. sliced fresh mushrooms
    ¼   cup chopped onion
    6   Tbsp. all-purpose flour
    ½   tsp. salt
    ⅛   tsp. pepper
    2   cans (14½ oz. each) chicken broth
    1   cup half-and-half cream

1. In a large saucepan, heat butter over medium-high heat; saute mushrooms and onion until tender.
2. Mix the flour, salt, pepper and one can broth until smooth; stir into mushroom mixture. Stir in the remaining broth. Bring to a boil; cook and stir until thickened, about 2 minutes. Reduce the heat; stir in the cream. Simmer soup, uncovered, until the flavors are blended, about 15 minutes, stirring occasionally.

SPINACH RICE

I serve this Greek-style rice dish alongside steaks with mushrooms. It's an elegant side that can easily be doubled if you're hosting guests for dinner.
—Jeanette Cakouros, Brunswick, ME

Takes: 20 min. • **Makes:** 2 servings

    2   Tbsp. olive oil
    ½   cup chopped onion
    ¾   cup water
    1   Tbsp. dried parsley flakes
    ¼   to ½ tsp. salt
    ⅛   tsp. pepper
    ½   cup uncooked instant rice
    2   cups fresh baby spinach

1. In a saucepan, heat oil over medium-high heat; saute onion until tender. Stir in water, parsley, salt and pepper; bring to a boil. Stir in rice; top with spinach.
2. Cover; remove from heat. Let stand until the rice is tender, 7-10 minutes. Stir to combine.

DID YOU KNOW?

Superfood Spinach

Easy to find, easy to grow and easy to love, spinach is one of the healthiest, most versatile vegetables out there. Cooked or raw, it has a mild flavor that's great mixed into salads, tossed in soup or added to smoothies, and it amps up nutrition without overpowering the flavor in your favorite dishes.

CAMPERS' COLESLAW

1. For dressing, mix first five ingredients until sugar is dissolved. Place fruit in a large bowl; toss gently with dressing.
2. Refrigerate, covered, until serving. Top with mint, if desired.

SWEET & TART LEMON GELATIN

I usually make two of these pretty citrus rings because they disappear so quickly.
—Patricia Ryzow, Thousand Oaks, CA

Prep: 15 min. + chilling • **Cook:** 5 min.
Makes: 12 servings

- 1   envelope unflavored gelatin
- 1   cup cold water
- 2   cups boiling water
- 2   pkg. (3 oz. each) lemon gelatin
- 1   can (12 oz.) frozen limeade concentrate, thawed
- 2   cups heavy whipping cream
- 3   Tbsp. confectioners' sugar
       Quartered fresh strawberries and fresh mint

1. In a small saucepan, sprinkle unflavored gelatin over cold water; let stand 1 minute. Heat and stir over low heat until gelatin is completely dissolved. Remove from heat.
2. In a large bowl, add boiling water to the lemon gelatin; stir 2 minutes to completely dissolve. Stir in unflavored gelatin mixture and limeade concentrate. Refrigerate until slightly thickened.
3. In a bowl, beat cream until it begins to thicken. Add confectioners' sugar; beat until soft peaks form. Beat gelatin mixture until frothy; fold in the whipped cream. Transfer to an 8-cup ring mold coated with cooking spray. Refrigerate gelatin mold, covered, until set.
4. To serve, unmold onto a large plate. Serve with strawberries and mint.

CAMPERS' COLESLAW

Crispy and crunchy, this no-fuss slaw makes a refreshing side dish for picnics, potlucks or any time you want to dine al fresco.
—Kimberly Wallace, Dennison, OH

Prep: 15 min. + chilling • **Cook:** 5 min.
Makes: 12 servings (¾ cup each)

- 1½ cups sugar
- ¾   cup white vinegar
- ¾   cup olive oil
- 1   Tbsp. salt
- 1   tsp. celery seed
- 1   medium head cabbage, shredded (about 10 cups)
- 1   large onion, chopped
- 1   medium green pepper, chopped

1. In a small saucepan, combine first five ingredients. Bring to a boil; cook and stir until the sugar is dissolved, 1-2 minutes. Remove from heat; cool completely.
2. In a large bowl, toss vegetables with dressing. Refrigerate, covered, until cold. Serve with a slotted spoon.

PINA COLADA FRUIT SALAD

Give friends a taste of the tropics with this bright fruit blend. Add fresh mint for an extra burst of flavor—or a splash of coconut rum for a grown-up kick.
—Carol Farnsworth, Greenwood, IN

Takes: 15 min. • **Makes:** 8 servings

- 1   can (10 oz.) frozen non-alcoholic pina colada mix, thawed
- ½   cup sugar
- ½   cup pineapple-orange juice
- ⅛   tsp. almond extract
- ⅛   tsp. coconut extract
- 1½ cups green grapes
- 1½ cups seedless red grapes
- 1½ cups fresh blueberries
- 1½ cups halved fresh strawberries
- 1   can (8 oz.) pineapple chunks, drained
- ½   cup fresh raspberries
       Thinly sliced fresh mint, optional

SWEET & TART
LEMON GELATIN

PINA COLADA
FRUIT SALAD

SPRING
ASPARAGUS

DILLY POTATO
& EGG SALAD

SPRING ASPARAGUS

This side dish is fresh and colorful whether it's served up warm or cold. I receive lots of compliments on the homemade dressing.
—Millie Vickery, Lena, IL

Takes: 25 min. • **Makes:** 8 servings

- 1½ lbs. fresh asparagus, trimmed and cut into 2-in. pieces
- 2 small tomatoes, cut into wedges
- 3 Tbsp. cider vinegar
- ¾ tsp. Worcestershire sauce
- ⅓ cup sugar
- 1 Tbsp. grated onion
- ½ tsp. salt
- ½ tsp. paprika
- ⅓ cup canola oil
- ⅓ cup sliced almonds, toasted
- ⅓ cup crumbled blue cheese, optional

1. In a large saucepan, bring 1 cup water to a boil. Add asparagus; cook, covered, until crisp-tender, for 3-5 minutes. Drain; place in a large bowl. Add the tomatoes; cover and keep warm.
2. Place vinegar, Worcestershire sauce, sugar, onion, salt and paprika in a blender; cover and process until smooth. While processing, gradually add oil in a steady stream. Toss with asparagus mixture. Top with almonds and, if desired, cheese.
Note: To toast nuts, bake in a shallow pan in a 350° oven for 5-10 minutes or cook in a skillet over low heat until lightly browned, stirring occasionally.

DILLY POTATO & EGG SALAD

As a young bride, I was eager to learn how to cook and make things that my husband would love. I tried combining my mom's potato salad recipe with his mom's recipe, and this is the delicious result.
—Angela Leinenbach, Mechanicsville, VA

Prep: 20 min. + chilling
Cook: 20 min. + cooling
Makes: 12 servings (¾ cup each)

- 4 lbs. medium red potatoes (about 14), peeled and halved
- 5 hard-boiled large eggs
- 1 cup chopped dill pickles
- 1 small onion, chopped
- 1½ cups mayonnaise
- 1 tsp. celery seed
- ½ tsp. salt
- ¼ tsp. pepper
  Paprika

1. Place potatoes in a large saucepan; add water to cover. Bring to a boil. Reduce the heat; cook, uncovered, until tender, 15-20 minutes. Drain; cool completely.
2. Cut potatoes into ¾-in. cubes; place in a large bowl. Peel and chop four eggs; peel and slice remaining egg. Add chopped eggs, pickles and onion to potatoes. Mix mayonnaise, celery seed, salt and pepper; stir gently into potato mixture.
3. Sprinkle with paprika; top with sliced egg. Refrigerate, covered, at least 2 hours before serving.

THREE-BEAN BAKED BEANS

I got this recipe from my aunt and made a few changes to suit our tastes. With ground beef and bacon mixed in, these satisfying beans are a big hit at backyard barbecues and church picnics.
—Julie Currington, Gahanna, OH

Prep: 20 min. • **Bake:** 1 hour
Makes: 12 servings (¾ cup each)

- ½ lb. ground beef
- 5 bacon strips, diced
- ½ cup chopped onion
- ⅓ cup packed brown sugar
- ¼ cup sugar
- ¼ cup ketchup
- ¼ cup barbecue sauce
- 2 Tbsp. molasses
- 2 Tbsp. prepared mustard
- ½ tsp. chili powder
- ½ tsp. salt
- 2 cans (16 oz. each) pork and beans, undrained
- 1 can (16 oz.) butter beans, rinsed and drained
- 1 can (16 oz.) kidney beans, rinsed and drained

1. Preheat oven to 350°. In a large skillet, cook and crumble beef with bacon and onion over medium heat until beef is no longer pink; drain.
2. Stir in sugars, ketchup, barbecue sauce, molasses, mustard, chili powder and salt until blended. Stir in beans. Transfer to a greased 2½-qt. baking dish. Bake, covered, until beans reach desired thickness, about 1 hour.
Freeze option: Freeze cooled bean mixture in freezer containers. To use, partially thaw in refrigerator overnight. Heat through in a saucepan, stirring occasionally and adding a little water to bean mixture if necessary.

Garden Beauty

Give your springtime decor a natural new look with this artichoke vase. Using a chef's knife, cut off an artichoke's stem and level its base. Using a serrated knife, cut about 1 in. from the artichoke top. Open the leaves slightly by gently pushing them outward. Use a melon baller to scoop out the interior of the artichoke just down to its base, deep enough to hold the stems of a small bouquet. If desired, rinse the inside of the artichoke with lemon juice to keep the flowers fresher longer. Add the flowers and adjust the arrangement as needed.

SPECIAL CELEBRATIONS

From a magical birthday party to a spooky soiree, the get-togethers found here make memories all year long. Get casual with a hearty menu perfect for the men in your life or invite folks over for a sip-and-see afternoon to meet the new baby. You'll also find sweets perfect for Independence Day, a finger-licking barbecue lineup, poolside snacks and more.

Unicorn Birthday Party

Is your little one dreaming of a magical unicorn birthday party? Unleash your creativity and playfulness to create a mythically magnificent celebration kids and adults won't soon forget. Frolic down the road of sweet surprises with these enchanted ideas for a whimsical menu, plenty of party fun and a unicorn cake that will be both a darling dessert and a sparkling centerpiece. Just follow the rainbows!

Unicorn Cake (p. 180) **Rainbow Shortbread Cookies** (p. 179)

KIDDIE
CRUNCH MIX

KIDDIE CRUNCH MIX

This no-bake snack mix is a real treat for kids, and you can easily increase the amount to fit your needs. Place in individual plastic bags or pour some into colored ice cream cones and cover with plastic wrap for a fun presentation.
—Kara de la Vega, Santa Rosa, CA

Takes: 10 min. • **Makes:** 6 cups

- 1 cup plain or frosted animal crackers
- 1 cup bear-shaped crackers
- 1 cup miniature pretzels
- 1 cup salted peanuts
- 1 cup M&M's
- 1 cup yogurt- or chocolate-covered raisins

In a bowl, combine all the ingredients. Store in an airtight container.

CARROT CABBAGE SLAW

This crunchy salad with a homemade honey mayonnaise dressing is light and complements almost any main dish.
—Geordyth Sullivan, Cutler Bay, FL

Takes: 20 min. • **Makes:** 12 servings

- 4 cups shredded cabbage
- 2 cups shredded carrots
- 2 medium Golden Delicious apples, chopped
- 1 cup raisins
- ½ cup chopped walnuts
- ½ cup honey
- 1 Tbsp. lemon juice
- 1 cup sour cream
- ¼ tsp. salt
- ⅛ tsp. pepper
- ⅛ to ¼ tsp. ground nutmeg, optional

1. In a large serving bowl, combine the cabbage, carrots, apples, raisins and walnuts.
2. In a small bowl, combine honey and lemon juice until smooth. Stir in the sour cream, salt and pepper; add nutmeg if desired. Stir into the cabbage mixture. Chill until serving.

MAGIC WANDS

MAGIC WANDS

These fun and colorul magic wands don't take a magician to make! You can change the colors to fit any party theme.
—Renee Schwebach, Dumont, MN

Prep: 25 min. + standing • **Makes:** 2 dozen

- 1½ cups white baking chips
- 1 pkg. (10 oz.) pretzel rods
  Colored candy stars or sprinkles
  Colored sugar or edible glitter

In a microwave, melt chips; stir until smooth. Dip each pretzel rod halfway into the melted chips; allow excess to drip off. Sprinkle with candy stars and colored sugar. Place on waxed paper; let stand until dry. Store in an airtight container.
Note: Edible glitter is available from Wilton Industries. Call 800-794-5866 or visit *wilton.com*.

APRICOT-RICOTTA STUFFED CELERY

This healthful protein filling can double as a dip for sliced apples. I often make it ahead of time, so kids can help themselves to an after-school snack.
—Larry Crowder, Grand Blanc, MI

Takes: 15 min. • **Makes:** about 2 dozen

- 3 dried apricots
- ½ cup part-skim ricotta cheese
- 2 tsp. brown sugar
- ¼ tsp. grated orange zest
- ⅛ tsp. salt
- 5 celery ribs, cut into 1½ in. pieces

Place apricots in a food processor. Cover and process until finely chopped. Add the ricotta cheese, brown sugar, orange zest and salt; cover and process until blended. Stuff or pipe into celery. Chill until serving.

How to Host a Magical Unicorn Party

Want to throw a bash as legendary as the mythical creature itself? Here are seven tips for hosting a truly amazing unicorn party.

DECORATE WITH RAINBOWS

Welcome unicorn lovers to a party room exploding into rainbows. Fill the air with streamers and balloons in traditional rainbow colors or a softer pastel palette.

START WITH A CUTE TREAT

For an appetizer that will impress guests of any age, whip up the cute and easy Little Dippers unicorn strawberries (right).

GIVE GUESTS TAILS AND HORNS

Get creative and transform the kids into unicorns! Fashion horns out of conical pieces of Styrofoam glued to simple headbands. Pompoms, shredded construction paper or raffia make great tails.

GET THE KIDS INVOLVED

Give each child a "horn" headband, and set up a craft table with glitter, paint, confetti and glue so they can decorate it. You can offer prizes for the most creative, too.

PIN THE HORN ON THE UNICORN

Reinvent the classic party game for your party. All it takes is a large poster printout of a unicorn, cutouts of a tail or horn, some Velcro and a blindfold for unicorn hunters.

CREATE A PHOTO BOOTH

Set up a colorful unicorn-themed backdrop, and arrange for a friend to help take pictures. You can print out photos while guests are playing games or eating cake, or email the photos after the party is over.

OFFER A MAGICAL TAKEAWAY

Goodie bags are always a treat! Decorate colorful paper bags with stickers, glitter and confetti. Stuff them with inexpensive toys, unicorn-shaped cookie cutters or colorful homemade candies.

RANCH BROCCOLI PASTA SALAD

Here's an easy summer salad for potlucks, luncheons and picnics. Tricolor spiral pasta and broccoli florets are coated with a mild dressing and bits of bacon.
—Margie Shaw, Americus, GA

Prep: 10 min. + chilling • **Makes:** 12 servings

- 1   pkg. (16 oz.) tricolor spiral pasta, cooked, rinsed and drained
- 3   cups broccoli florets
- ⅓   cup finely chopped onion
- ½   cup reduced-fat mayonnaise
- 2   Tbsp. fat-free milk
- 1   envelope reduced-fat ranch salad dressing mix
- ½   tsp. salt
- 6   bacon strips, cooked and crumbled

In a large bowl, combine pasta, broccoli and onion. In a small bowl, combine mayonnaise, milk, salad dressing mix and salt. Add to the pasta mixture; toss to coat evenly. Cover and refrigerate for at least 1 hour. Just before serving, stir in bacon.

STAR SANDWICHES

These star-shaped sandwiches are downright fun—and filled with savory egg salad. You can use whatever bread you like, but I prefer yellow egg bread.
—Pam Lancaster, Willis, VA

Takes: 25 min. • **Makes:** 8 sandwiches

- 4   hard-boiled large eggs, diced
- ½   cup mayonnaise
- 1   tsp. Dijon mustard
- ¼   tsp. dill weed
- ⅛   tsp. salt
- ⅛   tsp. pepper
- 16 slices egg bread or white bread

In a bowl, combine the eggs, mayonnaise, mustard, dill, salt and pepper. Using a large star-shaped cookie cutter, cut out 16 stars from the bread. Spread half of the star shapes with egg salad; top with remaining bread slices.

MARSHMALLOW FRUIT DIP

You can whip up this sweet and creamy dip in just 10 minutes. I like to serve it in a bowl surrounded by fresh-picked strawberries.
—Cindy Steffen, Cedarburg, WI

Takes: 10 min. • **Makes:** 5 cups

- 1   pkg. (8 oz.) cream cheese, softened
- ¾   cup cherry yogurt
- 1   carton (8 oz.) frozen whipped topping, thawed
- 1   jar (7 oz.) marshmallow creme
     Assorted fresh fruit

In a large bowl, beat cream cheese and yogurt until blended. Fold in whipped topping and marshmallow creme. Serve with fruit.

HOW-TO

Little Dippers

Get ready for big blue skies and sunny days with this fun lineup of rainbow-colored, candy-dunked strawberries. Sweet!

Dip berries in melted candy coating disks. Let dry on parchment. Add sprinkles or decorate as desired.

"Fruity and flavorful, these grab-and-go wraps are quick to assemble, easy to handle and low in calories."
—BOBBIE KEEFER, BYERS, CO

CRANBERRY
TURKEY WRAPS

CRANBERRY TURKEY WRAPS

Takes: 15 min. • **Makes:** 8 servings

- 1 can (11 oz.) mandarin oranges, drained
- 1 medium tart apple, peeled and diced
- 3 Tbsp. dried cranberries
- ¾ cup fat-free plain yogurt
- 2 Tbsp. fat-free mayonnaise
- 8 flour tortillas (8 in.)
- 8 lettuce leaves
- 1½ lbs. thinly sliced deli turkey
- 8 slices (1 oz. each) part-skim mozzarella cheese
- 2 Tbsp. chopped pecans, toasted

In a small bowl, combine the oranges, apple and cranberries. In another bowl, combine yogurt and mayonnaise; spread over tortillas. Layer each with lettuce, turkey, cheese, fruit mixture and pecans. Roll up tightly.

CHERRY PUNCH

Back in 1952, a co-worker gave me the recipe for this versatile rosy punch. It's not too sweet, so it really refreshes. My family and friends have sipped it at countless gatherings over the years.
—Davlyn Jones, San Jose, CA

Takes: 20 min. • **Makes:** about 6 qt.

- ¾ cup thawed lemonade concentrate
- 1 can (6 oz.) frozen limeade concentrate, thawed
- 1 can (20 oz.) pineapple chunks, undrained
- 2 cups water
- 2 liters cherry soda, chilled
- 2 liters ginger ale, chilled
  Lemon and lime slices, optional

In a blender, combine concentrates and pineapple; cover and blend until smooth. Pour into a gallon-size container; stir in water. Store in the refrigerator. To serve, pour the mixture into a punch bowl; add cherry soda and ginger ale. Garnish with lemon and lime slices if desired.

CRAZY-COLORED FRUIT POPS

Orange, pear, banana, raspberry, grape—the gang's all here! See if your party guests can guess the flavors in these summery rainbow pops.
—Vikki Spengler, Ocala, FL

Prep: 20 min. + freezing • **Makes:** 19 pops

- 1 cup orange-tangerine juice
- 2 cans (15 oz. each) reduced-sugar sliced pears, drained and divided
- 1 medium banana, sliced and divided
- 2 to 3 drops yellow food coloring, optional
- 4 drops red food coloring, optional, divided
- 1 cup red raspberry juice
- 1 cup grape juice
- 19 freezer pop molds or 19 paper cups (3 oz. each) and wooden pop sticks

1. In a blender, combine orange-tangerine juice, ¾ cup of the pears, a third of the banana slices, yellow food coloring and 1 drop of red food coloring if desired; cover and process until smooth. Fill each mold or cup with 1 Tbsp. of the mixture. Top molds with holders. If using cups, top with foil and insert sticks through foil. Freeze for 30 minutes or until firm.
2. In a blender, combine raspberry juice, ¾ cup of the pears, a third of the banana slices and the remaining red food coloring if desired; cover and process until smooth. If using pop molds, remove holders. If using cups, remove the foil. Pour the raspberry mixture over the orange layer. Return holders or foil. Freeze 30 minutes or until firm.
3. In a blender, combine grape juice, the remaining pears and the remaining banana slices; cover and process until smooth. If using pop molds, remove the holders. If using cups, remove the foil. Pour grape mixture over tops; replace holders or foil. Freeze for 30 minutes or until firm.

RAINBOW SHORTBREAD COOKIES

Everyone loves a classic shortbread cookie. Make them magical with a quick dip into melted baking chips and colored sprinkles. Your unicorns will love these rainbow bites.
—Angela Lemoine, Howell, NJ

Prep: 15 min. • **Bake:** 15 min.
Makes: 2 dozen

- ½ cup butter, softened
- ¾ cup confectioners' sugar
- 1 large egg
- 1½ cups all-purpose flour
- ¼ cup sprinkles
- ½ cup white baking chips, melted
  Additional sprinkles

1. In a large bowl, cream butter and sugar until light and fluffy. Beat in egg. Gradually add flour until blended. Stir in sprinkles. Form dough into a disc and wrap in plastic wrap; chill for 1 hour.
2. Preheat oven to 375°. Line a baking sheet with parchment paper. Place the dough on parchment and roll into a 12x8-in. rectangle. Score into 24 small rectangles. Bake until edges are golden brown, 10-15 minutes. Remove to cooling rack; cool.
3. Break or cut along the score marks. Dip one edge of each cookie into the melted chips, then dip in sprinkles; place on waxed paper until set.

UNICORN CAKE

UNICORN CAKE

This magical unicorn cake tastes as good as it looks. Baking the batter in smaller pans creates impressive height, and a few simple decorating tricks turn it into an Instagram-worthy dessert!
—Lauren Knoelke, Milwaukee, WI

Prep: 1 hour • **Bake:** 25 min. + cooling
Makes: 20 servings

- 2¼ cups cake flour
- 1½ cups sugar
- 3½ tsp. baking powder
- ½ tsp. salt
- ½ cup unsalted butter, cubed
- 4 large egg whites, room temperature
- ¾ cup 2% milk, divided
- 1 tsp. clear vanilla extract
- ½ tsp. almond extract
- ⅓ cup rainbow jimmies

BUTTERCREAM
- 6 oz. white baking chocolate, chopped
- ¼ cup heavy whipping cream
- 6 large egg whites
- 1½ cups sugar
- ½ tsp. cream of tartar
- ½ tsp. salt
- 2 cups unsalted butter, cubed
- 1½ tsp. vanilla extract
  Paste food coloring

1. Preheat the oven to 350°. Line the bottoms of three 6-in. round baking pans with parchment paper; grease and flour the baking pans.

2. In a large bowl, whisk the flour, sugar, baking powder and salt. Beat in butter until crumbly. Add egg whites, one at a time, beating well after each addition. Gradually beat in ¼ cup milk and extracts; beat on medium until light and fluffy, 2 minutes. Gradually beat in remaining milk. Gently fold in jimmies.

3. Transfer batter to the prepared pans. Bake until a toothpick inserted in center comes out clean, 25-30 minutes. Cool in pans 10 minutes before removing to wire racks; remove paper. Cool completely.

4. For buttercream, in a microwave, melt chocolate with cream until smooth; stir every 30 seconds. Set aside to cool slightly. In a heatproof bowl of a stand mixer, whisk egg whites, sugar, cream of tartar and salt until blended. Place over simmering water in a large saucepan over medium heat. Whisking constantly, heat mixture until a thermometer reads 160°, 8-10 minutes.

5. Remove from heat. With the whisk attachment of stand mixer, beat on high speed until cooled to 90°, about 7 minutes. Gradually beat in butter, a few tablespoonfuls at a time, on medium speed until smooth; beat in the vanilla and the white chocolate mixture.

6. Spread frosting between layers and over top and sides of cake. Divide the remaining buttercream into smaller portions; stir in food coloring to achieve desired colors for unicorn mane. Using the steps at right as a guide, decorate and pipe the mane as desired. Store in refrigerator.

Make Fancy Finishes

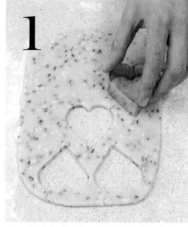

To make the ears, mix your favorite sugar cookie dough with jimmies; cut into 2-in. hearts and bake.

While the baked cookies are warm, mold them onto the curve of a large metal spoon; let stand until cooled.

Using an open star nozzle tip, fill in between the meringues with your first color of frosting.

2

For eyes, pipe melted white candy coating disks onto parchment; chill until set. (Make extra, just in case!)

3

Spray the piped eyes with edible gold glitter spray. (Available from Wilton Industries, *wilton.com*.)

4

To make the horn, spray a sugar ice cream cone with gold glitter spray.

6

Dip the straight edges of the cooled cookies into melted white chocolate; let set.

7

Gently push the horn and ears into place on the top of the cake.

8

To make the mane, gently press meringues (store-bought work great!) into the top and side of cake.

10

Add additional frosting in other colors around the outside of the meringues to fill in the mane.

11

Continue to add frosting to finish mane, switching frosting colors and decorating tips as desired.

12

Use tweezers to gently set each eye in place on the front of the cake; press gently to adhere.

Sip & See Party

Time to raise your glass, ya'll! A new baby has arrived, and the proud parents can't wait to introduce their darling bundle of joy to those nearest and dearest. But what exactly is a *sip and see*? A southern tradition that's making its way north and beyond, a sip and see party is a relaxed, intimate gathering where friends and family have the opportunity to snuggle, swaddle (and see!) the precious babe. After all the adoring coos and cuddles, guests sip a few drinks while enjoying some light refreshments. Cheers to the happy family!

Cucumber Party Sandwiches (p. 185) **Hazelnut Macarons** (p. 186) **Fruit Cooler** (p. 185)

Green Stamps

Use the end of a celery stalk to make fresh floral patterns on handmade party invitations or thank-you cards. Chop. Chop. Get inking!

WHAT YOU'LL NEED
Celery stalk
Ink pad
Plain wrapping paper and blank cards
Paper towels

DIRECTIONS

1. Cut the end of the celery crosswise to reveal the cross section. Stand, cut side down, on paper towels to blot up excess moisture.

2. Press cut side of celery into ink pad to cover the surface. Make a few practice stamps on scrap paper to determine how much ink you'll need and how much pressure to apply.

3. Lay a folded tea towel under the paper or card to be stamped. The layers of the towel soften the surface so that the vegetable can press evenly into the paper.

4. If desired, stamp a single motif onto a blank card for a matching tag or a repeated pattern over a large piece of paper for gift wrap.

BRIGHT IDEA!
If the stamping end of the vegetable becomes soggy, trim off a slice of the cross section to freshen the stamp.

FRUIT
COOLER

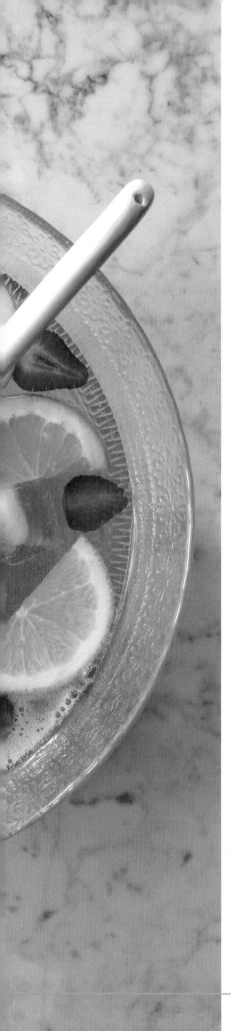

FRUIT COOLER

This punch looks so pretty with all the colorful fruit floating in the bowl. It's refreshing and easy to stir up.
—Dawn Shackelford, Fort Worth, TX

Takes: 10 min. • **Makes:** 2½ qt.

- ½ cup sugar
- ½ cup lemon juice
- 4 cups cold white grape juice
- 1 liter club soda, chilled
- 1 medium orange, halved and sliced
- ½ cup sliced strawberries
- ½ cup sliced fresh peaches
  Ice cubes, optional

1. In a punch bowl or pitcher, mix sugar and lemon juice until sugar is dissolved. Stir in grape juice.
2. To serve, stir in club soda and fruit. If desired, serve with ice.

CUCUMBER PARTY SANDWICHES

(SHOWN ON P. 183)
This is one of my favorite appetizers. We have lots of pig roasts here in Kentucky, and these small sandwiches are perfect to serve while the pig is cooking.
—Rebecca Rose, Mount Washington, KY

Prep: 20 min. + standing • **Makes:** 2½ dozen

- 1 pkg. (8 oz.) cream cheese, softened
- 2 Tbsp. mayonnaise
- 2 tsp. Italian salad dressing mix
- 30 slices cocktail rye or pumpernickel bread
- 60 thin cucumber slices
  Fresh dill sprigs and slivered red pearl onions, optional

1. Beat the cream cheese, mayonnaise and dressing mix until blended; let stand 30 minutes.
2. Spread cream cheese mixture on bread. Top with cucumber and, if desired, dill and red onion slivers. Cut diagonally in half if desired. Refrigerate, covered, until serving.

COCKTAIL CHEESE CRACKERS

My homemade crackers are delicious with your favorite sliced cheese or spread. For a change of pace, substitute cheddar cheese for the Swiss.

—Johnna Johnson, Scottsdale, AZ

Prep: 30 min.
Bake: 10 min./batch + cooling
Makes: 5 dozen

- 1¾ cups all-purpose flour
- 1 tsp. salt
- 1 tsp. baking powder
- 1 tsp. paprika
- ⅛ tsp. cayenne pepper
- 1 cup grated Parmesan cheese
- 1 cup shredded Swiss cheese
- ½ cup cold butter, cubed
- 1 large egg
- ½ cup heavy whipping cream
- 1 large egg yolk
- 1 tsp. 2% milk
  Optional toppings: poppy seeds, sesame seeds, caraway seeds and dried minced onion

1. Preheat oven to 375°. In a large bowl, whisk together first five ingredients; stir in cheeses. Cut in butter until crumbly. Whisk together egg and cream; gradually add to flour mixture, tossing with a fork until dough forms a ball.
2. Turn onto a floured surface; knead gently just until combined, about 10 times. Divide dough in half. Roll each portion into a 12x10-in. rectangle; cut dough into 2-in. squares. Pierce with a fork. Place 2 in. apart on parchment paper-lined baking sheets. In a small bowl, whisk together egg yolk and milk; brush over tops. If desired, sprinkle with choice of toppings.
3. Bake until golden brown, 9-12 minutes. Remove from pans to wire racks; cool completely. Store in an airtight container.

HAZELNUT MACARONS

The renowned chef Julia Child had a passion for life and French cooking as she and Alex Prud'homme described in the book *My Life in France*. The woman who introduced Americans to the delights of French cuisine most likely would have found these crispy French-style cookies a delight, too.
—*Taste of Home* Test Kitchen

Prep: 50 min.
Bake: 10 min./batch + cooling
Makes: about 5 dozen

- 6 **large egg whites**
- 1½ **cups hazelnuts, toasted**
- 2½ **cups confectioners' sugar**
  Dash salt
- ½ **cup superfine sugar**
- **COFFEE BUTTERCREAM**
- 1 **cup sugar**
- 6 **Tbsp. water**
- 6 **large egg yolks**
- 4 **tsp. instant espresso powder**
- 1 **tsp. vanilla extract**
- 1½ **cups butter, softened**
- 6 **Tbsp. confectioners' sugar**

1. Place egg whites in a bowl; let stand at room temperature for 30 minutes.
2. Preheat the oven to 350°. Place the hazelnuts and confectioners' sugar in a food processor; pulse until the nuts are finely ground.
3. Add salt to egg whites; beat on medium speed until soft peaks form. Gradually add superfine sugar, 1 Tbsp. at a time, beating on high until stiff peaks form. Fold in the hazelnut mixture.
4. Pipe 1-in.-diameter cookies about 2 in. apart onto parchment paper-lined baking sheets. Bake until the cookies are lightly browned and firm to the touch, 9-12 minutes. Transfer the cookies on the parchment paper to wire racks and cool completely.
5. For buttercream, in a heavy saucepan, combine sugar and water. Bring to a boil; cook over medium-high heat until sugar is dissolved. Remove from heat. In a small bowl, whisk a small amount of hot syrup into egg yolks; return all to pan, whisking constantly. Cook mixture until thickened, 2-3 minutes, stirring constantly; remove from heat. Stir in espresso powder and vanilla; cool completely.
6. Attach the whisk attachment to a stand mixer and beat the butter until creamy. Gradually beat in cooled syrup. Beat in the confectioners' sugar until fluffy. Refrigerate until the mixture firms to a spreading consistency, about 10 minutes.
7. Spread about 1½ tsp. buttercream onto the bottom of each of half of the cookies; top with remaining cookies. Store in airtight containers in the refrigerator.
To toast whole hazelnuts: Bake in a shallow pan in a 350° oven until fragrant and lightly browned, 7-10 minutes, stirring occasionally. To remove the skins, wrap hazelnuts in a tea towel; rub with towel to loosen skins.

GREEN TOMATO SALSA

I came up with this fresh salsa so I could use all the green tomatoes in my garden before the weather turned cold. It's one of my go-to dishes for parties.
—Vanessa Moon, Tucson, AZ

Prep: 20 min. + standing • **Cook:** 10 min.
Makes: 24 servings (¼ cup each)

- 1 **medium green pepper**
- 1 **serrano pepper**
- 5 **medium green tomatoes or**
  5 large tomatillos, husks removed
- 1 **medium onion, chopped**
- 2 **garlic cloves, minced**
- ⅓ **cup lime juice**
- 2 **Tbsp. olive oil**
- 4 **tsp. agave nectar**
- 1 **tsp. coarsely ground pepper**
- ½ **tsp. salt**
- 3 **Tbsp. fresh cilantro leaves**
- 1 **medium ripe avocado, peeled,**
  pitted and quartered
  Tortilla chips

1. Preheat broiler. Place peppers on a foil-lined baking sheet. Broil 3-4 in. from heat until skins blister, about 5 minutes. With tongs, rotate peppers a quarter turn. Broil and rotate until all sides are blistered and blackened. Immediately place in a bowl; let stand, covered, 20 minutes.
2. Using tongs, place the tomatoes, a few at a time, in a pot of boiling water for 5 minutes. Remove tomatoes; cool slightly. Peel and finely chop tomatoes; place in a large bowl.
3. Remove skin, stems and seeds from charred peppers. Finely chop peppers; add to tomatoes. Stir in onion and garlic.
4. Place all remaining ingredients except chips in a blender; cover and process until smooth. Add to tomato mixture, stirring to combine. Serve with chips.
Note: Wear gloves when cutting hot peppers; the oils can burn skin. Avoid touching your face.

GINGER MINT JULEP

Mint juleps aren't just for Kentucky Derby day. Enjoy one while gathering with friends for a baby shower or luncheon.
—Ellen Riley, Murfreesboro, TN

Prep: 15 min. + chilling
Cook: 5 min. + cooling • **Makes:** 10 servings

- 2 **cups sugar**
- 2 **cups water**
- 2 **cups loosely packed chopped**
  fresh spearmint
- **EACH SERVING**
- ½ **to ¾ cup crushed ice**
- 1 **oz. bourbon**
- 2 **tsp. lime juice**
- 1½ **oz. ginger beer**

1. For mint syrup, place sugar, water and chopped mint in a large saucepan; bring to a boil over medium heat. Cook until sugar is dissolved, stirring occasionally. Remove from heat; cool completely.
2. Strain the syrup through a fine-mesh strainer; discard the mint. Refrigerate, covered, until cold, at least 2 hours.
3. For each serving, place ice in a mint julep cup or rocks glass. Add bourbon, lime juice and ¼ cup mint syrup; stir until mixture is cold. Top with beer.

GINGER
MINT JULEP

HAM SALAD

HAM SALAD

I first made this for a shower, and everyone raved about it. It's a favorite sandwich at church suppers and family gatherings, and a perfect way to make use of leftover ham.
—Patricia Reed, Pine Bluff, AR

Takes: 15 min. • **Makes:** 10 servings

- ¾ cup mayonnaise
- ½ cup finely chopped celery
- ¼ cup sliced green onions
- 2 Tbsp. minced fresh chives
- 1 Tbsp. honey
- 2 tsp. spicy brown mustard
- ½ tsp. Worcestershire sauce
- ½ tsp. seasoned salt
- 5 cups diced fully cooked ham or turkey
- ⅓ cup chopped pecans and almonds, toasted
  Slider buns, split, optional

1. Mix first eight ingredients. Stir in ham. Refrigerate, covered, until serving.
2. Stir in pecans before serving. If desired, serve on buns.

CAYENNE PECANS

These toasted nuts are crunchy and mildly seasoned. The cayenne pepper adds a little zing everyone is sure to love.
—Phyllis Stanley, Avery, TX

Takes: 20 min. • **Makes:** 4 cups

- ¼ cup butter, cubed
- 3 Tbsp. Worcestershire sauce
- ¾ tsp. salt
- ¾ tsp. cayenne pepper
- 4 cups pecan halves (about 15 oz.)

1. Preheat oven to 350°. In a microwave, melt butter; stir in Worcestershire sauce, salt and cayenne. Toss pecans with butter mixture; spread evenly in an ungreased 15x10x1-in. pan.
2. Bake pecans until lightly toasted, about 15 minutes, stirring occasionally. Cool in pan on a wire rack. Store cooled nuts in an airtight container.

BUTTER POUND CAKE

Whether garnished with fresh berries and sprigs of rosemary or just served plain, this rich cake is fabulous. It bakes to a beautiful golden brown and it's definitely a keeper!
—Edgar Wright, Silver Spring, MD

Prep: 15 min. • **Bake:** 50 min. + cooling
Makes: 12 servings

- 1 cup butter, softened
- 2 cups sugar
- 1 tsp. vanilla extract
- 5 large eggs
- 2¼ cups all-purpose flour
- ¼ tsp. baking powder
- ⅛ tsp. salt
- 3 Tbsp. water
  GARNISH, OPTIONAL
- 3 Tbsp. light corn syrup
- 1 pkg. fresh rosemary sprigs
- ¼ cup sugar, divided
- ¼ cup fresh cranberries
- 2 Tbsp. fresh blueberries
  Confectioners' sugar, optional

1. Preheat oven to 350°. Grease and flour a 10-in. fluted tube pan.
2. Cream butter and sugar until light and fluffy. Beat in vanilla and eggs, one at a time. Whisk together the flour, baking powder and salt. Add to creamed mixture alternately with water, beating after each addition. Transfer to prepared pan.
3. Bake until a toothpick inserted in center comes out clean, 50-55 minutes. Cool 10 minutes before removing from pan; cool completely on a wire rack.
4. If desired, for garnish, place corn syrup in a small microwave-safe bowl. Microwave, uncovered, 10 seconds or until warm. Brush corn syrup lightly over rosemary. Sprinkle sugar to coat; place on waxed paper to dry. Reheat remaining corn syrup until warm; gently toss the cranberries and blueberries in syrup. Toss in remaining sugar to coat. Place on waxed paper; let stand until set, about 1 hour.
5. Just before serving, top cake with sugared rosemary and berries. If desired, dust with confectioners' sugar.
Note: To remove cakes easily, use solid shortening to grease plain and fluted tube pans.

ROASTED GARLIC DEVILED EGGS

I love incorporating new flavors into old classics, and this twist was a big hit. The garlic can be roasted and the eggs can be hard-boiled up to three days in advance. The yolk filling can be whipped up the night before so you don't have any last-minute fuss before the party.
—Ellen Weaver, Denver, CO

Prep: 15 min. • **Bake:** 50 min. + cooling
Makes: 2 dozen

- 1 whole garlic bulb
- 1 Tbsp. olive oil
- 12 hard-boiled large eggs
- ½ cup mayonnaise
- 2 Tbsp. grated Parmesan cheese
- 1 tsp. paprika
  Chopped fresh chives, optional

1. Preheat oven to 350°. Remove papery outer skin from garlic bulb, but do not peel or separate the cloves. Cut off top of garlic bulb, exposing individual cloves. Drizzle the cut cloves with oil. Wrap in foil. Bake until the cloves are soft and light golden, 50-60 minutes. Unwrap; cool completely.
2. Meanwhile, cut eggs lengthwise in half. Remove yolks to a bowl; reserve whites. Squeeze garlic from skins and add to yolks; mash yolks and garlic with a fork. Stir in the mayonnaise, cheese and paprika.
3. Pipe or spoon filling into egg whites. If desired, sprinkle with chives. Refrigerate, covered, until serving.

TEST KITCHEN TIP

How To Peel Fresh Garlic

Using the blade of a chef's knife, crush garlic clove. Peel away skin.

STRAWBERRY
CHEESECAKE BITES

PEACHES & CREAM RASPBERRY TART

Fresh peach slices and big, juicy raspberries crown this beautiful tart. An almond-flavored cream filling and macaroon crust complement the fruits. It's the perfect dessert for company during peach season.
—Brenda Harmon, Hastings, MN

Prep: 30 min. • **Bake:** 15 min. + cooling
Makes: 10 servings

- 2 cups crumbled soft coconut macaroons (about 9 cookies)
- 1 cup ground pecans
- 3 Tbsp. butter, melted
- ½ cup heavy whipping cream
- 1 pkg. (8 oz.) cream cheese, softened
- ⅓ cup sugar
- 2 tsp. orange juice
- 1 tsp. vanilla extract
- ¼ tsp. almond extract
- ¼ cup apricot preserves
- 2 tsp. honey
- 4 medium peaches, peeled and sliced or 3 cups frozen sliced peaches, thawed
- 2 Tbsp. lemon juice
- ½ cup fresh raspberries

1. Preheat oven to 350°. Place cookies, pecans and melted butter in a food processor; process until blended. Press onto bottom and up sides of an ungreased 11-in. fluted tart pan with removable bottom. Place pan on a baking sheet.
2. Bake until the crust is golden brown, 12-14 minutes. Cool crust completely on a wire rack.
3. For filling, in a small bowl, beat whipping cream until soft peaks form. In another bowl, beat cream cheese and sugar until smooth. Beat in orange juice and extracts. Fold in whipped cream. Spread over crust.
4. For glaze, in a small saucepan, mix preserves and honey. Cook and stir over low heat until melted; press through a strainer. Toss peaches with lemon juice. Arrange the peaches and raspberries over the filling; brush with glaze. Store in the refrigerator.

STRAWBERRY CHEESECAKE BITES

The only thing more exquisite than a bright, red strawberry is a strawberry filled with cream cheese. If you don't have a cake decorating bag, use a spoon to fill the berries, then use a plastic sandwich bag with just the tip of one corner cut off to drizzle the chocolate.
—Linda Baldt, Croydon, PA

Takes: 30 min. • **Makes:** 20 servings

- 1 pkg. (8 oz.) cream cheese, softened
- ⅓ cup confectioners' sugar
- ¼ tsp. vanilla extract
- 20 large fresh strawberries (about 1½ lbs.)
- ¼ cup semisweet chocolate chips
- 1 tsp. shortening
  Graham cracker crumbs, optional

1. For filling, beat the cream cheese, confectioners' sugar and vanilla extract until smooth.
2. Remove stems from strawberries. Using a paring knife or small melon baller, cut a 1-in.-deep opening in the stem end of strawberries. Pipe or spoon cream cheese mixture into openings. Place on a waxed paper-lined baking sheet.
3. In a microwave, melt chocolate and shortening; stir until smooth. Drizzle over the strawberries; if desired, sprinkle with graham cracker crumbs. Refrigerate the strawberries until set.

PEACHES & CREAM
RASPBERRY TART

Red, White & Blue Desserts

Bring on the red, white and blue with these very berry-liscious desserts. Perfect for Memorial Day, Fourth of July or any day in the great USA, each one is fabulous, fuss-free and guaranteed to be an all-American knockout. We're certain you'll make (and eat) these star-spangled treats with patriotic pride!

Berry-Patch Brownie Pizza (p. 197)

STARS & STRIPES PARFAITS

Show your stripes with berry-filled rice pudding parfaits. They're ideal for patriotic celebrations or any time you crave a cool and refreshing dessert.
—Mrs. Fred Stacy, Big Rock, VA

Prep: 30 min. + cooling • **Makes:** 6 servings

- 2 cups cooked rice
- 1 cup 2% milk
- 1 cup heavy whipping cream
- ¼ cup sugar
- 2 large egg yolks
- 1 Tbsp. butter
- 1 tsp. vanilla extract
- 1 cup fresh blueberries
- 1 cup fresh raspberries
  Sweetened whipped cream and toasted chopped almonds, optional

1. In a heavy saucepan, combine the rice, milk, cream and sugar; bring to a boil over medium heat. Reduce heat to maintain a low simmer. Cook, uncovered, until rice is soft, about 20 minutes, stirring frequently.
2. Remove from heat. In a small bowl, stir a small amount into egg yolks; return all to pan, stirring constantly. Bring to a boil; cook and stir 2 minutes. Remove from heat; stir in butter and vanilla. Cool rice pudding completely.
3. Layer half the blueberries, half the pudding mixture and half the raspberries in six parfait glasses. Repeat the layers. Refrigerate until serving. If desired, top with whipped cream and almonds.

TEST KITCHEN TIP

Rice Pudding

Rice puddings are made with cooked rice, a custard mixture, flavoring and spices. They can be served warm or cold. Store in the refrigerator for 1 to 2 days.

BLACKBERRY-LEMON PUDDING CAKE

I grew up in Texas, where every summer I looked forward to picking dewberries. The berries were so good that not even the threat of snakebite could scare me away. Now I live in Colorado and have since fallen in love with the state's sweet blackberries. I combined the berries with a light and airy lemon meringue batter to create this world-class dessert.
—Karen Harris, Littleton, CO

Prep: 30 min. • **Bake:** 45 min.
Makes: 9 servings

- 2 large eggs, separated
- 2 cups fresh blackberries
- 1¼ cups sugar, divided
- 1 cup all-purpose flour
- 2 tsp. baking powder
- ½ tsp. salt
- ½ cup 2% milk
- ⅓ cup butter, melted
- 2 tsp. grated lemon zest
- ¼ cup lemon juice
- 1 tsp. vanilla extract
- ½ cup packed brown sugar
- ½ tsp. ground cinnamon
- 1¼ cups boiling water
- ½ cup sliced almonds
  Vanilla ice cream

1. Preheat oven to 350°. Place the egg whites in a small bowl; let stand at room temperature while preparing batter. Place blackberries in a greased 8-in. square baking dish.
2. In a large bowl, whisk together 1 cup sugar, flour, baking powder and salt. In another bowl, whisk together milk, melted butter, egg yolks, lemon zest and juice, and vanilla; add to dry ingredients, stirring just until moistened. With a clean bowl and clean beaters, beat egg whites until stiff peaks form; fold into batter. Spoon over blackberries.
3. Mix brown sugar, cinnamon and the remaining sugar; sprinkle over batter. Slowly pour boiling water over top of the batter. Sprinkle with almonds.
4. Bake until a toothpick inserted into cake portion comes out clean. 45-50 minutes. Serve warm with ice cream.

BLUEBERRY
LATTICE BARS

BLUEBERRY LATTICE BARS

Our area has an annual blueberry festival, and my daughters and I are always looking for new berry recipes to enter in the cooking contest. These lovely bars won a blue ribbon one year.
—Debbie Ayers, Baileyville, ME

Prep: 25 min. + chilling
Bake: 30 min. + cooling • **Makes:** 2 dozen

1⅓	cups butter, softened
⅔	cup sugar
¼	tsp. salt
1	large egg
½	tsp. vanilla extract
3¾	cups all-purpose flour

FILLING

3	cups fresh or frozen blueberries
1	cup sugar
3	Tbsp. cornstarch

1. Cream the butter, sugar and salt until light and fluffy; beat in the egg and vanilla. Gradually beat in flour. Divide dough in half; shape each into a 1-in.-thick rectangle. Wrap in plastic; refrigerate dough 2 hours or overnight.

2. Preheat oven to 375°. Place blueberries, sugar and cornstarch in a small saucepan. Bring to a boil over medium heat, stirring frequently; cook and stir until thickened, about 2 minutes. Cool slightly.

3. Roll each portion of dough between two sheets of plastic wrap into a 14x10-in. rectangle. Place rectangles on separate baking sheets; freeze until firm, for 5-10 minutes. Place one rectangle in a greased 13x9-in. baking pan, pressing onto bottom and about ½-in. up the sides. Add filling.

4. Cut the remaining rectangle into ½-in. strips; freeze 5-10 minutes to firm. Arrange the strips over filling in crisscross fashion. If desired, press edges with a fork to seal strips. Bake until top crust is golden brown, 30-35 minutes. Cool on a wire rack. Cut into bars.

BERRY
PISTACHIO PIE

BERRY PISTACHIO PIE

My grandmother used to make this pie when I was a small child. A woman from Brooklyn gave her the recipe, but my grandmother could never remember the woman's name or the name of the pie, comically dubbing it Lady from Brooklyn's Pie. Feel free to use any flavored gelatin, or try walnuts or pecans instead of pistachios. I use a store-bought graham cracker crust, but you can also use a chocolate graham cracker crust.

—Judy DeGrottole, New York, NY

Prep: 25 min. + chilling • **Makes:** 10 servings

- 1 cup boiling water
- 1 pkg. (3 oz.) lemon gelatin
- ¾ cup cold water
- 1 tsp. grated lemon zest
- 2 Tbsp. lemon juice, divided
- 1 carton (12 oz.) whipped topping, divided
- ¾ cup pistachios, chopped
  One 10-in. graham cracker crust (about 9 oz.)
- 1½ cups fresh strawberries, quartered
- 1 cup fresh blueberries
  Sweetened shredded coconut, toasted
  Additional chopped pistachios

1. In a large bowl, add boiling water to gelatin; stir for 2 minutes to completely dissolve. Stir in cold water, lemon peel and 1 Tbsp. lemon juice. Refrigerate, covered, until almost firm, 1½ to 2 hours.
2. Fold 2 cups whipped topping into gelatin. Beat until smooth, 1-2 minutes. Fold in pistachios. Transfer to crust. Refrigerate, covered, at least 4 hours.
3. To serve, spread 1½ cups whipped topping over gelatin mixture. Toss berries with remaining lemon juice; spoon over pie. Sprinkle with coconut and, if desired, additional pistachios. Serve with remaining whipped topping.

STRAWBERRY BALSAMIC FILLED CUPCAKES

Here's a twist on traditional strawberry shortcake. This combination of classic and sophisticated flavors is a perfect summer dessert. Be sure to refrigerate the remaining berry-balsamic reduction to use on toast.

—Kate Brown, St. Michael, MN

Prep: 45 min. + cooling
Bake: 20 min. + cooling
Makes: 2 dozen

- 1 pkg. yellow cake mix (regular size) or angel food cake mix
- 2 cups fresh strawberries, sliced
- ¼ cup sugar
- 3 Tbsp. balsamic vinegar
- ¾ tsp. dried thyme
TOPPING
- 1 carton (8 oz.) mascarpone cheese
- 1 cup heavy whipping cream
- ¾ cup confectioners' sugar
- 1 tsp. vanilla or almond extract

1. Prepare and bake cake mix according to package directions for cupcakes. Let cupcakes cool completely.
2. Place strawberries, sugar, vinegar and thyme in a small saucepan; bring to a boil. Reduce heat to medium; cook, uncovered, until thickened, 12-15 minutes, stirring occasionally. Cool completely.
3. Beat topping ingredients on medium speed until stiff peaks form, for 2 minutes (do not overmix). Refrigerate, covered, while filling cupcakes.
4. To fill cupcakes, cut a 1-in. circle (1-in. deep) in the top of each cupcake; remove cut portion and set aside. Spoon 1 tsp. strawberry mixture into each opening; replace cutout portions. Refrigerate the filled cupcakes for 10 minutes.
5. Pipe or dollop topping over cupcakes. Refrigerate until serving.

BERRY-PATCH BROWNIE PIZZA

Fruit, almonds and chocolate make this pie-shaped brownie stand apart from basic square brownies. The berries add fresh flavor and a nutritional boost.

—Sue Kauffman, Columbia City, IN

Prep: 20 min. + chilling
Bake: 15 min. + cooling
Makes: 12 servings

- 1 pkg. fudge brownie mix (13x9-in. pan size)
- ⅓ cup chopped unblanched almonds
- 1 tsp. almond extract
TOPPING
- 1 pkg. (8 oz.) cream cheese, softened
- 1 Tbsp. sugar
- 1 tsp. vanilla extract
- ½ tsp. grated lemon zest
- 2 cups whipped topping
  Assorted fresh berries
  Fresh mint leaves and coarse sugar, optional

1. Preheat oven to 375°. Prepare brownie batter according to package directions for fudge-like brownies, adding almonds and almond extract. Spread into a greased 14-in. pizza pan.
2. Bake until a toothpick inserted in the center comes out clean, 15-18 minutes. Cool completely on a wire rack.
3. Beat the first four topping ingredients until smooth; fold in whipped topping. Spread over crust to within ½ in. of edges; refrigerate, loosely covered, 2 hours.
4. To serve, cut into slices; top with berries of choice. If desired, top with mint and sprinkle with coarse sugar.

SUPER STRAWBERRY SHORTCAKE

People will say *wow* when you set this dessert on the table. It bursts with fresh berry flavor and is not overly sweet.
—Renee Bisch, Wellesley, ON

Prep: 20 min. • **Bake:** 15 min. + cooling
Makes: 8 servings

- 4 cups fresh strawberries, sliced
- 2 Tbsp. sugar

SHORTCAKE
- 1¾ cups all-purpose flour
- 2 Tbsp. sugar
- 1 tsp. baking powder
- ½ tsp. baking soda
- ½ tsp. salt
- ¼ cup cold butter, cubed
- 1 large egg, lightly beaten
- ¾ cup sour cream

WHIPPED CREAM
- 1 cup heavy whipping cream
- 2 Tbsp. sugar
- 1 tsp. vanilla extract

1. Preheat oven to 425°. Toss the sliced strawberries with sugar; let stand, allowing juices from berries to release.
2. For shortcake, whisk together the flour, sugar, baking powder, baking soda and salt; cut in butter until mixture resembles coarse crumbs. In another bowl, whisk together egg and sour cream. Add to the flour mixture; stir just until moistened.
3. On a lightly floured surface, gently knead dough 8-10 times. Transfer dough to a lightly greased baking sheet; roll or pat to a 7½-in. circle. Bake until golden brown, 13-17 minutes. Remove to a wire rack; cool completely.
4. In a bowl, beat cream until it begins to thicken. Add sugar and vanilla; beat until stiff peaks form.
5. Using a long serrated knife, cut the shortcake horizontally in half. Spoon half the strawberries (including juices) over top; spread with half the whipped cream. Add the top of shortcake; layer with the remaining whipped cream and berries.

BERRY TARTLETS

Raspberries and blueberries pair nicely with the lemon curd in these delectable miniature tarts. The treats are fantastic for a ladies tea, brunch or any warm-weather celebration.
—Mary Walters, Westerville, OH

Prep: 25 min. • **Bake:** 25 min. + cooling
Makes: 1 dozen

- Pastry for double-crust pie (9 in.)
- 2 Tbsp. sugar
- 1 Tbsp. cornstarch
- 1 pkg. (12 oz.) frozen unsweetened mixed berries, thawed
- 1 Tbsp. lemon juice

TOPPING
- ⅓ cup heavy whipping cream
- ¼ cup lemon curd
- 1 tsp. sugar
- ¼ tsp. vanilla extract
- Fresh berries, optional

1. Preheat oven to 400°. On a lightly floured surface, roll the pastry dough to ⅛-in. thickness. Using a 4-in. round cookie cutter, cut 12 circles, rerolling scraps as necessary. Press circles onto bottoms and up sides of ungreased muffin cups.
2. Mix sugar and cornstarch; toss with berries and lemon juice. Spoon 2 Tbsp. filling into each cup. Bake on a lower oven rack until pastry is golden brown and filling is bubbly, 24-26 minutes. Cool 10 minutes before removing from pan to a wire rack; cool completely.
3. For topping, beat cream until soft peaks form. In another bowl, mix lemon curd, sugar, vanilla and 1 Tbsp. whipped cream; fold in remaining whipped cream. Spoon topping onto filling. If desired, top with fresh berries. Refrigerate until serving.
Pastry for double-crust pie (9 in.): Combine 2½ cups all-purpose flour and ½ tsp. salt; cut in 1 cup cold butter until crumbly. Gradually add ⅓ to ⅔ cup ice water, tossing with a fork until dough holds together when pressed. Divide dough in half. Shape each into a disk; wrap in plastic. Refrigerate 1 hour or overnight.

BERRY
TARTLETS

STRAWBERRY CITRUS ICE

Daiquiri fans will love this frozen blend of strawberries, lime juice and orange juice.
—Robin Keane, Framingham, MA

Prep: 15 min. + freezing
Makes: about 3½ cups

¾	**cup sugar**
½	**cup water**
3	**cups fresh strawberries, hulled**
¼	**cup lime juice**
¼	**cup orange juice**

1. For sugar syrup, place sugar and water in a small saucepan; bring to a boil, stirring constantly until sugar is dissolved. Remove syrup to a bowl; cool slightly. Refrigerate, covered, until cold.

2. Process strawberries and juices in a blender until smooth. Add sugar syrup; pulse to blend.

3. Pour into cylinder of ice cream maker; freeze according to the manufacturer's directions. Serve immediately or store in freezer containers, allowing headspace for expansion.

TEST KITCHEN TIP

Hulling Strawberries

Here's a quick and easy way to hull strawberries. Simply insert a straw into the tip of the berry and push it through the other end.

STRAWBERRY CITRUS ICE

MIXED BERRY TIRAMISU

Because I love tiramisu, I came up with this deliciously refreshing twist on the traditional coffee-flavored Italian dessert. Fresh macerated berries star with crisp ladyfinger cookies and mascarpone cheese. Serve it from a glass bowl or in clear dishes to show off the luscious layers.
—Najmussahar Ahmed, Ypsilanti, MI

Prep: 35 min. + chilling • **Makes:** 12 servings

- 3 cups fresh raspberries
- 3 cups fresh blackberries
- 2 cups fresh blueberries
- 2 cups fresh strawberries, sliced
- 1⅓ cups sugar, divided
- 4 tsp. grated orange zest
- ½ cup orange juice
- 1 cup heavy whipping cream
- 2 cartons (8 oz. each) mascarpone cheese
- 1 tsp. vanilla extract
- 1 pkg. (7 oz.) crisp ladyfinger cookies
  Additional fresh berries, optional

1. Place berries in a large bowl. Mix ⅓ cup sugar, orange zest and orange juice; toss gently with berries. Refrigerate, covered, 45 minutes. Beat cream until soft peaks form. In another bowl, mix mascarpone cheese, vanilla and remaining sugar. Fold in whipped cream, one third at a time.
2. Drain the berries over a shallow bowl, reserving juices. Dip 12 ladyfingers in the reserved juices, allowing excess to drip off. Arrange in a single layer on bottom of a 13x9-in. dish. Layer with half the berries and half the mascarpone mixture; repeat the layers.
3. Refrigerate, covered, overnight. If desired, top with additional berries before serving tiramisu.
Note: This recipe was prepared with Alessi brand ladyfinger cookies.

COOL & CREAMY RASPBERRY DELIGHT

This fruity and creamy dessert tasted like a winner. A few summers ago, I got the chance to confirm that when it took first place in a contest at work. It remains a wonderful finale to any festive occasion.
—Mary Olson, Albany, OR

Prep: 20 min. + chilling
Bake: 20 min. + cooling
Makes: 12 servings

- 2¼ cups all-purpose flour
- 2 Tbsp. sugar
- ¾ cup cold butter, cubed

FILLING
- 1 pkg. (8 oz.) cream cheese, softened
- 1 cup confectioners' sugar
- 1 tsp. vanilla extract
- ¼ tsp. salt
- 2 cups whipped topping

TOPPING
- 2 cups boiling water
- 2 pkg. (3 oz. each) raspberry gelatin
- 2 pkg. (10 oz. each) frozen sweetened raspberries or sliced strawberries
  Additional whipped topping, optional

1. Preheat oven to 300° In a large bowl, mix flour and sugar; cut in butter until crumbly. Press onto the bottom of an ungreased 13x9-in. pan. Bake until set, 20-25 minutes (crust will not brown). Cool completely on a wire rack.
2. Beat first four filling ingredients until smooth. Fold in whipped topping; spread over crust.
3. For topping, add boiling water to the gelatin; stir for 2 minutes to completely dissolve. Add the raspberries; stir until blended. Refrigerate until mixture begins to thicken, about 20 minutes. Spoon over filling. Refrigerate until set. If desired, serve with additional whipped topping.

Backyard Pool Party

Splash, splash, it's time for a pool party bash! Grab your beach towel and get ready for some fun in the sun. With this lineup of easy, breezy outdoor eats—including ideas for homemade ice cream floats—you and your guests will have it made in the shade.

CILANTRO TOMATO
BRUSCHETTA

CILANTRO TOMATO BRUSCHETTA

If you want to a capture summer in an appetizer, try this easy bruschetta. The garden-fresh ingredients combine in an hors d'oeuvre that sets the stage for a variety of main dishes.
—Lisa Kane, Milwaukee, WI

Takes: 25 min. • **Makes:** about 2 dozen

- 1 loaf (1 lb.) French bread, cut into 1-in. slices
- ½ cup olive oil, divided
- 1 Tbsp. balsamic vinegar
- 3 small tomatoes, seeded and chopped
- ¼ cup finely chopped onion
- ¼ cup fresh cilantro leaves, coarsely chopped
- ¼ tsp. salt
- ¼ tsp. pepper
- ¼ cup shredded part-skim mozzarella cheese

1. Preheat oven to 325°. Place bread slices on ungreased baking sheets; brush with ¼ cup oil. Bake until bread is golden brown, 10-12 minutes.
2. In a small bowl, whisk together vinegar and remaining oil. Stir in tomatoes, onion, cilantro, salt and pepper.
3. To serve, spoon scant 1 tablespoon tomato mixture onto each slice of bread. Top with cheese.

FRESH VEGETABLE DIP

Our family loves this cool and creamy dip for snacking. The kids are all smiles while they munch on their crunchy veggies.
—Denise Goedeken, Platte Center, NE

Prep: 5 min. + chilling
Makes: about 2¼ cups

- 1½ cups (12 oz.) sour cream
- ¾ cup mayonnaise
- 1 Tbsp. dried minced onion
- 1 tsp. garlic salt
- 1 tsp. dill weed
- 1 tsp. dried parsley flakes
  Dash Worcestershire sauce
  Assorted fresh vegetables

In a small bowl, mix first seven ingredients. Refrigerate, covered, at least 1 hour. Serve with vegetables.

CHICKEN SALAD PARTY SANDWICHES

CHICKEN SALAD PARTY SANDWICHES

My famous chicken salad arrives at the party chilled in a plastic container. When it's time to set out the food, I stir in the pecans and assemble the sandwiches. They're great for buffet-style potlucks.
—Trisha Kruse, Eagle, ID

Takes: 25 min. • **Makes:** 16 servings

- 4 cups cubed cooked chicken breast
- 1½ cups dried cranberries
- 2 celery ribs, finely chopped
- 2 green onions, thinly sliced
- ¼ cup chopped sweet pickles
- 1 cup fat-free mayonnaise
- ½ tsp. curry powder
- ¼ tsp. coarsely ground pepper
- ½ cup chopped pecans, toasted
- 16 whole wheat dinner rolls
  Leaf lettuce

1. In a large bowl, combine first five ingredients. Mix mayonnaise, curry powder and pepper; stir into chicken mixture. Refrigerate until serving.
2. To serve, stir in pecans. Spoon onto lettuce-lined rolls.

Note: To toast nuts, bake in a shallow pan in a 350° oven for 5-10 minutes or cook in a skillet over low heat until lightly browned, stirring occasionally.

CHEDDAR BROCCOLI SALAD

This salad is often on our Sunday dinner menu. The flavors and textures blend so nicely that we never tire of this standby, and judging by the compliments, it seems like our friends enjoy it just as much.
—Melody Mellinger, Myerstown, PA

Prep: 15 min. + chilling • **Makes:** 8 servings

- 6 cups fresh broccoli florets
- 1½ cups shredded cheddar cheese
- ⅓ cup chopped onion
- 1½ cups mayonnaise
- ¾ cup sugar
- 3 Tbsp. red wine vinegar
- 12 bacon strips, cooked and crumbled

1. Place broccoli, cheese and onion in a large bowl. Mix mayonnaise, sugar and vinegar; toss with broccoli mixture.
2. Refrigerate, covered, at least 4 hours. Stir in bacon just before serving.

ORANGE
LEMONADE

ORANGE LEMONADE

I came up with this sipper when I was looking for a way to sweeten lemonade without adding more sugar. It became a favorite way to cool down on a hot day. I'll often double the batch and send a jar next door to my mother-in-law.
—Wendy Masters, Grand Valley, ON

Prep: 15 min. + chilling
Cook: 5 min. + cooling
Makes: 12 servings

- 1¾ cups sugar
- 2½ cups water
- 2 Tbsp. grated lemon zest
- 2 Tbsp. grated orange zest
- 1½ cups lemon juice (about 10 lemons)
- 1½ cups orange juice (about 5 oranges)
- 6 cups cold water

1. In a large saucepan, combine sugar and 2½ cups water; cook and stir over medium heat until sugar is dissolved. Cool slightly.
2. Stir in citrus zest and juices. Let stand, covered, 1 hour. Strain syrup; refrigerate, covered, until cold.
3. To serve, fill glasses or pitcher with an equal amount of fruit syrup and water. Add ice and serve.

ITALIAN SUBMARINE

My Italian husband grew up eating this flavorful sandwich. His mother used to make it after the Saturday chores were finished. Put the sub together a few hours ahead and refrigerated, then serve with chips, veggies and dip for a delicious meal.
—Christine Lupella, Fifty Lakes, MN

Takes: 15 min. • **Makes:** 8 servings

- 1 loaf (1 lb.) unsliced Italian bread
- 2 to 3 Tbsp. olive oil
- 2 to 4 Tbsp. shredded Parmesan cheese
- 1 to 1½ tsp. dried oregano
- 1 medium tomato, thinly sliced
- ½ lb. thinly sliced deli ham
- ¼ lb. sliced provolone cheese
- ¼ lb. thinly sliced hard salami

1. Cut Italian bread horizontally in half. Hollow out bottom half, leaving a ¼-in. shell (save removed bread for another use or discard). Brush cut surfaces of bread with oil; sprinkle with Parmesan cheese and oregano.
2. Layer bottom half with the remaining ingredients. Replace bread top. Cut into eight slices.

ITALIAN
SUBMARINE

SWEET
MACARONI SALAD

SWEET MACARONI SALAD

A sweet dressing makes this macaroni salad out of the ordinary. My aunt gave me the recipe. I occasionally leave out the green pepper, and it still tastes great.
—Idalee Scholz, Cocoa Beach, FL

Prep: 20 min. + chilling
Makes: 16 servings

- 1 pkg. (16 oz.) elbow macaroni
- 4 medium carrots, shredded
- 1 large green pepper, chopped
- 1 medium red onion, chopped
- 2 cups mayonnaise
- 1 can (14 oz.) sweetened condensed milk
- 1 cup cider vinegar
- ½ cup sugar
- 1 tsp. salt
- ½ tsp. pepper

1. Cook macaroni according to package directions. Drain and rinse in cold water; drain well.
2. In a large bowl, combine macaroni and vegetables. Whisk together the remaining ingredients until smooth and the sugar is dissolved; stir into the macaroni mixture. Refrigerate, covered, overnight.

CAJUN PARTY SNACK MIX

This crisp snack mix packs a punch. Once you start eating, it's hard to stop.
—Miriam Hershberger, Holmesville, OH

Prep: 10 min. • **Bake:** 40 min.
Makes: about 2 qt.

- 2½ cups Corn Chex
- 2 cups Rice Chex
- 2 cups Crispix
- 1 cup miniature pretzels
- 1 cup mixed nuts
- ½ cup butter, melted
- 1 Tbsp. dried parsley flakes
- 1 tsp. celery salt
- 1 tsp. garlic powder
- ¼ to ½ tsp. cayenne pepper
- ¼ tsp. hot pepper sauce

1. Preheat oven to 250°. Place first five ingredients in a large bowl. Mix remaining ingredients; toss with cereal mixture. Spread into an ungreased 15x10x1-in. pan.
2. Bake 40-60 minutes, stirring every 15 minutes. Store in airtight containers.

PINA COLADA FLOAT

What's better than an ice cream float? One that takes you to the tropics. Here the fresh taste of pineapple and coconut offer up a little bit of paradise in every sip. Add a splash of rum to make it a grown-up float.
—Deirdre Cox, Kansas City, MO

Takes: 5 min. • **Makes:** 1 serving

- ½ cup vanilla ice cream
- 1 cup chilled pineapple soda

TOPPINGS
- ¼ cup sweetened whipped cream
- 1 Tbsp. toasted unsweetened coconut flakes
- 1 maraschino cherry

Place ice cream and soda in a tall glass. Add toppings; serve immediately.
Note: We tested this recipe with Jarritos pineapple soda. Other brands of pineapple soda include Fanta, Sunkist, Crush, Goya and Canada Dry.

STRAWBERRY TOSSED SALAD

I love this summertime salad because it is so versatile. It's full of fresh berry flavor and pairs especially well with grilled entrees. Or add chopped chicken or steak to make it a meal on its own.
—Patricia McNamara, Kansas City, MO

Takes: 20 min. • **Makes:** 8 servings

- ½ cup canola oil
- ⅓ cup sugar
- ¼ cup cider vinegar
- 1 garlic clove, minced
- ¼ tsp. salt
- ¼ tsp. paprika
  Pinch white pepper
- 8 cups torn romaine
- 4 cups torn Bibb or Boston lettuce
- 2½ cups sliced fresh strawberries
- 1 cup shredded Monterey Jack cheese
- ½ cup chopped walnuts, toasted

1. For dressing, place the first seven ingredients in a jar with a tight-fitting lid; shake until sugar is dissolved.
2. In a large bowl, combine remaining ingredients. Just before serving, shake dressing again and toss with salad.

FRUIT & CHEESE KABOBS

Here's a fruity snack that's easy to make ahead and carry to the ballpark, beach or playing field. The cinnamon-spiced yogurt dip adds that special touch!
—*Taste of Home* Test Kitchen

Takes: 20 min.
Makes: 12 kabobs (1½ cups dip)

- 1 cup (8 oz.) vanilla yogurt
- ½ cup sour cream
- 2 Tbsp. honey
- ½ tsp. ground cinnamon
- 2 cups fresh strawberries, halved
- 1½ cups green grapes
- 8 oz. cubed cheddar or Monterey Jack cheese, or a combination of cheeses

For dip, mix first four ingredients. On 12 wooden skewers, alternately thread strawberries, grapes and cheese cubes. Refrigerate until serving.

Cool Pool

Here's a party-perfect way to chill drinks. First, fill water balloons with water, tie them off and place in the freezer until frozen solid. Then add the frozen water balloons to a kiddie pool, nestle in the beverages and invite your guests to grab and sip as they please.

Float On

Create a custom float bar for your summertime shindig. Assemble fruit-flavored sodas like clementine, grapefruit and pomegranate plus colorful ice creams like Blue Moon or black cherry. Then take it over the top with a few rainbow sprinkles and gummy candies.

CATCH-A-WAVE COOKIES

Use this basic sugar cookie recipe to make the perfect poolside treat.
—Coleen Walter, Bancroft, MI

Prep: 30 min.
Bake: 10 min/batch + cooling
Makes: about 2½ dozen

1 cup butter, softened
¾ cup sugar
1 tsp. vanilla extract
½ tsp. almond extract
2 large eggs
2¼ cups all-purpose flour
1 tsp. cream of tartar
½ tsp. baking soda
¼ tsp. salt
¼ tsp. ground nutmeg
FROSTING
¼ cup butter, softened
3 cups confectioners' sugar
1 tsp. almond extract
2 to 4 Tbsp. hot water
Blue food coloring
Optional decorations: bear-shaped crackers, fish-shaped graham crackers, AirHeads candies, gummy sour rings, white sugar pearls and palm tree party picks

1. Preheat oven to 350°. Cream butter and sugar until light and fluffy; beat in the extracts and eggs, one at a time. In another bowl, whisk together flour, cream of tartar, baking soda, salt and nutmeg; gradually beat into creamed mixture.
2. Drop dough by rounded tablespoonfuls 3 in. apart onto parchment paper-lined baking sheets; flatten slightly with bottom of a glass dipped in sugar. Bake until edges begin to brown, 8-10 minutes. Remove from pan to wire racks; cool completely.
3. For frosting, beat butter, confectioners' sugar, extract and enough water to reach desired consistency; tint blue with food coloring. Spread frosting over cookies and decorate as desired.
Note: Cream of tartar is an acid. When it's combined with baking soda, it creates carbon dioxide, helping these cookies puff up just a bit. It also gives them their signature soft texture. Vanilla extract can be used in place of almond extract in both the cookie dough and frosting.

Songs for Summertime

Here are some tunes for the perfect poolside party.

SUMMER OF '69
Bryan Adams

CHEESEBURGER IN PARADISE
Jimmy Buffett

CALIFORNIA GIRLS
The Beach Boys

HOT FUN IN THE SUMMERTIME
Sly and the Family Stone

**(SITTIN' ON)
THE DOCK OF THE BAY**
Otis Redding

SUMMERTIME BLUES
Eddie Cochran

WIPE OUT
The Surfaris

WALKING ON SUNSHINE
Katrina and the Waves

CATCH-A-WAVE
COOKIES

Texas Barbecue

Here's a scrumptious roundup of Lone Star State barbecue classics in all their finger-licking glory. Get ready to dig into pulled pork, brisket, potato salad, banana cream pie and more. Some even come from the recipe boxes of Texas home cooks!

Spiced Pulled Pork Sandwiches and **Cleo's Potato Salad** (p. 219)

MELON-BERRY
SALAD

MELON-BERRY SALAD

The best way to cool down on a warm day is a chilled fruit salad. Serve this one for breakfast, brunch or dessert. Yogurt and coconut milk make the creamy dressing even more decadent.
—Carrie Hirsch, Hilton Head Island, SC

Prep: 15 min. • **Makes:** 12 servings (¾ cup)

- 1 cup fat-free vanilla Greek yogurt
- ½ cup coconut milk
- ½ cup orange juice
- 4 cups cubed cantaloupe (½-in.)
- 4 cups cubed watermelon (½-in.)
- 2 medium navel oranges, sectioned
- 1 cup fresh raspberries
- 1 cup fresh blueberries
- ½ cup sweetened shredded coconut, toasted

1. For dressing, whisk together yogurt, coconut milk and orange juice. Refrigerate until serving.
2. To serve, place the fruit in a large bowl; toss gently with dressing. Sprinkle with the shredded coconut.

Note: To toast coconut, bake in a shallow pan in a 350° oven for 5-10 minutes or cook in a skillet over low heat until golden brown, stirring occasionally.

LEMONY PINEAPPLE ICED TEA

TEST KITCHEN TIP

Fast Fruit Salad

To save time on the day of the barbecue, prepare the dressing for Melon-Berry Salad the night before and store in a covered container in the refrigerator. Also, cut up the melons and store in separate containers in the refrigerator. Just before guests arrive, combine all the fruit. Wait until just before serving to garnish the salad, otherwise the toasted coconut will get soggy.

LEMONY PINEAPPLE ICED TEA

Take a sip of iced tea with a Hawaiian twist. I garnish each glass with some of our fresh, sweet pineapple.
—Beverly Toomey, Honolulu, HI

Prep: 20 min. + chilling • **Cook:** 10 min.
Makes: 20 servings (1 cup each)

- 16 cups water
- 24 tea bags
- 6 fresh mint sprigs
- 3⅓ cups sugar
- 3 cups unsweetened pineapple juice
- 1 cup lemon juice

1. In a stockpot, bring water to boil; remove from heat. Add tea bags; steep, covered, 10 minutes. Discard tea bags. Add mint; steep 5 minutes; discard mint. Add remaining ingredients, stirring to dissolve sugar.
2. Transfer to pitchers or a large covered container. Refrigerate, covered, until cold. If desired, serve with ice.

SWEET PEPPER CABBAGE SLAW

A simple cooked dressing and red pepper give this cabbage mixture a delightful sweet flavor. It's perfect for parties and pairs well with any grilled meat.
—Jackie Deibert, Klingerstown, PA

Prep: 15 min. • **Cook:** 10 min. + cooling
Makes: 12 servings

- 1 cup sugar
- ½ cup water
- ¼ cup cider vinegar
- ¼ cup olive oil
- 10 cups shredded cabbage
- 2 medium sweet red peppers, chopped

1. For dressing, place sugar, water and vinegar in a small saucepan; bring to a boil, stirring to dissolve sugar. Cook, uncovered, 5 minutes. Cool completely. Stir in oil.
2. To serve, place vegetables in a large bowl. Add dressing; toss to coat.

FRESH PEACH SALSA

Whether scooped up on chips or spooned onto tacos, this peachy salsa packs the bright taste of summer into every bite. It also makes a tasty garnish for chicken or fish. Make it in the food processor in almost no time at all.
—Shawna Laufer, Fort Myers, FL

Takes: 15 min.
Makes: 16 servings (¼ cup each)

- 4 medium peaches, peeled and quartered
- 2 large tomatoes, seeded and cut into wedges
- ⅔ cup chopped sweet onion
- ½ cup fresh cilantro leaves
- 2 garlic cloves, peeled and sliced
- 2 cans (4 oz. each) chopped green chilies
- 4 tsp. cider vinegar
- 1 tsp. lime juice
- ¼ tsp. pepper
  Baked tortilla chip scoops

1. Place first five ingredients in a food processor; pulse until peaches are coarsely chopped. Add chilies, vinegar, lime juice and pepper; pulse just until blended.
2. Remove to a bowl; refrigerate, covered, until serving. Serve with chips.

TEXAS-STYLE BRISKET

This is hands down the quintessential Texas-style brisket. Even my husband's six-generation Texas family is impressed! Grilling with wood chips takes a little extra effort, but I promise, you'll be glad you did. Each bite tastes like heaven on a plate.
—Renee Morgan, Taylor, TX

Prep: 35 min. + chilling
Cook: 6 hours + standing
Makes: 20 servings

- 1 whole fresh beef brisket (12 to 14 lbs.)
- ½ cup pepper
- ¼ cup kosher salt
  Large disposable foil pan
  About 6 cups wood chips, preferably oak

1. Trim fat on brisket to ½-in. thickness. Rub brisket with pepper and salt; place in a large disposable foil pan, fat side up. Refrigerate, covered, several hours or overnight. Meanwhile, soak the wood chips in water.
2. To prepare the grill for slow indirect cooking, adjust the grill vents so the top vent is half open and the bottom vent is open only one-quarter of the way open. Make two arrangements of 45 unlit coals on opposite sides of the grill, leaving the center of the grill open. Light 20 additional coals until ash-covered; distribute over unlit coals. Sprinkle 2 cups soaked wood chips over lit coals.
3. Replace grill rack. Close grill and allow temperature in grill to reach 275°, about 15 minutes.
4. Place foil pan with brisket in center of grill rack; cover grill and cook 3 hours (do not open grill). Check temperature of grill periodically to maintain a temperature of 275° throughout cooking. Heat level may be adjusted by opening vents to raise temperature and closing vents partway to decrease temperature.
5. Add an additional 10 unlit coals and 1 cup wood chips to each side of the grill. Cook brisket, covered, 3-4 hours longer or until fork tender (a thermometer inserted in brisket should read about 190°); add additional coals and wood chips as needed to maintain a grill temperature of 275°.
6. Remove brisket from grill. Cover tightly with foil; let stand 30-60 minutes. Cut brisket across the grain into slices.

SHRIMP TOSTADAS WITH LIME-CILANTRO SAUCE

I love shrimp and veggies marinated in citrus juice, also known as ceviche. This recipe starts with cooked shrimp and those same fresh ceviche flavors. Enjoy these tostadas as a make-ahead appetizer or dinner entree.
—Leslie Kelley, Dorris, CA

Prep: 35 min. + standing
Makes: 10 servings

- 1½ lbs. peeled and deveined cooked shrimp (26-30 per lb.), coarsely chopped
- 1½ cups chopped, peeled English cucumber
- 8 radishes, thinly sliced
- 4 plum tomatoes, chopped
- 4 green onions, chopped
- 2 jalapeno peppers, seeded and minced
- 2 Tbsp. minced fresh cilantro
- 2 Tbsp. lime juice
- 3 garlic cloves, minced
- 1 tsp. salt
- ¼ tsp. pepper
- 1 medium ripe avocado, peeled and cubed

SAUCE
- 1 cup sour cream
- 2 Tbsp. minced fresh cilantro
- 1 tsp. grated lime zest
- 1 Tbsp. lime juice
- ¼ tsp. salt
- ¼ tsp. ground cumin
- ⅛ tsp. pepper

ASSEMBLY
- 10 tostada shells

1. Place first 11 ingredients in a large bowl; toss to combine. Gently stir in avocado; let stand 15 minutes.
2. In a small bowl, mix sauce ingredients. To serve, spread tostada shells with sauce. Top with shrimp mixture.

SHRIMP TOSTADAS WITH
LIME-CILANTRO SAUCE

CLEO'S
POTATO
SALAD

CLEO'S POTATO SALAD

My mom, Cleo Lightfoot, loved cooking all kinds of different recipes, but her favorite meal was one she made when hosting backyard barbecues in the summer. She would make her famous ribs, baked beans and this delicious potato salad.
—Joan Hallford, North Richland Hills, TX

Prep: 25 min. • **Cook:** 20 min.
Makes: 12 servings (¾ cup each)

- 3½ lbs. red potatoes (about 12 medium), cut into 1-in. cubes
- 6 bacon strips, chopped
- ¼ cup sugar
- 1 Tbsp. all-purpose flour
- ½ cup water
- 1 large egg, lightly beaten
- 3 Tbsp. cider vinegar
- 1 Tbsp. grated onion
- 1 tsp. celery seed
- 1 tsp. salt
- ½ tsp. pepper
- 1 cup heavy whipping cream, whipped
- 4 hard-boiled large eggs, chopped
- 2 medium celery ribs, chopped

1. Place potatoes in a large saucepan; cover with water. Bring to a boil. Reduce heat; cook, uncovered, until tender, 10-15 minutes. Drain; cool completely.
2. Meanwhile, in a saucepan, cook bacon over medium heat until crisp. Remove with a slotted spoon; drain on paper towels. Remove all but 1 Tbsp. drippings from pan.
3. Stir sugar and flour into drippings until smooth. Gradually stir in water; cook and stir over medium-high heat until thickened and bubbly. Remove from heat. Stir a small amount of hot mixture into beaten egg; return all to pan, stirring constantly. Slowly bring to a boil, stirring constantly; remove from heat. Transfer to a large bowl; cool completely.
4. Gently stir in vinegar, onion and seasonings. Fold in whipped cream. Stir in eggs, celery, potatoes and bacon. Refrigerate, covered, until serving.

SPICED PULLED PORK SANDWICHES

(SHOWN ON P. 213)
A fabulous spiced rub flavors this tender pulled pork. It's my sweetie's favorite main dish, and I love that it's so easy. Add more or less salt to taste.
—Katie Citrowske, Bozeman, MT

Prep: 30 min. • **Cook:** 6 hours
Makes: 10 servings

- 1½ tsp. salt
- 1½ tsp. garlic powder
- 1½ tsp. ground cumin
- 1½ tsp. ground cinnamon
- 1½ tsp. chili powder
- 1½ tsp. coarsely ground pepper
- 1 boneless pork shoulder butt roast (3 to 4 lbs.), halved
- 2 Tbsp. olive oil
- 2 medium onions, halved and sliced
- 8 garlic cloves, coarsely chopped
- 1½ cups water
- 1 Tbsp. liquid smoke, optional
- 10 hamburger buns, split and toasted
  Barbecue sauce
  Sliced jalapenos, optional

1. Mix seasonings; rub over pork. In large skillet, heat oil over medium heat. Brown pork on all sides. Transfer to a 5- or 6-qt. slow cooker.
2. In same pan, cook and stir onions over medium heat until lightly browned, for 4-5 minutes. Add the garlic; cook and stir 1 minute. Add the water; bring to a boil, stirring to loosen browned bits from pan. If desired, stir in liquid smoke. Add to pork.
3. Cook, covered, on low until meat is tender, 6-8 hours. Remove roast; discard onion mixture. Shred pork with two forks; return to slow cooker and heat through. Serve on buns with barbecue sauce. If desired, garnish with sliced jalapenos.

SOUTHWEST LAYERED CORNBREAD SALAD

With no last-minute assembly needed, this layered salad is ready for a spot on the party buffet.
—Rod & Sue Brusius, Omro, WI

Prep: 20 min. • **Bake:** 15 min. + cooling
Makes: 12 servings (¾ cup each)

- 1 pkg. (8½ oz.) cornbread/muffin mix
- 2 cans (15 oz. each) black beans, rinsed and drained
- 1 can (15¼ oz.) whole kernel corn, drained
- 3 medium tomatoes, chopped
- 1 medium onion, chopped
- 1½ cups ranch salad dressing
- 2 cups shredded cheddar cheese

1. Prepare and bake cornbread according to package directions. Cool completely on a wire rack. Break into crumbles.
2. In a 3-qt. bowl, layer half of each of the following: cornbread, black beans, corn, tomatoes, onion, dressing and cheese. Repeat layers. Refrigerate salad, covered, until serving.

HOW-TO

How to Easily Shred Pork for Sandwiches

Remove cooked pork from the slow cooker or pan with a slotted spoon if necessary. Reserve cooking liquid if needed. Place meat in a shallow pan to catch any drippings. With two forks, pull the meat into thin shreds. Return the shredded meat to the pan or slow cooker to warm or use as recipe directs.

PEACH CRUMBLE BARS

My favorite way to enjoy these bars is to eat them while sitting on the porch with iced tea in hand. They're great for any occasion and will be gobbled up quickly.
—Ally Billhorn, Wilton, IA

Prep: 20 min. • **Bake:** 50 min. + cooling
Makes: 9 servings

- ½ cup butter, softened
- ¾ cup packed brown sugar
     Dash salt
- 1⅓ cups all-purpose flour

FILLING
- 2 Tbsp. all-purpose flour
- 1 Tbsp. brown sugar
- 1 tsp. ground cinnamon
- 4½ cups fresh or frozen sliced peeled peaches (about 20 oz.), thawed and drained
- ½ cup chopped pecans, toasted

1. Preheat oven to 350°. Beat the butter, brown sugar and salt until blended; beat in flour until crumbly. Reserve 1 cup mixture for topping. Press remaining mixture onto bottom of a greased 8-in. square baking pan. Bake until lightly browned, 12-15 minutes. Cool on a wire rack.
2. For filling, mix flour, brown sugar and cinnamon; toss with peaches. Spread over crust; sprinkle with pecans. Top with the reserved topping.
3. Bake until topping is golden brown, 35-40 minutes. Cool on a wire rack. Cut into bars.
Note: To toast nuts, bake in a shallow pan in a 350° oven for 5-10 minutes or cook in a skillet over low heat until lightly browned, stirring occasionally.

TEST KITCHEN TIP

Using Frozen Peaches for Fresh

The peak season for fresh peaches is June through September. But you can always substitute frozen peaches (thawed and drained) or well-drained canned peaches in equal amounts for fresh peaches. One pound of frozen or canned peaches is equal to approximately three medium peaches.

PECAN-CHOCOLATE CHIP COCONUT COOKIES

When my four children were young, everyone wanted different kinds of cookies. After I came up with this recipe, everyone was happy, and it's still a cookie they ask for. Thanks to the cream cheese, these cookies bake up soft and fluffy.
—Linda Brown, Hooker, OK

Prep: 35 min.
Bake: 10 min./batch + cooling
Makes: about 9 dozen

- 1 cup butter, softened
- 1 pkg. (8 oz.) cream cheese, softened
- 1 cup packed brown sugar
- 1 cup sugar
- 2 large eggs
- 1 tsp. vanilla extract
- 2½ cups all-purpose flour
- 1 tsp. baking soda
- 1 tsp. salt
- 2 cups (12 oz.) semisweet chocolate chips
- ⅔ cup sweetened shredded coconut
- 1½ to 2 cups pecan halves

1. Preheat oven to 350°. Beat first four ingredients until blended. Beat in eggs and vanilla. Whisk together flour, baking soda and salt; gradually beat into the butter mixture. Stir in the chips and coconut.
2. Drop by rounded teaspoonfuls 2 in. apart onto greased baking sheets. Top each with a pecan half.
3. Bake cookies until lightly browned, 9-11 minutes. Remove from pans to wire racks to cool.

NUTELLA BANANA CREAM PIE

Here's a banana cream pie with a little Italian flair. The chocolate and hazelnut go well with the banana, and the rolled chocolate pie crust makes it extra-special. If you don't have time to melt and pipe the chocolate stars, just sprinkle the top of the pie with grated chocolate or cocoa powder instead.
—Crystal Schlueter, Babbitt, MN

Prep: 45 min. + chilling
Bake: 20 min. + cooling
Makes: 10 servings

- 1¼ cups all-purpose flour
- 2 Tbsp. baking cocoa
- 1 Tbsp. sugar
- ½ cup cold butter, cubed
- 3 to 4 Tbsp. cold brewed coffee

DECORATIONS
- ¼ cup semisweet chocolate chips
- ¼ tsp. shortening

FILLING
- 1 carton (8 oz.) mascarpone cheese
- ¾ cup Nutella
- 2 medium bananas, thinly sliced
- 2 cups heavy whipping cream
- 3 Tbsp. instant banana cream pudding mix
- 2 Tbsp. chopped hazelnuts, toasted

1. In a small bowl, mix flour, cocoa and sugar; cut in the butter until crumbly. Gradually add cold coffee, tossing with a fork until dough holds together when pressed. Shape into a disk; wrap in plastic. Refrigerate 1 hour or overnight.
2. On a lightly floured surface, roll dough to a ⅛-in.-thick circle; transfer to a 9-in. pie plate. Trim pastry to ½ in. beyond rim of plate; flute edge. Refrigerate 30 minutes. Preheat oven to 425°.
3. Line pastry with a double thickness of foil. Fill with pie weights, dried beans or uncooked rice. Bake on a lower oven rack until set, 15-20 minutes. Remove foil and weights; bake until edges are browned, about 5 minutes. Cool completely on a wire rack.
4. For decorations, in a microwave, melt chocolate chips and shortening; stir until smooth. Transfer to a food-safe plastic bag. Cut a small hole in a corner of bag; pipe designs over a waxed paper-lined baking sheet. Freeze designs until set, about 5 minutes.
5. For filling, mix mascarpone cheese and Nutella until blended; spread into crust. Top with bananas.
6. In another bowl, beat cream until it begins to thicken. Add pudding mix; beat until stiff peaks form. Cut a small hole in the tip of a pastry bag or in a corner of another plastic bag; insert a 1M star tip. Fill with cream mixture; pipe rosettes over pie. Sprinkle with chopped hazelnuts. Top with chocolate decorations.
Note: Let pie weights cool before storing. Beans and rice may be reused for pie weights, but not for cooking.

NUTELLA BANANA
CREAM PIE

Celebrate
Back to School

Whether they're learning the alphabet or typing a history paper, kids are making school-day memories that will last a lifetime. To keep them fueled all day long, turn to these fun, kid-friendly ideas for quick and easy breakfasts, school lunches, cute snacks and delicious dinners that will get the entire family excited to start a brand new year.

Chocolate Chip, PB & Banana Sandwiches (p. 228)

FRENCH TOAST FINGERS

2. In a small saucepan, whisk milk, almonds, oats, cocoa and ¼ cup date puree until blended. (Save remaining puree for another use.) Bring to a boil over medium heat, stirring occasionally. Remove from the heat; stir in the butter and vanilla.

To make pureed dates: In a heat safe container, pour boiling water over whole pitted dates. Allow to soak for 10 minutes. Drain off water and reserve. Puree dates in food processor until creamy, add as little water as needed to obtain smooth texture.

CHEESEBURGER OMELET SLIDERS

Prep: 25 min. • **Cook:** 25 min.
Makes: 6 servings (2 sliders per serving)

- 1   lb. lean ground beef (90% lean)
- 1   tsp. salt, divided
- ½   tsp. pepper, divided
- 8   large eggs
- ½   cup water
- 1   cup shredded Havarti cheese
- 12 dinner rolls, split
- 12 tomato slices
     Optional ingredients: ketchup, sliced onion and pickle slices

1. Combine beef, ½ tsp. salt and ¼ tsp. pepper; mix lightly but thoroughly. Shape into twelve 2-in. patties. In a large skillet, cook the burgers over medium heat until cooked through, 2-3 minutes per side. Remove from heat; keep warm.
2. Whisk together eggs, water and the remaining salt and pepper. Place a small nonstick skillet coated with cooking spray over medium-high heat; pour in ½ cup egg mixture. Mixture should set immediately at edges. As eggs set, push cooked edges toward the center, letting the uncooked eggs flow underneath. When the eggs are thickened and no liquid egg remains, sprinkle ⅓ cup cheese on one side. Top with three burgers, spacing evenly; fold the omelet in half. Slide onto a cutting board; tent with foil to keep warm. Repeat to make three more omelets.
3. To serve, cut each omelet into three wedges; place each wedge on a roll. Add the tomatoes and, if desired, remaining ingredients.

FRENCH TOAST FINGERS

Kids love anything on a stick. Bite-sized French toast skewers make a fun breakfast to munch before heading out the door.
—Mavis Diment, Marcus, IA

Takes: 20 min. • **Makes:** 4 servings

- 2   large eggs
- ¼   cup 2% milk
- ¼   tsp. salt
- ½   cup strawberry preserves
- 8   slices day-old white bread
     Confectioners' sugar, optional

1. In a shallow bowl, whisk together the eggs, milk and salt. Spread preserves on four slices of bread; top with remaining bread. Trim crusts; cut each sandwich into three strips.
2. Preheat griddle over medium heat. Lightly grease griddle. Dip both sides of the strips in egg mixture; place on griddle. Toast until golden brown, about 2 minutes per side. Dust with confectioners' sugar if desired.

BROWNIE BATTER OATMEAL

We've all grown up eating piping hot bowls of lumpy oatmeal for breakfast, and everyone has favorite toppings to make porridge more palatable. My recipe transforms a ho-hum morning staple into something you'll jump out of bed for!
—Kristen Moyer, Bethlehem, PA

Takes: 30 min. • **Makes:** 2 servings

- 1   cup pitted dates, chopped
- 1   cup 2% milk
- ½   cup ground almonds
- ⅓   cup old-fashioned oats
- 2   Tbsp. baking cocoa
- 1   tsp. butter
- 1   tsp. vanilla extract

1. Place dates in a heatproof bowl; cover with boiling water. Let stand until softened, about 10 minutes. Drain, reserving ⅓ cup liquid. Place dates and reserved liquid in a food processor; process until smooth.

"A cheeseburger inside an omelet? Yes, please! This fun twist on both breakfast and dinnertime faves is easy to assemble and delicious any time of day."

—DENISE LAROCHE, HUDSON, NH

CHEESEBURGER
OMELET SLIDERS

GUAC CROCS & VEGGIES

Apple Dippers

Gather your apple dunkin' gang to try these easy-to-make, easy-to-eat chocolate apple treats.

TO MAKE:
Place chocolate chips in a microwave-safe bowl, then microwave in 30-second intervals, stirring in between, until melted. Slice apples into wedges, then dunk, sprinkle and munch.

FUN COMBOS:
- chocolate + marshmallows + crushed graham crackers
- chocolate + chopped peanuts
- chocolate + popcorn
- chocolate + sea salt
- chocolate + flaked coconut
- chocolate + toffee
- chocolate + granola

GUAC CROCS & VEGGIES

I'm all grown-up, but I still love to play with my food. Garbanzo beans in the guacamole add taste, texture and nutrition. The croc part is just plain fun.
—Kallee Krong-McCreery, Escondido, CA

Takes: 20 min. • **Makes:** 2 cups dip

- 1 can (15 oz.) garbanzo beans or chickpeas, rinsed and drained
- 3 Tbsp. mayonnaise
- 1 Tbsp. lemon juice
- ½ tsp. garlic salt
- 2 large ripe avocados
  Decoration options: red and yellow pepper pieces, sliced miniature cucumbers, radishes and ripe olives
  Assorted fresh vegetables

1. For dip, place first four ingredients in a food processor; process until smooth. Cut avocados lengthwise in half around the seed; remove seeds. Reserving skins, carefully scoop out avocado and add to bean mixture; process until blended.
2. For crocodile heads, fill avocado skins with dip. As desired, add pepper pieces for teeth, radish and olive slices for eyes, and olives for noses. Serve with vegetables.

CHEWY GRANOLA BARS

These bars manage to be both soft and crispy at the same time. They make a nutritious portable treat.
—Virginia Krites, Cridersville, OH

Prep: 10 min. • **Bake:** 25 min. + cooling
Makes: 2 dozen

- ½ cup butter, softened
- 1 cup packed brown sugar
- ¼ cup sugar
- 1 large egg
- 2 Tbsp. honey
- ½ tsp. vanilla extract
- 1 cup all-purpose flour
- 1 tsp. ground cinnamon
- ½ tsp. baking powder
- ¼ tsp. salt
- 1½ cups quick-cooking oats
- 1¼ cups Rice Krispies
- 1 cup chopped nuts
- 1 cup raisins or semisweet chocolate chips, optional

1. Preheat oven to 350°. Cream butter and sugars until light and fluffy. Beat in egg, honey and vanilla. Whisk together flour, cinnamon, baking powder and salt; gradually beat into creamed mixture. Stir in oats, Rice Krispies, nuts and, if desired, raisins or chocolate chips.
2. Press into a greased 13x9-in. pan. Bake until light brown, 25-30 minutes. Cool on a wire rack. Cut into bars.

TEST KITCHEN TIP

Cutting Granola Bars

Cutting granola bars can be a sticky business. To make it easier, spritz the knife with nonstick cooking spray before cutting bars, repeating as needed.

CRESCENT MAC & CHEESE BITES

My kids go crazy for macaroni and cheese, and they love anything wrapped up in a crescent roll. With the help of my daughter, Lula, I decided to put the two together in one yummy recipe. These are delicious as either an appetizer or a main entree.
—Katherine Gerrety, Jacksonville, FL

Takes: 30 min. • **Makes:** 8 servings

- ½ cup shredded cheddar cheese
- 3 Tbsp. 2% milk
- 2 Tbsp. cream cheese
- 1 Tbsp. butter
  Dash salt
  Dash pepper
- ¾ cup cooked elbow macaroni
- ¼ cup bacon bits
- 1 tube (8 oz.) refrigerated crescent rolls

1. Preheat oven to 375°. Place first six ingredients in a microwave-safe bowl; microwave on high until blended, about 1 minute, stirring every 30 seconds. Stir in macaroni and bacon bits. Refrigerate 5 minutes.
2. Unroll crescent dough and separate into eight triangles. Place 2 Tbsp. macaroni mixture on the wide end of each triangle. Roll into crescents; place on an ungreased baking sheet.
3. Bake until golden brown, 10-13 minutes. Serve warm.

CHOCOLATE CHIP, PB & BANANA SANDWICHES

One of my favorite combos is peanut butter, chocolate and bananas. These sammies make a quick, easy and healthy lunch youngsters can take to school.
—Charlotte Gehle, Brownstown, MI

Takes: 10 min. • **Makes:** 2 servings

- ¼ cup creamy peanut butter
- 2 Tbsp. honey
- ¼ tsp. ground cinnamon
- 2 Tbsp. miniature semisweet chocolate chips
- 4 slices whole wheat bread
- 1 medium banana, thinly sliced

Mix peanut butter, honey and cinnamon; stir in chocolate chips. Spread over bread. Layer two bread slices with banana slices; top with remaining bread. If desired, cut into shapes using cookie cutters.

MUFFIN-CUP CORN DOGS

Bring a little bit of summer back with a county fair favorite. Little ones are sure to enjoy this take on traditional corn dogs.
—Grace Bryant, Merritt Island, FL

Prep: 15 min. • **Bake:** 20 min.
Makes: 6 servings

- 1 cup all-purpose flour
- 1 cup yellow cornmeal
- 2 Tbsp. sugar
- 2 tsp. baking powder
- 2 tsp. ground mustard
- 1 tsp. salt
- 2 large eggs
- 1 cup 2% milk
- 3 Tbsp. canola oil
- 6 hot dogs, each cut into 4 pieces
  Ketchup or honey mustard, if desired

1. Preheat oven to 375°. Whisk together first six ingredients. In another bowl, whisk together the egg, milk and oil. Add to the flour mixture; stir just until moistened.
2. Fill 12 greased muffin cups three-fourths full with batter. Add two hot dog pieces to each muffin.
3. Bake until a toothpick inserted in center of muffin comes out clean, 17-20 minutes. Cool for 5 minutes before removing from pan. Serve warm with ketchup if desired.

CHOCOLATE CHIP,
PB & BANANA
SANDWICHES

Fruit Punch

MUFFIN-TIN
CHICKEN POTPIES

MUFFIN-TIN CHICKEN POTPIES

I made these personalized chicken pot pies in muffin tins for my kids, and they gobbled them up. For the record, the grown-ups did, too!
—Melissa Haines, Valparaiso, IN

Prep: 30 min. • **Bake:** 15 min.
Makes: 10 servings

- 1 Tbsp. butter
- 2 celery ribs, sliced
- ½ cup chopped onion
- 3 cups frozen mixed vegetables (about 15 oz.)
- 1 can (10¾ oz.) condensed cream of chicken soup, undiluted
- ½ cup 2% milk
- ½ tsp. onion powder
- ¼ tsp. garlic salt
- ⅛ tsp. dried thyme
- ⅛ tsp. pepper
- 2 cups cubed cooked chicken breast
- 4 tubes (6 oz. each) small refrigerated flaky biscuits (5 count)

1. Preheat oven to 375°. In a large skillet, heat butter over medium heat; saute the celery and onion until tender, 4-5 minutes. Stir in the mixed vegetables, soup, milk and seasonings; heat through, stirring mixture occasionally. Stir in the cooked chicken; remove from heat.
2. On a lightly floured surface, roll each biscuit into a 5-in. circle. Press each onto the bottom and up sides of a greased muffin cup, allowing edges to extend above cup. Fill with about 3 Tbsp. chicken mixture. Pull up edges of dough and fold partway over filling, pleating as needed.
3. Bake until golden brown and filling is bubbly, 15-18 minutes. Cool 1 minute before serving.

HAM & CHEESE MINI MEAT LOAVES

I came up with a meat loaf recipe for my son who doesn't like meatloaf. I was looking for a variation with a comfort-food feel and kid-friendly flavor. The small loaves are ideal for children trying something new.
—Jan Charles, Greeneville, TN

Prep: 25 min. • **Bake:** 30 min.
Makes: 8 servings

- 1 cup quick-cooking oats
- 1 medium onion, quartered
- 1 small tomato, seeded and quartered
- ¼ cup packed fresh parsley sprigs
- 2 Tbsp. Worcestershire sauce
- 2 garlic cloves, minced
- 1 tsp. salt
- ½ tsp. pepper
- 3 dashes hot pepper sauce
- 1 large egg, lightly beaten
- 2½ lbs. ground beef
- 8 thin slices deli ham
- 8 slices Gruyere or Swiss cheese

GLAZE
- 1 cup ketchup
- ¼ cup Dijon mustard
- 1 tsp. balsamic vinegar

1. Preheat oven to 350°. Place first nine ingredients in a food processor; process until blended. Transfer to a large bowl; stir in egg. Add beef; mix lightly but thoroughly (mixture will be soft).
2. Divide the mixture into eight portions. On a piece of parchment paper, pat each portion into a 5-in. square; layer with ham and cheese to within 1 in. of edges. Roll up jelly-roll style, starting with a short side and peeling away paper while rolling. Pinch the seam and ends to seal. Place on a rack in a roasting pan, seam side down.
3. Mix glaze ingredients; brush over meat loaves. Bake until a thermometer inserted in meat loaf reads 160°, 30-40 minutes.

BEEF TACO MUFFINS

Who doesn't love tacos? I decided to recreate a beefy classic as muffins. We love the baked sour cream and cheese on top. Just add your favorite toppings!
—Melissa Haines, Valparaiso, IN

Prep: 25 min. • **Bake:** 15 min.
Makes: 8 servings

2   tubes (8 oz. each) refrigerated crescent rolls
1   lb. lean ground beef (90% lean)
1   envelope taco seasoning
¾   cup water
3   Tbsp. sour cream
1   cup shredded Colby-Monterey Jack cheese
    Optional toppings: shredded lettuce, chopped green onions, chopped tomatoes and sliced ripe olives

1. Preheat oven to 375°. Unroll tubes of crescent dough; separate each into eight triangles. Press each triangle onto the bottom and up the sides of an ungreased muffin cup. Prick bottoms with a fork. Bake until light golden, 4-6 minutes. Using a spoon, press gently to reshape cups.
2. In a large skillet, cook and crumble beef over medium heat until no longer pink, 5-7 minutes. Stir in taco seasoning and water; bring to a boil. Reduce the heat; simmer, uncovered, until thickened, 3-4 minutes.
3. In individual muffin cup, place about 1½ tablespoons beef mixture, about ½ teaspoon sour cream and 1 tablespoon cheese. Bake until cheese is melted and crust is golden brown, 10-12 minutes. Top as desired.

CRUNCHY ORANGE CHICKEN STRIPS

Take a first piece for the crunch. Take a second for the sweetly spicy orange flavor. Or try substituting apricot nectar for the orange juice and apricot jam for the marmalade.
—Nicole Filizetti, Stevens Point, WI

Prep: 20 min. + marinating • **Cook:** 35 min.
Makes: 6 servings

1½ lbs. boneless skinless chicken breasts, cut into 1-in.-thick strips
⅔   cup plus 1 Tbsp. orange juice, divided
½   cup all-purpose flour
1   tsp. salt
½   tsp. pepper
⅛   tsp. cayenne pepper
2   large eggs, lightly beaten
4   cups Rice Krispies, slightly crushed
3   Tbsp. olive oil
⅓   cup orange marmalade
2   Tbsp. honey

1. Toss chicken with ⅔ cup orange juice; refrigerate, covered, 1-4 hours.
2. In a shallow bowl, mix the flour and seasonings. Place eggs and Rice Krispies in separate shallow bowls. Dip chicken in flour mixture to coat both sides; shake off excess. Dip in eggs, then cereal, patting to help coating adhere.
3. In a large skillet, heat oil over medium-high heat. Add chicken in batches; cook until golden brown and no longer pink, 5-6 minutes per side. Drain chicken on paper towels.
4. Wipe skillet clean if necessary. In same pan, mix marmalade, honey and remaining orange juice; cook and stir over low heat until slightly thickened. Add chicken; heat through, turning to coat. Serve chicken strips immediately.

GARLIC BREAD PIZZA SANDWICHES

I love inventing new ways to make grilled cheese sandwiches for my kids. This version tastes like pizza. Using frozen garlic bread is a time-saver.
—Courtney Stultz, Weir, KS

Takes: 20 min. • **Makes:** 4 servings

1   pkg. (11¼ oz.) frozen garlic Texas toast
¼   cup pasta sauce
4   slices provolone cheese
16 slices pepperoni
8   slices thinly sliced hard salami
    Additional pasta sauce, warmed, optional

1. Preheat griddle over medium-low heat. Add the garlic toast; cook until lightly browned, about 3-4 minutes per side.
2. Spoon 1 tablespoon sauce over each of four toasts. Top with cheese, pepperoni, salami and remaining toasts. Cook until crisp and cheese is melted, 3-5 minutes, turning as necessary. If desired, serve with additional sauce.

TEST KITCHEN TIP

Clean Cutting

To easily slice Garlic Bread Pizza Sandwiches cleanly without making a mess of the gooey melted cheese, use a pizza cutter instead of a knife.

**GARLIC BREAD
PIZZA SANDWICHES**

Guys' Night In

Boys' night in is no buttoned-down affair. Heck, *no*. When hungry fellas gather, they want mancave staples like chili, corn chips, bacon, beef and beer. Whipping up hot and hearty pleasers is easy with these stick-to-the-ribs recipes boasting big bold flavors. Whether it's for Saturday night entertaining, poker night, the day of the big game or just a hungry man looking for something satisfying to pair with his favorite ale or lager, dude food is king!

Picadillo Sliders (p. 240)

GAME-STOPPER
CHILI

BACON
CHEESEBURGER
SOUP

BACON CHEESEBURGER SOUP

This recipe brings two of my favorite foods—soup and burgers—together in one. The fresh lettuce, chopped tomato and crisp bacon make this taste just like an all-American burger.
—Geoff Bales, Hemet, CA

Prep: 20 min. • **Cook:** 4 hours
Makes: 6 servings

- 1½ lbs. lean ground beef (90% lean)
- 1 large onion, chopped
- ⅓ cup all-purpose flour
- ½ tsp. pepper
- 2½ cups chicken broth
- 1 can (12 oz.) evaporated milk
- 1½ cups shredded cheddar cheese
- 8 slices process American cheese, chopped
- 1½ cups shredded lettuce
- 2 medium tomatoes, chopped
- 6 bacon strips, cooked and crumbled

1. In a large skillet, cook and crumble beef with onion over medium-high heat until no longer pink, 6-8 minutes; drain. Stir in flour and pepper; transfer mixture to a 5-qt. slow cooker.

2. Stir in broth and milk. Cook, covered, on low until flavors are blended, 4-5 hours. Stir in cheeses until melted. Top servings with remaining ingredients.

GAME-STOPPER CHILI

A hearty chili with sausage, beef, beans and barley is perfect for the half-time food rush. People actually cheer when they see me coming with my slow cooker!
—Barbara Lento, Houston, PA

Prep: 25 min. • **Cook:** 6 hours
Makes: 12 servings (4 qt.)

- 1 can (28 oz.) diced tomatoes, undrained
- 1 can (15 oz.) black beans, rinsed and drained
- 1 can (15 oz.) kidney beans, rinsed and drained
- 1 lb. boneless beef chuck steak, cut into 1-in. cubes
- 1 lb. bulk spicy pork sausage, cooked and drained
- 2 medium onions, chopped
- 1 medium sweet red pepper, chopped
- 1 medium green pepper, chopped
- 1 cup hot chunky salsa
- ⅓ cup medium pearl barley
- 2 Tbsp. chili powder
- 2 tsp. jarred roasted minced garlic
- 1 tsp. salt
- 1 tsp. ground cumin
- 4 cups beef stock
- 2 cups shredded Mexican cheese blend
  Corn chips

1. Place all ingredients except shredded cheese and chips in a 6-qt. slow cooker. Cook, covered, on low until beef is tender, 6-8 hours.

2. Stir in cheese until melted. Serve chili with chips.

Freeze option: Freeze the cooled chili in freezer containers. To use, partially thaw in refrigerator overnight. Heat through in a saucepan, stirring occasionally.

CUBAN SLIDERS

Bake sliders until lightly toasted with melty cheese. Leftovers keep well in the fridge and make a lovely cold snack. Followers of my blog, *houseofyumm.com*, go nuts for these!
—Serene Herrera, Dallas, TX

Takes: 30 min. • **Makes:** 2 dozen

- 2 pkg. (12 oz. each) Hawaiian sweet rolls
- 1¼ lbs. thinly sliced deli ham
- 9 slices Swiss cheese (about 6 oz.)
- 24 dill pickle slices
TOPPING
- ½ cup butter, cubed
- 2 Tbsp. finely chopped onion
- 2 Tbsp. Dijon mustard

1. Preheat oven to 350°. Without separating rolls, cut each package of rolls in half horizontally; arrange the bottom halves in a greased 13x9-in. baking pan. Layer with the ham, cheese and pickles; replace top halves of rolls.

2. In a microwave, melt the butter; stir in chopped onion and mustard. Drizzle over rolls. Bake, covered, 10 minutes. Uncover pan; bake until golden brown and heated through, 5-10 minutes longer.

Test Your Recall

How many slogans can you pair with the frothy brand each describes?
Answers on page 240.

1. BUDWEISER
2. COORS
3. CORONA
4. FOSTER'S
5. GUINNESS
6. MILLER HIGH LIFE
7. OLD MILWAUKEE
8. SCHLITZ
9. STELLA ARTOIS

A. The Champagne of Beers
B. Good Things Come to Those Who Wait
C. Brewed with Pure Rocky Mountain Spring Water
D. Reassuringly Expensive
E. Miles Away from Ordinary
F. The Beer That Made Milwaukee Famous
G. The King of Beers
H. Tastes as Great as Its Name
I. Australian for Beer

RAMEN SLIDERS

I grew up eating ramen and love it to this day. These sliders are a fun spin on my favorite type of noodle soup, which is topped with an egg and kimchi.
—Julie Teramoto, Los Angeles, CA

Prep: 40 min. • **Bake:** 20 min.
Makes: 10 servings

- 1 pkg. (3 oz.) beef or pork ramen noodles
- 1 lb. ground beef
- 4 green onions, thinly sliced
- 2 hard-boiled large eggs, sliced
  Sriracha Asian hot chili sauce
  Kimchi, optional

1. Preheat oven to 350°. Grease 20 muffin cups. Cook noodles according to package directions, saving seasoning packet for meat mixture. Drain; divide the noodles among prepared muffin cups. Bake until noodles are crisp and light golden brown, 20-25 minutes. Remove from pans to wire racks to cool.
2. Meanwhile, combine the beef, green onions and reserved seasoning packet, mixing lightly but thoroughly. Shape into ten 2½-in. round patties.
3. In a large nonstick skillet, cook burgers over medium heat 4-6 minutes on each side until a thermometer reads 160°. Cut each egg into five slices. Serve burgers on ramen buns with egg slices, chili sauce and, if desired, kimchi.

OATMEAL RAISIN COOKIES

These old-fashioned cookies are an all-time favorite. A friend gave me the recipe many years ago. The secret is to measure exactly and to not overbake.
—Wendy Coalwell, Abbeville, GA

Takes: 30 min. • **Makes:** about 3½ dozen

- 1 cup shortening
- 1 cup sugar
- 1 cup packed light brown sugar
- 3 large eggs
- 1 tsp. vanilla extract
- 2½ cups all-purpose flour
- 2 tsp. baking soda
- 1 tsp. salt
- 1 tsp. ground cinnamon
- 2 cups old-fashioned oats
- 1 cup raisins
- 1 cup coarsely chopped pecans, optional

1. In a large bowl, cream the shortening and sugars until light and fluffy. Beat in eggs, one at a time, beating well after each addition. Beat in vanilla. Combine the flour, baking soda, salt and cinnamon. Add to the creamed mixture, stirring just until combined. Stir in oats, raisins and pecans if desired.
2. Shape into 1-in. balls. Place 2 in. apart on ungreased baking sheets. Flatten with a greased glass bottom.
3. Bake at 350° until golden brown, 10-11 minutes. Do not overbake. Remove to wire rack to cool.

RAMEN SLIDERS

HEARTY BAKED POTATO SOUP

My aunt, who is an amazing cook, gave me this recipe. With its bacon, cheese and chives, the soup tastes just like a loaded baked potato. My husband and I love it on chilly nights.
—Molly Seidel, Edgewood, NM

Prep: 25 min. • **Cook:** 6 hours
Makes: 10 servings (3½ qt.)

- 5 lbs. baking potatoes, cut into ½-in. cubes (about 13 cups)
- 1 large onion, chopped
- ¼ cup butter
- 4 garlic cloves, minced
- 1 tsp. salt
- ½ tsp. pepper
- 3 cans (14½ oz. each) chicken broth
- 1 cup shredded sharp cheddar cheese
- 1 cup half-and-half cream
- 3 Tbsp. minced fresh chives
  Optional toppings: shredded cheddar cheese, sour cream, crumbled cooked bacon and minced chives

1. Place first seven ingredients in a 6-qt. slow cooker. Cook, covered, on low until potatoes are very tender, 6-8 hours.
2. Mash potatoes slightly to break up and to thicken soup. Add 1 cup cheese, cream and chives; heat through, stirring until blended. Serve with toppings as desired.
Freeze option: Freeze cooled soup in freezer containers. To use, partially thaw in refrigerator overnight. Heat through in a saucepan, stirring occasionally.

PICADILLO SLIDERS

When I'm pressed for time, these beefy sandwiches are my go-to. Any leftover picadillo makes for great nachos or queso dip. It freezes well, too!
—Patterson Watkins, Philadelphia, PA

Prep: 15 min. • **Cook:** 25 min.
Makes: 1½ dozen

1 Tbsp. canola oil
1 medium yellow onion, diced
2 garlic cloves, minced
2 lbs. ground beef
½ cup pimiento-stuffed olives, halved
2 cans (14½ oz. each) diced tomatoes, drained
1 cup beef broth
¼ cup red wine vinegar
¼ cup raisins
2 Tbsp. tomato paste
1 Tbsp. chili powder
2 tsp. ground cumin
1 tsp. ground cinnamon
1½ tsp. salt
18 potato dinner rolls

1. In a large skillet, heat oil over medium heat. Saute the onion until translucent, 6-8 minutes; add garlic, and cook 1 minute more. Add ground beef; cook, crumbling meat, until no longer pink, 6-8 minutes. With a slotted spoon, remove meat; drain excess fat.
2. Return meat to skillet. Add the next 10 ingredients. Stir over medium heat until well blended. Reduce heat; simmer until sauce has thickened, 10-15 minutes.
3. Toast rolls. Spoon the beef mixture on each roll (they may be juicy). Serve sliders immediately.

PEANUT BUTTER SWIRL BROWNIES

Peanut butter and chocolate are always a delicious duo, but they really play well together in this tempting treat. Even with a sizable collection of brownie recipes, I reach for this one often. The marbled look attracts curious tasters...the flavor brings them back for seconds.
—Linda Craig, Edmonton, AB

Prep: 15 min. • **Bake:** 25 min. + cooling
Makes: 3 dozen

½ cup butter, softened
⅔ cup sugar
½ cup packed brown sugar
2 large eggs
2 Tbsp. milk
¾ cup all-purpose flour
½ tsp. baking powder
¼ tsp. salt
¼ cup creamy peanut butter
⅓ cup peanut butter chips
⅓ cup baking cocoa
½ cup semisweet chocolate chips

1. In a large bowl, cream butter and sugars. Add the eggs and milk; mix well. Combine the flour, baking powder and salt; add to creamed mixture and mix well.
2. Divide batter in half. To one portion, add peanut butter and peanut butter chips; mix well. To the other portion, add the cocoa and chocolate chips; mix well.
3. In a greased 9-in. square baking pan, spoon chocolate batter in eight mounds in a checkerboard pattern. Spoon seven mounds of peanut butter batter between the chocolate batter. Cut through batters with a knife to swirl.
4. Bake at 350° for 25-30 minutes or until a toothpick inserted in the center comes out clean. Cool on a wire rack. Cut into bars to serve.

PIZZA SOUP WITH GARLIC TOAST CROUTONS

This comforting soup will satisfy your deepest pizza cravings. I sometimes substitute Italian sausage for chicken or add a little Parmesan cheese. Go nuts and add all your favorite pizza toppings!
—Joan Hallford, North Richland Hills, TX

Prep: 10 min. • **Cook:** 6 hours
Makes: 10 servings (about 4 qt.)

1 can (28 oz.) diced tomatoes, drained
1 can (15 oz.) pizza sauce
1 lb. boneless skinless chicken breasts, cut into 1-in. pieces
1 pkg. (3 oz.) sliced pepperoni, halved
1 cup sliced fresh mushrooms
1 small onion, chopped
½ cup chopped green pepper
¼ tsp. pepper
2 cans (14½ oz. each) chicken broth
1 pkg. (11¼ oz.) frozen garlic Texas toast
1 pkg. (10 oz.) frozen chopped spinach, thawed and squeezed dry
1 cup shredded part-skim mozzarella cheese

1. In a 6-qt. slow cooker, combine first nine ingredients. Cook, covered, on low until chicken is tender, 6-8 hours .
2. For the croutons, cut Texas toast Into cubes; bake according to package directions. Add the spinach to soup; heat through, stirring occasionally. Top servings with cheese and warm croutons.
Freeze option: Freeze cooled soup in freezer containers. To use, partially thaw in refrigerator overnight. Heat through in a saucepan, stirring occasionally. Prepare croutons as directed. Top soup with cheese and croutons.

Beer Slogans, p. 238: 1-G, 2-C, 3-E, 4-I, 5-B, 6-A, 7-H, 8-F, 9-D

PIZZA SOUP WITH
GARLIC TOAST CROUTONS

Special Celebrations

MINI HOT BROWNS

Here's my take on the famous Hot Brown sandwich. Guests quickly line up for juicy turkey slices and crispy bacon, piled on toasted rye bread and then topped with a rich cheese sauce.
—Annette Grahl, Midway, KY

Takes: 30 min. • **Makes:** 1½ dozen

- 1 tsp. chicken bouillon granules
- ¼ cup boiling water
- 3 Tbsp. butter
- 2 Tbsp. all-purpose flour
- ¾ cup half-and-half cream
- 1 cup shredded Swiss cheese
- 18 slices snack rye bread
- 6 oz. sliced deli turkey
- 1 small onion, thinly sliced and separated into rings
- 5 bacon strips, cooked and crumbled
- 2 Tbsp. minced fresh parsley

1. Preheat oven to 350°. Dissolve bouillon in water; set aside.
2. In a saucepan, melt butter over medium heat. Stir in flour until smooth; add cream and bouillon. Bring to a boil; cook and stir until thickened, 1-2 minutes. Stir in cheese until melted. Remove from heat.
3. Place bread slices on two baking sheets. Layer each slice with the turkey, onion and cheese mixture. Bake until heated through, 10-12 minutes. (Or preheat broiler and broil until the edges of bread are crisp and sauce is bubbly, 3-5 minutes.) Sprinkle with bacon and parsley.

Try them as sliders: Double the number of bread slices but only put toppings on half the slices. After assembling, use remaining bread slices to top your mini sandwiches.

CHICKEN FAJITA CHOWDER

For south-of-the-border flavor, I head for my slow cooker and this favorite chowder recipe. It's always a winner at family dinners and potlucks, especially topped with fresh avocado, shredded cheddar cheese and chili cheese corn chips.
—Nancy Heishman, Las Vegas, NV

Prep: 20 min. • **Cook:** 4 hours
Makes: 10 servings (3½ qt.)

- 3 large tomatoes, chopped
- 1 can (15 oz.) black beans, rinsed and drained
- 6 oz. fully cooked Spanish chorizo links, sliced
- 2 lbs. boneless skinless chicken breasts, cut into 1-in. cubes
- 1 envelope fajita seasoning mix
- 1½ cups frozen corn, thawed
- 1 medium sweet red pepper, chopped
- 1 medium green pepper, chopped
- 6 green onions, chopped
- ¾ cup salsa
- ½ cup chopped fresh cilantro
- 2 cans (14½ oz. each) reduced-sodium chicken broth
- 1 can (10¾ oz.) condensed nacho cheese soup, undiluted
  Cubed avocado and additional cilantro, optional

1. Place first twelve ingredients in a 6-qt. slow cooker. Cook, covered, on low until chicken is tender, 4-5 hours.
2. Stir in cheese soup; heat through. If desired, top servings with avocado and additional cilantro.

SAUSAGE & CHICKEN GUMBO

This recipe for the classic southern comfort food was the first thing I ever cooked for my girlfriend. It was simple to make, but tasted gourmet. Lucky for me, it was love at first bite.
—Kael Harvey, Brooklyn, NY

Prep: 35 min. • **Cook:** 6 hours
Makes: 6 servings

- ¼ cup all-purpose flour
- ¼ cup canola oil
- 4 cups chicken broth, divided
- 1 pkg. (14 oz.) smoked sausage, cut into ½-in. slices
- 1 cup frozen sliced okra, thawed
- 1 small green pepper, chopped
- 1 medium onion, chopped
- 1 celery rib, chopped
- 3 garlic cloves, minced
- ½ tsp. pepper
- ¼ tsp. salt
- ¼ tsp. cayenne pepper
- 2 cups coarsely shredded cooked chicken
  Hot cooked rice

1. In a heavy saucepan, mix flour and oil until smooth; cook and stir over medium heat until light brown, about 4 minutes. Reduce heat to medium-low; cook and stir until dark reddish brown, about 15 minutes (do not burn). Gradually stir in 3 cups broth; transfer to a 4- or 5-qt. slow cooker.
2. Stir in sausage, vegetables, garlic and seasonings. Cook, covered, on low until flavors are blended, 6-8 hours. Stir in the chicken and remaining broth; heat gumbo through. Serve with rice.

Freeze option: Freeze cooled soup in freezer containers. To use, partially thaw in refrigerator overnight. Heat through in a saucepan, stirring occasionally and adding a little broth if necessary.

Haunted House Halloween Treats

This year pull out all the scary stops with a fearsomely festive haunted house Halloween party. It's easy to turn your home into a place where anything eerie can—and probably will—happen. Treat guests to this ghoulishly delicious spread of boo-riff-ic tricks and treats, including a haunted house brownie. Pick and choose from the following spine-tingling ideas, or use them all, to create a spooktacular night of fright. Enter if you dare!

Brownie Haunted House (p. 249)

HOT DOG MUMMIES
WITH HONEY
MUSTARD DIP

SPIDER SLIDERS

We're always trying to do fun things with food to make meals memorable. Better grab one of these creepy, crawly spiders before it walks away!

—Frank Millard, Edgerton, WI

Prep: 20 min. • **Bake:** 25 min.
Makes: 12 servings

- 2 large sweet potatoes (about 12 oz. each)
- ½ tsp. salt
- ¼ tsp. ground cumin
- ¼ tsp. dried thyme
- ⅛ tsp. ground cinnamon
- ⅛ tsp. pepper
- ¼ cup canola oil
- 1 lb. ground beef
- ¼ cup dried minced onion
- ½ tsp. seasoned salt
- 6 slices American cheese
- 12 dinner rolls, split
- 24 pimiento-stuffed olive slices

1. Adjust oven racks to upper-middle and lower-middle position. Preheat oven to 400°. Peel and cut sweet potatoes into ¼-in. julienne strips. Place in a greased 15x10x1-in. baking pan. Mix salt, cumin, thyme, cinnamon and pepper. Drizzle the sweet potatoes with oil; sprinkle with spice mixture. Toss to coat.

2. Bake on the bottom oven rack 25-30 minutes or until golden brown and tender, turning once. Meanwhile, in a large bowl, combine beef, onion and seasoned salt, mixing lightly but thoroughly. Press onto bottom of a greased 13x9-in. baking dish. Bake on top oven rack 15-20 minutes or until a thermometer reads 160°.

3. Drain fat from baking dish; place cheese slices evenly over meat. Bake 2-3 minutes longer or until cheese is melted. Cut into 12 patties. Place one patty on each roll bottom; arrange eight fries to form spider legs. Replace tops. Press two olive slices onto cheese to form eyes.

HOT DOG MUMMIES WITH HONEY MUSTARD DIP

Kids can't get enough of these flaky, golden mummy sandwiches. The accompanying mustard dip adds just the right kick.

—Jessie Sarrazin, Livingston, MT

Prep: 25 min. • **Bake:** 10 min.
Makes: 20 appetizers (about 1 cup dip)

- 1 tube (8 oz.) refrigerated crescent rolls
- 20 miniature hot dogs
- 1 large egg
- 2 tsp. water
  Dijon mustard

DIP
- ½ cup mayonnaise
- 3 Tbsp. Dijon mustard
- 3 Tbsp. honey
- 1 Tbsp. cider vinegar
  Dash hot pepper sauce

1. Separate crescent roll dough into two rectangles; seal seams and perforations. Cut each rectangle horizontally into 10 strips. Wrap one dough strip around each miniature hot dog.

2. Place 1 in. apart on an ungreased baking sheet. In a small bowl, whisk the egg and water; brush over tops. Bake at 375° for 10-15 minutes or until golden brown. Using mustard, add eyes to mummies. In a small bowl, combine the dip ingredients; serve with mummies.

Utensil Packets

Set the table with these fun, simple utensil packets. Fold a paper napkin in half and slide it into a waxed paper bag. Tuck in plastic utensils, then tie a coordinating ribbon around the center of the bag, finishing it off with a simple knot.

SPIDER
SLIDERS

GHOSTLY CHICKEN
& PEPPER PIZZA

GHOSTLY CHICKEN & PEPPER PIZZA

This friendly ghost pizza won't scare folks away from the dinner table. My family loves Halloween, so we like creating fun recipes like this one. Fill the pizza with whatever toppings you like best.
—Francine Boecher, Queensbury, NY

Prep: 50 min. + marinating • **Bake:** 10 min.
Makes: 6 pieces

- ⅔ cup plus 2 Tbsp. olive oil, divided
- ¼ cup lemon juice
- 4 garlic cloves, minced
- 1 Tbsp. Dijon mustard
- 2 tsp. dried oregano
- ¾ tsp. dried thyme
- ¾ tsp. pepper
- ½ lb. boneless skinless chicken breasts
- ¾ cup chopped green pepper
- ¾ cup chopped sweet red pepper
- 1 loaf (1 lb.) frozen pizza dough, thawed
- 1½ cups shredded part-skim mozzarella cheese
- ¼ tsp. salt

1. Whisk together ⅔ cup oil with next six ingredients. Reserve 3 Tbsp. marinade for pizza. Add chicken to remaining marinade; toss in a shallow dish to coat. Refrigerate, covered, 2 hours.
2. Preheat oven to 375°. Place chicken mixture in a greased 8-in. square baking dish. Bake until a thermometer reads 165°, 22-27 minutes. When cool enough to handle, cut chicken into bite-sized pieces.
3. Meanwhile, in a small skillet, heat about 1 Tbsp. oil over medium heat. Cook and stir peppers until tender, 4-6 minutes. Increase oven heat to 450°.
4. Divide pizza dough in half. On a lightly floured surface, roll each piece into a 12x9-in. rectangle. Transfer one rectangle to a greased baking sheet. Brush reserved marinade over rectangle to within ½ in. of edges. Top with chicken, peppers and cheese. Sprinkle with salt. Place second dough rectangle over pizza and pinch edges to seal. Using a kitchen scissors, cut out eyes and mouth. Cut bottom to form a jagged edge; pinch edges of dough to reseal. Brush with remaining oil.
5. Bake pizza for 10-15 minutes or until golden brown.

BROWNIE HAUNTED HOUSE

(SHOWN ON P. 245)
Don't worry about getting this sweet showstopper to stand upright. The fudgy brownies are the perfect foundation for building a tasty haunted house. Trick-or-treaters beware!
—Sarah Farmer, Waukesha, WI

Prep: 20 min. • **Bake:** 30 min. + cooling
Makes: 16 servings

- 1 cup sugar
- ½ cup packed brown sugar
- ⅔ cup butter, cubed
- ¼ cup water
- 2 tsp. instant coffee granules, optional
- 1¾ cups semisweet chocolate chips
- 4 large eggs
- 2 tsp. vanilla extract
- 1½ cups all-purpose flour
- ½ tsp. baking soda
- ½ tsp. salt
    Vanilla frosting
    Chocolate frosting
    Paste food coloring
    Assorted sprinkles
    Assorted candies

1. Preheat oven to 325°. Line a 13x9-in. baking pan with foil, letting ends extend up sides. In a large heavy saucepan, combine sugars, butter, water and, if desired, coffee granules; bring to a boil, stirring constantly. Remove from heat; add chocolate chips and stir until melted. Cool slightly.
2. Whisk the eggs until foamy, about 3 minutes. Add vanilla; gradually whisk in chocolate mixture. In another bowl, whisk flour, baking soda and salt; stir into the chocolate mixture.
3. Pour into prepared pan. Bake on a lower oven rack until a toothpick inserted in center comes out with moist crumbs (do not overbake), 30-40 minutes. Cool in pan on a wire rack.
4. Lifting with foil, remove brownies from pan; let cool completely. Discard foil. Cut off the corners of brownie to resemble a house. If desired, cut scraps into pumpkins and ghosts using cookie cutters. Tint the frosting as desired with food coloring. Decorate brownie house with frosting and candies.

JACK-O'-LANTERN EMPANADAS

Your trick-or-treaters will love these spooktacular pockets with goofy grins. The savory filling is perfectly spiced, and the refrigerated pastry makes prep easy.
—Matthew Hass, Franklin, WI

Prep: 45 min. • **Bake:** 15 min.
Makes: 2½ dozen

- 1 Tbsp. canola oil
- ½ cup frozen corn
- ¼ cup finely chopped onion
- ¼ cup finely chopped sweet red pepper
- 2 garlic cloves, minced
- 1 can (15 oz.) solid-pack pumpkin
- ½ cup black beans, rinsed and drained
- 2 tsp. chili powder
- ¾ tsp. salt
- ¾ tsp. ground cumin
- ½ tsp. dried oregano
- 2 pkg. (14.1 oz. each) refrigerated pie pastry
- 1 large egg
- 1 Tbsp. water

1. Preheat oven to 425°. In a large skillet, heat oil over medium heat. Add corn, onion and pepper; cook and stir 2-3 minutes or until tender. Add the garlic; cook 1 minute longer. Stir in pumpkin, black beans and seasonings; heat through. Cool slightly.
2. On a lightly floured surface, unroll pastry sheets. Cut 60 pumpkins with a 3-in. floured pumpkin-shaped or round cookie cutter, rerolling dough as necessary. Place half the cutouts 2 in. apart on parchment paper-lined baking sheets; top each with about 1 Tbsp. pumpkin mixture. Using a knife, cut jack-o'-lantern faces or slits out of the remaining pastries. Place over the top of the pumpkin mixture; press edges with a fork to seal.
3. In a small bowl, whisk egg and water; brush over pastries. Bake until golden brown, 12-15 minutes. Remove from pan to wire racks.

Soul Tunes

Here are some spellbinding
songs to set the mood.

I PUT A SPELL ON YOU
Screamin' Jay Hawkins

TIME WARP
Little Nell, Patricia Quinn
& Richard O'Brien

SOMEBODY'S WATCHING ME
Rockwell

THRILLER
Michael Jackson

WEREWOLVES OF LONDON
Warren Zevon

THIS IS HALLOWEEN
The Citizens of Halloween Town

THE MUNSTERS THEME
Jack Marshall

MONSTER MASH
Bobby "Boris" Pickett &
the Crypt-Kickers

THE TWILIGHT ZONE
The Ventures

(DON'T FEAR) THE REAPER
Blue Öyster Cult

SUPERSTITION
Stevie Wonder

THE PURPLE PEOPLE EATER
Sheb Wooley

**SCARY MONSTERS
(AND SUPER CREEPS)**
David Bowie

EYES ON YOU CUPCAKES

Look out! This crazy cupcake only has eyes for you. Don't worry though, he's delicious!
—Karen Tack, Riverside, CT

Takes: 30 min. • **Makes:** 6 cupcakes

- 1   can (16 oz.) vanilla frosting
       Neon green food coloring
- 6   prepared vanilla or chocolate cupcakes, baked in liners
- ¼   cup purple sprinkles
- 1   tube (4.25 oz.) brown decorating frosting
- 8   to 10 large marshmallows
- 25   miniature marshmallows
- 35   M&M's minis

1. Tint vanilla frosting with neon green food coloring. Spread a generous mound of frosting on each cupcake. Before the frosting dries, top with purple sprinkles.
2. Pipe a small dot of brown decorating frosting onto a marshmallow. Lightly press an M&M's mini into frosting dot to create an eye. Repeat with remaining marshmallows; let dry.
3. Pierce each marshmallow eye with a toothpick; insert opposite end of the toothpick into cupcake as desired.

SPOOKY JOES

I serve these sloppy joes open-faced and cut the cheddar cheese into fun Halloween shapes. They pair nicely with crispy potato wedges and sliced fruit.
—Darla Wester, Meriden, IA

Takes: 20 min. • **Makes:** 8 servings

- 2   lbs. ground beef
- 2   cans (10¾ oz. each) condensed tomato soup, undiluted
- 1   tsp. onion salt
- 2   cups shredded cheddar cheese
- 8   hamburger buns, split
- 8   slices cheddar cheese

In a large skillet, cook beef over medium heat until no longer pink; drain. Stir in the soup and onion salt; heat through. Stir in shredded cheddar cheese until melted. Spoon about ½ cup onto the bottom of each bun. Cut cheese slices with 2½-in. Halloween cookie cutters; place over beef mixture. Serve bun tops on the side.

BEWITCHING STUFFED POTATOES

I livened up my cheesy stuffed potatoes by giving each a silly face and hat. These creepy spuds will be a hit at dinner.
—Mary Shenk, DeKalb, IL

Prep: 25 min. • **Bake:** 15 min.
Makes: 8 servings

- 4   medium potatoes (about 8 oz. each)
- ½   cup mayonnaise
- 1   cup shredded cheddar cheese
- 8   bacon strips, cooked and crumbled
- ⅓   cup oil-packed sun-dried tomatoes, patted dry and chopped
- 1   green onion, thinly sliced
- ½   tsp. salt
- ¼   tsp. pepper
- 8   slices Monterey Jack cheese

TOPPINGS
     Sliced ripe olives, drained
     Roasted sweet red peppers, drained and sliced
     Blue corn tortilla chips

1. Preheat oven to 400°. Scrub the potatoes; pierce several times with a fork. Microwave, uncovered, on high until tender, 12-15 minutes, turning once.
2. When the potatoes are cool enough to handle, cut in half lengthwise. Scoop out pulp, leaving ¼-in.-thick shells. Mash the pulp with mayonnaise, adding next six ingredients.
3. Spoon into potato shells. Place on a baking sheet; top with a piece of cheese. Bake until heated through, 12-15 minutes. Decorate, as desired, with the olives and peppers; serve potatoes with blue corn tortilla chips.

TOMBSTONE
TREATS

MUMMY POPPERS

I wrapped these spicy jalapeno poppers in puff pastry to look like a mummy. You can tame the heat by adjusting the amount of chipotle peppers.

—Nick Iverson, Denver, CO

Prep: 30 min. • **Bake:** 30 min.
Makes: 32 appetizers

- 1 pkg. (8 oz.) cream cheese, softened
- 2 cups shredded cheddar cheese
- 2 green onions, finely chopped
- 1 to 2 chipotle peppers in adobo sauce, finely chopped
- 2 Tbsp. lime juice
- 1 Tbsp. honey
- ½ tsp. salt
- ½ tsp. ground cumin
- ¼ tsp. pepper
- 16 jalapeno peppers, halved lengthwise and seeded
- 1 pkg. (17.3 oz.) frozen puff pastry, thawed and cut lengthwise into 32 strips

1. Preheat oven to 400°. Beat first nine ingredients until blended. Spoon or pipe the cheese mixture into pepper halves.
2. Wrap puff pastry strips around pepper halves. Transfer the wrapped peppers to parchment paper-lined baking sheets. Bake poppers until golden brown and cheese is melted, 30-40 minutes.

TEST KITCHEN TIP

Popper Pointers

When making Mummy Poppers, there's no need to use peppers of the same size and shape. Varying them creates visual interest. A measuring teaspoon is a great tool for removing seeds. Use a food-safe plastic bag to pipe the filling. Snip off a corner, insert the cheese mixture and pipe away.

TOMBSTONE TREATS

My brother loves rice cereal squares, and my mom loves sugar cookies. This is a Halloween treat that both of them like.
—Jill Wright, Dixon, IL

Prep: 45 min. • **Bake:** 10 min. + cooling
Makes: 16 servings

- 3 Tbsp. butter
- 4 cups miniature marshmallows
- 7½ cups crisp rice cereal
- 1 tube (16½ oz.) refrigerated sugar cookie dough
- ⅔ cup all-purpose flour
- 1 tsp. water
- 4 drops green food coloring
- 1½ cups sweetened shredded coconut
     Black paste food coloring
     Vanilla frosting
     Brown decorating icing
- 1 cup (6 oz.) semisweet chocolate chips, melted
     Candy pumpkins

1. In a large saucepan over low heat, melt butter. Stir in marshmallows until melted. Remove from heat. Stir in cereal until well coated. With a buttered spatula, press into a greased 13x9-in. pan. Cool.
2. Beat the cookie dough and flour until combined. On a lightly floured surface, roll out dough to ¼-in. thickness. Draw or trace a tombstone pattern onto waxed paper; using the pattern as a guide, cut out 16 tombstones from dough. Place cutouts 2 in. apart on ungreased baking sheets.
3. Along bottom edge of each cookie, insert two toothpicks halfway into dough. Bake at 350° until golden brown, 8-10 minutes. Remove to wire racks to cool.
4. In a large resealable plastic bag, combine water and green food coloring. Add coconut; seal bag and shake to coat. Toast coconut; set aside. Using black paste food coloring, tint frosting gray. Frost sugar cookies; add words using brown decorating icing.
5. Cut cereal bars into 3x2-in. rectangles; spread with melted chocolate chips. Using toothpicks, insert cookies into cereal bars. Decorate tombstones with coconut and candies as desired.

Creepy Cottage

This miniature scene is big on frightful fun. Craft by Christina Spalatin, Wauwatosa, Wisconsin

WHAT YOU'LL NEED

Ceramic house
Black matte spray paint
Acrylic paints
Hollow carvable foam pumpkin
Battery-operated mini LED light string
Fairy garden bench
Spice jar lids, optional
Moss
Paintbrushes
Drill
Glue gun

DIRECTIONS

1. Spray-paint ceramic house. Dry thoroughly. Using acrylic paints, paint house details, if desired. Paint pumpkin interior using acrylic paint; let dry thoroughly before adding any additional details.

2. Using ¼-in. drill bit, drill a hole in the back of the pumpkin near the bottom. Insert light string through hole and spread lights on the pumpkin floor.

3. Arrange the house and bench inside pumpkin. Glue to the floor, using jar lids underneath to add height if needed. Glue moss to floor and around the jar lids. Display the finished pumpkin on a cake pedestal.

BONES & BLOOD

Like a zombie, you'll be desperate for more of these bone-shaped cookies and dip. Fight nicely over them—no biting!
—*Taste of Home* Test Kitchen

Prep: 45 min.
Bake: 25 min./batch + cooling
Makes: 40 cookies (2 cups sauce)

  5 **large egg whites**
  ½ **cup cake flour**
  ½ **cup ground almonds**
  ¼ **tsp. ground cinnamon**
  ⅛ **tsp. ground cloves**
  ⅛ **tsp. ground nutmeg**
  1 **tsp. vanilla extract**
  ¼ **tsp. cream of tartar**

      Dash salt
  4 **drops yellow food coloring, optional**
  ¾ **cup plus 2 Tbsp. sugar**
SAUCE
  1¼ **cups heavy whipping cream**
  ½ **cup semisweet chocolate chips**
  ½ **cup strawberry jelly**
      Red food coloring, optional

1. Place the egg whites in a large bowl; let stand at room temperature about 30 minutes. Meanwhile, combine the flour, almonds, cinnamon, cloves and nutmeg.
2. Add the vanilla, cream of tartar, salt and, if desired, food coloring to the egg whites. Beat on medium speed until soft peaks form. Gradually add sugar, 1 Tbsp. at a time, beating on high until stiff glossy peaks form and sugar is dissolved. Fold in flour mixture.
3. Fill a pastry bag with the egg white mixture. Pipe 4-in. logs onto parchment-lined baking sheets. Pipe two ½-in. balls at both ends of each log to make a bone shape. Bake at 300° for 25-30 minutes or until firm to the touch. Remove to wire racks. Store in an airtight container.
4. In a microwave-safe bowl, combine the cream, chips and jelly. Microwave on high for 30-second intervals until melted; stir until smooth. Tint red if desired. Cool sauce to room temperature and serve with bones. Refrigerate leftover sauce.

Index

SHARE YOUR **MOST-LOVED RECIPES**

Do you have a special tradition that has become part of your family's holiday tradition? Are homemade gifts and crafts included in your celebrations? We want to hear from you. Visit **tasteofhome.com/submit** to submit a recipe or craft for editorial consideration.

PAGE 105

PAGE 71

PAGE 197

PAGE 161